ANAL

❖

G000150743

KAREL WILLIAMS, COLIN HASLAM,
JOHN WILLIAMS, SUKHDEV JOHAL
with ANDY ADCROFT

Berghahn Books
Providence

First published in 1994 by

Berghahn Books Inc.

© Karel Williams, Colin Haslam, John Williams, Sukhdev Johal 1994

Library of Congress Cataloging in Publication Data
Cars: analysis, history, cases / Karel Williams . . . [et al.]; with
research assistance by Andy Adcroft.
p.   cm.
Includes bibliographical references and index.
ISBN 1-57181-850-2 : $49.95 — ISBN 1-57181-851-0 (pbk.) : $22.95
1. Automobile industry and trade — United States. 2. Automobile
industry and trade — Japan. 3. Automobile industry and trade —
Europe. I Williams, Karel.
HD9710.U52C26   1994
338.4'76292—dc20   94-29657
                                                    CIP

British Library Cataloging in Publication Data
A catalogue record for this book is available from the British Library.

Printed in the USA.

"Slowly we are learning,

We at least know this much

That we have to unlearn

Much that we are taught

And are growing chary

Of emphatic dogmas"

W. H. Auden

Karel Williams is a Reader in the Department of Accounting and Finance at the University of Manchester (Oxford Road, Manchester M13 9PL tel. UK 61 275 4016 • fax UK 61 275 4023).

Colin Haslam is a Reader in the Business Policy Section at East London University (Longbridge Road, Dagenham, Essex, RM8 2AS tel. UK 81 590 7722 • fax UK 81 849 3538).

Contents

——— ❖ ———

List of Tables

—— ❖ ——

List of Abbreviations

--- ❖ ---

AACP	Anglo American Council on Productivity.
ATM	Automatic Transfer Machines.
BEP	Break-even point.
BL	British Leyland.
BLMC	British Leyland Motor Corporation.
BMC	British Motor Corporation.
BMW	Bavarian Motor Works.
cpe	Corrected cars per employee.
CPRS	Central Policy Review Staff.
CV's	Commercial vehicles.
D & D	Design and Development.
EC	European Community.
EC12	The twelve members of the European Community.
ERM	Exchange Rate Mechanism.
EU	The European Union.
Ford UK	Ford operations based in the United Kingdom.
Ford US	Ford operations based in the United States.
GDP	Gross Domestic Product.
GM	General Motors.
GM Europe	General Motors, European operations.
GMAC	General Motors Acceptance Corporation, the finance division of General Motors.
GM US	General Motors, American operations.
HMSO	Her Majesty's Stationary Office.
hp	Horse power.
ILO	International Labor Office.
IMVP	International Motor Vehicle Program.

IMWF	International Metalworkers Federation.
JAMA	Japanese Automobile Manufacturers Association.
MAL	The moving assembly line.
MB	Mercedes-Benz.
MIT	Massachusetts Institute of Technology.
M-Form	A divisionalised organizational structure where power and autonomy are devolved.
MVP	Motor Vehicle Project.
NUMMI	The joint venture between General Motors and Toyota based in Freemont, California.
OE	Original Equipment.
OECD	Organization of Economic and Cultural Development.
Opel	The German division of General Motors.
PSA	The parent of Peugeot, Citroen and Peugeot-Talbot.
SIA	Subaru-Isuzu Automotive Inc., the joint venture in the United States.
SIC	Standard Industrial Classification.
SMMT	Society of Motor Manufacturers and Traders of Great Britain.
TMC	Toyota Motor Corporation.
TMS	Toyota Motor Sales.
TPS	Toyota Production System.
UAW	United Auto Workers.
UK	United Kingdom.
UN	United Nations.
UMTRI	University of Michigan Transportation Research Institute.
US	United States.
VA	Value Added.
VAG	Volkswagen-Audi-Group.
VAPE	Value Added per Employee.
VDA	Verband der Automobilindustrie.
VW	Volkswagen.
WIP	Work in Progress.

1
Introduction
Cars: Analysis, History and Cases.

———— ❖ ————

In popular culture cars signify the product, not the business activity of making and selling the product. This is because cars are potent symbols and accessories which are consumed world wide in image if not in substance; according to marketing legend, Mercedes Benz challenges Coca Cola for the title of world's most recognized brand although most of the world's consumers will never drive or own a car which carries the three-pointed star. The status of cars as product is indicated again by the proliferation of popular car magazines which sell to mainly male enthusiasts in all the advanced countries; their glossy pictures and overwritten text create a pornography of 'what will she do', 0 to 60 times, maximum speeds and all the rest. All this is slightly bizarre when most of the cars in the world's park are functional mobility boxes with as much inherent glamour as the fridge which provides the cool box in our kitchens. This point was captured by Paul Simon when he observed with uncharacteristic sharpness that 'cars are cars all over the world'.

For intellectuals who are concerned with popular culture, the product-centered semiotics which attach desire and fantasy to the mundane product is an obvious and privileged object of analysis. Hence, the famous Barthes essay in *Mythologies* which discusses the newly introduced and futurist Citroen DS model of the mid 1950s whose distinctive shark-like profile will be familiar to all of Barthes' older European readers. Those intellectuals who are concerned with the activity of making and selling cars cannot compete in this game. A scholarly history of the Citroen car company or a consultant's report on the competitiveness of the French industry would not and could not have the same appeal because these texts must renounce the element of desire and fantasy which sustains popular interest and because they must take responsibility for constituting an intellectual object which is not pregiven and obvious. The car factory and the car market simply do not have the same powerful, immediate appeal as the product. Thus, most print shops sell images of cars amongst the Monet and the Manet but few sell reproductions of the heroic Detroit Industry murals by Rivera which memorialize Rouge, the world's greatest car factory, and only scholarly pedants would be able to identify the figures of Charlie Sorensen and Edsel Ford who stare down from the South Wall mural.

The activity of making and selling cars is nevertheless of massive practical importance and considerable intellectual interest. It is of practical importance because cars sustain personal mobility and threaten to create urban gridlock; as we observe in Chapter 9, the EC 'park' now includes 135 million cars or roughly one car for every economically active person. The business of car manufacturing alone employs between 10-25 percent of the manufacturing workforce in all the advanced countries. The location of that manufacturing activity is of considerable macro importance because cars, as the only 'big-ticket' item which enters into international trade, are an important generator of trade deficits and surpluses; as Chapter 6 observes, cars and car parts account for 40 percent of the German and Japanese trade surpluses and 40 percent of the British and American trade deficits. Intellectually, the good news is that the activity is of considerable intellectual interest exactly because it is opaque and complex in a way that the product is not. The bad news is that this activity is generally constructed within intellectual frameworks which simplify and misrepresent it.

An activity as diverse and multi-dimensional as car making cannot of course be contained within one framework. The shelves of academic libraries show how the activity can be used to illustrate a wide range of discursive and real world processes and mechanisms. The Marxisant theory of the labor process would have existed with or without the car factory; but the literature which illustrates the problems and potential of labor process control in the twentieth century draws heavily on car factory examples. Equally, mainstream organization theory constructs categories like M-form, where power and authority is devolved to the different divisions, which are then illustrated using car firm examples; for generations of students, General Motors (GM) under Sloan has provided the classic example of the benefits of divisional organization. The same is true of organizing concepts like mass production which have become increasingly influential in recent years; the concept of mass production is always illustrated with the example of Ford and the Model T. Illustrations like this which sample the activity and invariably confirm discursive pre-conceptions should obviously be treated with some caution. But there is little scope for testing them against reliable independent knowledge because our modern understanding of the activity is generally constructed through the two frameworks of orthodox economics and management discourse.

The starting point of our book is that neither of these frameworks provides an adequate basis for understanding the activity and this position is developed in a running critique which threads through subsequent chapters. As a preliminary, it is useful to indicate the key texts and positions which we reject.

From the 1950s to the 1970s, the activity of car manufacture was represented as part of applied economics and the economic theory of the firm and the industry was dominant. The discursive incorporation of the activity into applied economics began in the 1940s with studies by Rostas and others of the productivity deficit with America; the enduring legacy was an (unjustified) combinatorial production function concept of production and a (problematic) set of measurement techniques focused on physical labor input which have been appropriated by all subsequent analysts. The most effective exponents of the applied economics approach were Maxcy and Silbertson (1959) who modestly and rigorously brought the theory of the firm to life by adding empirical information on costs and recent technical developments such as the automatic transfer machine. Theirs was the economics of the cost curve which supported the idea of semi-automatic reductions in cost as volume increased at the same time as it introduced the idea of a minimum-efficient scale which prevented the adoption of sophisticated high volume technology by small producers. In the 1970s, this style of descriptive empirical work (e.g. Rhys, 1972) was increasingly displaced by the new style of econometrics and modeling which used algebra, equations and plugged in data sets. The new approach was occasionally applied to cars where it could generate interesting results; but papers such as those of Fuss and Waverman (1992), which rightly emphasized the importance of capacity utilization, were so technical that they were primarily of interest only to other economists.

When the economists preferred to talk amongst themselves, their place in interpreting the activity of car manufacture was increasingly taken during the 1980s by business school academics who represented the discourse of management and tackled the new problem of Japanese success against the Americans who had hitherto led the world industry. The new approach was epitomized by the Massachusetts Institute of Technology (MIT) based International Automobile Project which subsequently became the International Motor Vehicle Project (IMVP); this project produced Altshuler et al. *The Future of the Automobile* (1984) which was billed as 'the most comprehensive assessment ever conducted of the world's largest industry' and Womack et al. *The Machine that Changed the World* (1990), a popular business book that became an international bestseller. New discourses are constructed partly out of the bits and pieces of the old and so it was in this case. The business-school professors borrowed the old productivity measurement techniques and some of the old themes which they used in an increasingly loose and rhetorical way which we criticize in Chapters 7 and 10; the Altshuler et al. book included an unsupported argument about flexible new technology and the end of scale while plant level productivity comparisons were the only statistical exhibit in the Womack et al. book. They added their own managerialist assumption that all problems could be solved by more and better management. While economics had effectively denied management agency, the new discourse presented management as the heroic actor which could always save the firm; thus Womack et al.'s book introduced the concept of 'lean production', an assembly of originally Japanese manufacturing techniques which all managements could imitate and through which all firms and industries could succeed.

The manifest absurdity of this evangelical Japanolatory inevitably provoked a critical reaction which included our own extended review of the Womack et al. book and its supporting research papers (Williams et al., 1992b). Our review established the weakness of the evidence which Womack et al. cited to support the hypothesis of a massive discontinuity between old-style mass production and new-style lean production; the review also observed that Womack et al. ignored the statistical evidence from company accounts and official sources which controverted their assertion that the Japanese had a huge 2 to 1 physical-efficiency advantage over the American car firms. This negative work was worthwhile as a ground-clearing exercise not least because it established that the IMVP could not meet these criticisms; their only response to date has been an article which does not deal with our criticisms but uses benchmarking comparisons to support their original position (Oliver et al., 1993). But a critical reading and secondary commentary on the illusions and errors of the IMVP could only have a limited effect because it provided no positive alternative. The statement of an alternative position was difficult because it involved reconceptualizing the activity of manufacturing and selling cars. This book represents a sustained attempt at reconceptualization, and in the rest of this introduction we will briefly comment on the form of the book which is divided into three major sections, and on the content of the nine different chapters which make up those sections.

The form of the book is relatively straightforward because it is divided into three sections labeled analysis, history and cases. The Analysis section consists of six relatively short chapters which provide a loose framework for the rest of the book. This first section identifies the basic similarities which unite the firms engaged in the business from Ford (Highland Park) to Toyota. The historical section consists of two longer chapters which separately examine Ford (Highland Park) and Toyota, the motor industry's two great productionist success stories, as well as British Motor Corporation/British Leyland Motor Corporation/British Leyland (BMC/BLMC/BL), the largest failure in the industry's history. This second section challenges the misappropriation of the industry's history through imaginary stereotypes such as mass and lean production. The third section again includes two longer chapters on three contemporary cases (the EC, Japan and America) which cover all the current major car producing regions. This section provides our interpretation of the competition between America and Japan as well as a sustained analysis of the interesting and neglected case of the EC industry.

The book took this form partly in response to the difficulty and intractability of the source material and the limits of our team's resources. While we dispute some of the results of recent work on the car industry, more fundamentally we reject the basis of those results in research methods which construct the past entirely through secondary sources and construct the present without exploiting the resources of company reports and accounts and of official statistics. One of our central aims was to extend the range and depth of our analysis by rectifying these deficiencies of research method and technique. Thus, the second historical section was based on archive research into primary sources on Ford as well as a comprehensive and exhaustive review of neglected secondary material on Toyota and BMC. The first and third sections are based on close, forensic analysis of the measures and ratios which can be extracted from company accounts and official sources. Wherever possible we used databases such as Eurostat on the European industry but the limits of Datastream coverage of the Japanese assemblers were such that much of the work on company accounts had to be done the hard way. Tables such as those on assembler value-added per employee or cash flow per vehicle produced (Tables 10.3 and 10.4) were obtained by extracting raw figures year by year from the hard copy accounts of six assemblers; several sub totals (plus the calculative formula for adding and subtracting sub totals to obtain the end result required) were then put into our own data base before we could press the key and obtain the appropriate result.

The decision to go for a method-driven research project was inevitable and correct. Our team uniquely included historians with long experience of primary research and accountants who were convinced that the kind of ratio analysis which figures in brokers' circulars could be developed so that it gave a broader view of the activity; like General Booth, their motto was 'why should the devil have the best tunes?' The only practical problem was that our research was unfunded hence considerable effort and sacrifice were required to sustain the commitment to time consuming traditional research methods and to hold the focus on interpreting the results. In terms of expense, this book cost less than $5,000 or 0.1 percent of the $5 million which the IMVP spent and all the rest was authors' time. As a way of motivating and holding together a team which was burdened with other commitments, we worked collectively on one section at a time. The initial research and final drafting of individual chapters was usually undertaken by one or two of the authors; but the interpretation and story line in each chapter was invariably the result of intense (and sometimes heated) internal discussion which involved all the authors. The individual chapters embody an ongoing argument with each chapter representing an interim solution which was then superseded by further research.

At the same time, the three-section form of our book is a device which solves the problem of the absence of development that bedevils so many business school texts where the thesis is stated, empirically illustrated and then recapitulated in a way which sentences readers to twenty years of boredom. The basic function of the archive research and ratio analysis is to generate an unpredictable, supplementary knowledge which is essential to any serious attempt to explore and define a complex object such as the activity of car manufacturing.

The form of our book is designed to allow us to incorporate the supplementary knowledge generated by these techniques into an open and developing book. Thus, the history and cases are not simply applications or illustrations of the analysis. This point should be self evident in the third Cases section which was drafted last and include a range of concepts, issues and theoretical references, from Machiavelli to social settlement, which are absent from the analysis section which was the first to be drafted. In our view the conceptual drift between sections one and three is not a defect but an intellectual virtue although we do accept that it makes the book more 'difficult'.

As the authors began to articulate and develop this project, they reluctantly accepted that *Cars* was another of their worthy books which would not sell on airport bookstands; this was a matter of personal regret because all the authors are well past the stage where too much success too soon would turn their heads. A difficult book will inevitably lose readers who are accustomed to prepackaged knowledge where 'Big Ideas' are clearly labelled and ideally set up in a binary way so that everything is conveniently one thing or the other; similarly, a book which is concerned to generate interesting knowledge with social value will not appeal to those who want useful knowledge which has a managerial 'how to do it' value. Our response is that these are sales well lost insofar as our aim was always to establish an intellectual knowledge which was worthy of the complex object of car making and selling. In military terms, our aim was not to take as much ground as possible but to establish a bridgehead position from which further advance could be sustained. The book will have succeeded if it opens up the possibility of future work by ourselves and others who draw on the research techniques, concepts and results; our book is deliberately written in a way which does not prescribe the form and content of this work. In many ways the key test is whether others find our work useful; in this introduction, like Yeats in his last afternoon as himself, we can only hope to become our admirers.

If we turn now to content, it is fairly easy to summarize the themes and findings of the different sections. Thus, the first analysis section aims to characterize production and to establish the connection between the conceptually distinct domains of production, market and finance. Our characterization of the productive process as repetitive manufacturing is different because we put the main emphasis on standardization of the process path; car manufacturing since Henry Ford has involved the movement of a bulky, heavy and awkward object incorporating some 15,000 parts through a multiplicity of short-cycle processes along a standardized conversion path. The analysis section also emphasizes the connection to the market much more strongly than in most other accounts of the activity; in repetitive manufacturing, the basic aim of flow cannot be sustained against market restriction. As for the financial results of cash flow and profit, these are not represented as objectives but as results which drop out for those firms and industries which solve their productive problems and line up a suitable market.

The order of exposition in successive chapters of the first section is however different from this order of analysis. Because the activity is so widely misunderstood, Chapter 2 (the first of the analysis chapters) opens with an analysis of financial ratios in major assembler firms which shows that in car manufacturing, as in other kinds of manufacturing, labor typically takes 70 percent of value-added, leaving a relatively small residual available as free cash for product renewal and profit for shareholders. This point establishes the basic importance of taking labor hours and cost out of the product as a way of improving or maintaining financial ratios. The physical problems of car manufacturing as repetitive manufacturing are then introduced; the key physical problem is that a multiplicity of heterogeneous operations must be repeated on short cycles.

Chapter 3 considers whether and how labor can be taken out through investment in fixed capital equipment or by what we call productive intervention. Investment in fixed capital equipment is generally emphasized in economics and fits the popular stereotype of manufacturing as a machine-centered activity. It is easy to show that car manufacturing is different because the largest object of investment is not machines but tools, dies and fixtures which allow the machines to be reused for the manufacture of new models. Productive intervention is our own concept for other more effective kinds of intervention during the design and manufacturing phases. In design and development the objective is product simplification and in production the aim is to take labor out by improving materials flow and recomposing labor tasks. This argument about productive intervention, like all the rest in Chapters 2 and 3, represents the activity in simplified, static terms; Chapters 4, 5 and 6 relax various assumptions and introduce ever increasing complexity.

Chapter 4 explores the conditions of improved manufacturing flow inside and outside the factory; the internal and external conditions include technical control over production, social control over the workforce and sustained market demand. Against this background, when most firms cannot achieve or maintain improved flow, Chapter 4 emphasizes that wage levels are just as important as sectoral hours to build; we totally reject any analysis which, like the IMVP, emphasizes physical differences in hours to build without considering the financial effects of differences in wage levels. Chapter 5 explores the impact of the market by analyzing the different home market environments within which American, European and Japanese firms have operated over the past twenty years. This analysis is continued in Chapter 6 which shows how unbalanced international trade intensifies disadvantage for the unsuccessful just as it represents escape from home market constraints for the successful. The most important and striking conclusion is that most assemblers (including all the Japanese except Toyota) are weak firms with a limited ability to stand market downturn; as Chapter 5 shows, the average car firm has considerable difficulty in generating the cash for model renewal and the profit to keep shareholders content.

The second historical section of the book aims to destroy currently fashionable attempts to characterize the activity of car manufacture in terms of opposed modern and post-modern production systems; on the one hand mass production is supposedly exemplified by Ford (Highland Park) and the Model T while its successor is variously termed lean production or Toyota production system because it is universally supposed to have originated inside the Toyota company. For those who believe in such concepts, the history of car manufacturing becomes the story of the diffusion of these systems; while failures, like those of BMC and the British industry, are attributed to incomplete adoption of the best practice system. Against this, the second historical section piles up evidence against the identification of Ford and Toyota as system prototypes and reinforces this by presenting an alternative explanation of BMC's failure. If the technical problems of repetitive manufacturing are always much the same, the technical factory solutions are much more similar than most social scientists suppose. It is above all the external market conditions which underwrite the temporary success of firms like Ford and Toyota and guarantee the failure of firms like BMC.

Chapter 7 discusses the success of Ford (Highland Park) and of Toyota and presents these firms as heroic exceptions rather than system prototypes. The argument begins by questioning the standard identification of Ford with mass production; the stereotype of Fordism as semi-skilled workers and dedicated machines producing a standardized product is tested against the archive evidence and found to be wanting. We have published these arguments before (Williams et al., 1992c and 1993c), but our attack on the mythology of the Toyota production system is entirely new. It begins by registering the ambiguities about the nature and extent of a system which would be better called the Toyota assembly system because it has always relied on the feed of cheap components from a low wage supplier system. The myth of 'Ohnoism' and the autodidactic Japanese is then displaced in an account which for the first time weighs the contribution of Ohno in production against that of Kamiya who headed Toyota Motor Sales. A final long-run comparison of Ford and Toyota's measurable achievements suggests that Toyota did not realize an unprecedented level of efficiency.

Chapter 8 considers the failure of BMC/BLMC/BL which is the obverse of Toyota and Ford's success. Failure, which is seldom carefully analyzed in the management literature, is quite as instructive as success. Against accounts which emphasize BMC's failure to adopt the full mass-production system we argue that BMC's failure was market led. Woollard, whose grasp of flow manufacturing equals that of Ohno, provided the company with world-class manufacturing facilities just as Issigonis provided class-leading product designs. The company's problem was its failure to develop a product range which could surmount market limitations and generate the cash for product renewal. From the early 1960s these problems were intensified by slower growth in a maturing car market. And from the late 1960s they were intensified by an increasing reliance on managers who understood much less about the business than their car-making predecessors. Generally, we are fairly skeptical about the role of management which so often struggles ineffectually against structural limitations and constraints, but in this case management did make a difference by failing to recognize the force of these limitations and constraints.

The third section on contemporary cases aims to open out the analysis in new directions. The analysis of Europe, America and Japan, the three main producing regions, works by incorporating concepts, issues and evidence. This section introduces the idea of two alternative strategies of cost reduction and cost recovery; it reinforces and articulates the concept of an arc-like trajectory which is introduced in our treatment of Ford and Toyota; and it places much emphasis on the concept of social settlement which encapsulates the structurally determined variables around wages and hours which are generally beyond management control. On issues, the theme of grid-lock and the growing contradiction between urbanism and car use is introduced in a way which complements the earlier treatment of saturated and cyclical markets. On evidence, this section provides a synthesis of earlier points and positions because Chapter 9 reviews European performance and Chapter 10 systematically contrasts the American and Japanese industries.

Chapter 9 on the European industry is written in a Machiavellian framework which puts the main emphasis on power without responsibility. The EC producers make up a weak and divided industry whose nationally-based assemblers have lost the protection of their national governments without gaining the protection of the supranational EC which has misguidedly ceded market space to the Japanese producers. This chapter refutes interpretations which assume or assert that the European industry has done nothing in the face of the impending threat of Japanese competition; the Germans and Swedes pursued strategies of cost recovery by moving the product up market and forced the rest of the European industry into cost reduction and taking out labor hours. The financial results were disappointing because everybody took the hours out so that the chronically loss-making industry is now unable to satisfy the interests of the different stakeholders and must look after its shareholders by sacrificing its workers. The most likely outcome is predatory restructuring, whose mechanisms and results are examined through an analysis of the Renault-Volvo merger. Although the merger was derailed by Swedish opposition, the calculations of both sides are 'extremely interesting. For Volvo the merger was a way of exiting an unprofitable auto business while Renault was hoping to strengthen its commitment to its auto business whose profit could have been improved by rationalization at the expense of Swedish workers who have enjoyed the world industry's highest wages and shortest working hours.

Chapter 10 considers the competition between the American and Japanese industries. The (unexpected) success of the Japanese firms against the American Big Three, who had traditionally led the world industry, is important in itself and as an intellectual puzzle; most of the work on cars over the past fifteen years or more has been trying to answer the question of how and why the Japanese won out in this competitive struggle. The current orthodoxy supposes that the

Japanese won because their management practices and choices were superior. Against this we argue that the Americans were doomed to fail (regardless of the quality of their management) because their national social settlement imposed a series of cost handicaps which we illustrate and quantify; in the period up to 1985, the Japanese had the advantage of low wages and long hours as well as the benefit of a home market which was largely immune to the cyclical fluctuations which punished the American majors. We have chosen to present this material as the last chapter of our book because it explicitly raises the issue of what the product and the activity embody and represent. Within the two orthodox frameworks of economics and management the answer to the question is that product and activity represent efficiency or inefficiency and good management or bad management. Our own rather different answer is that the product and the activity both represent social relations; the contest between America and Japan was and is the contest between different social settlements.

In this way we hope, through our work, to reinforce a certain political and moral sensibility. The most offensive aspect of the IMVP position was the 'win win' position that more efficient production of cheaper cars could come through the spread of management practices and forms of work which employees actually preferred; in this respect the IMVP did no more than echo the business school rhetoric of human resource management about liberated and empowered workers. Like other critics we noted that the IMVP cited no empirical evidence to support its position. But we did not believe that it was useful to oppose this position directly with our own politics and morality which includes terms like intensification and exploitation nor did we believe that it was easy to measure these realities in ways which were convincing. Instead we have concentrated throughout this book on the technical and the measurable so as to establish an empirical basis for the moral point that, in the words of the Book of Ecclesiastes, the race is not to the swift nor yet riches to men of understanding. The car companies and industries which failed were not generally slow or stupid; they were, like most of the unsuccessful since biblical times, only in the wrong place at the wrong time. As the American, Swedish and German cases show the key misfortune is often to pay wages which are higher and work hours which are shorter than those of competitors; the Japanese, who now pay relatively high wages are increasingly exposed to this risk which increasingly afflicts all the advanced countries in cars and electronics. And the implications are of course political; if our analysis is correct, the problems of the average car company like Renault, Ford or Nissan cannot be solved by management attempts to emulate the heroic exceptions who have captured the available market space or to reduce costs to the level of low wage competitors; the problems of the average car company can only be solved by political regulation.

January 1994

✦ ✦ ✦

2
Financial and Physical Characteristics

———— ❖ ————

If we wish to understand the activity of car manufacture, we must appreciate the similarities which unite, and the differences which separate, the various firms and national industries. In this chapter we begin by considering the similarities in the form of financial and physical characteristics which have given the cars business since Ford and the Model T its distinctive identity. Some basics have not changed in eighty years and all car manufacturers and component makers face certain recurrent problems which are defined by the characteristics of the business. This position does not imply seamless continuity because later chapters will analyze differences, especially differences in external circumstances which separate different firms and national industries.

Financial Characteristics

We will begin by considering financial ratios, especially those relating to the composition of costs and to the distribution of value-added. These ratios provide a general basis for understanding any business activity and may provide a basis for demarcating one activity from others which have different ratios. In terms of the average composition of costs and distribution of value-added, the cars business is not so very different from many other kinds of manufacturing. The most important distinguishing characteristic of the cars business is the unusually severe cyclical fluctuations in labor's share of value-added; these fluctuations afflict those car firms which have large exposure to cyclical car markets and therefore suffer wide variations in volume and capacity utilization. For purposes of this chapter's initial exposition of the overall characteristics of the activity we will ignore this complication which is addressed in later chapters.

The activity of car manufacture shares many fundamental financial characteristics with other forms of manufacturing, but these characteristics are nevertheless frequently neglected or misunderstood in management discourse, industrial economics or management accounting. Business school graduates can reproduce key concepts from Michael Porter's oeuvre (1985, 1990), but often cannot generalize about the composition of costs or the distribution of value-added in manufacturing or any other kind of activity. They use 'added value' as a management slogan but cannot calculate value-added by either the additive or subtractive method. Those who have studied management accounting will have been confused by textbook examples which reinforce the occasional assertion that labor cost is relatively small and unimportant in modern manufacturing.

This confusion about whether labor costs matter arises partly because in cars, as in most other mechanical engineering activity, firms producing finished cars or major components buy in half or more of the value of the product in the form of components. This basic fact is encapsulated in Table 2.1 which gives the purchases-to-sales ratio for twelve major car firms; like the two succeeding tables, Table 2.1 removes the effects of cyclicality by presenting averages for the decade 1980 to 1991 which runs from one cyclical downturn to the next. Purchases include raw materials and services as well as components, but components are by far and away the largest item in the bill for purchases. For all the American and European firms, the purchases-to-sales ratio ranges between an average of 62 to 69 percent. The only current exceptions are the Japanese who are very much less vertically integrated. One major firm, General Motors , used to be an exception of a different kind: its traditional US policy of vertical integration meant that about 45 percent of the value of the GM car originated in its own factories. The Japanese have consistently been (and remain) at the other end of the spectrum: firms like Toyota, Nissan and Honda buy in around 80 percent or more of the value of the car from suppliers.

Table 2.1: Purchases-to-Sales Ratio for Twelve Major Car Companies, Average of 1980-1991.

Company	Purchases-to-Sales Ratio (percent)
Toyota	86.3
Nissan	80.7
Honda	79.5
Mazda	86.8
GM	65.6
Ford	62.2
Chrysler	64.9

Table 2.1 (*continued*)

Company	Purchases-to-Sales Ratio (percent)
VAG	61.6
BMW	65.4
Fiat	62.2
PSA	66.3
Ford UK	69.4

Notes: 1. The purchases-to-sales ratio is calculated as sales minus value-added (calculated as labor costs including social charges plus depreciation plus net income or pre-tax profits). In a year when a company makes a loss this is not included in the value-added calculation: instead conversion costs (value-added) are taken as labor plus depreciation costs;

2. In all cases the period covered by the above calculation is 1980–1991 except as follows: Fiat 1987–1991; PSA 1984–1990; Ford UK 1982–1991; Mazda 1982–1991.

Source: Consolidated Company Reports and Accounts, various years.

The implication is that manufacturing is only a loose description of what most car and major component firms do: assembly and manufacture is a more accurate way of describing their activity. This is especially so in the case of the Japanese industry where an unusually large part of the conversion work is undertaken by suppliers. One of the paradoxes of the activity is that the end product is very strongly identified with an assembler's brand name; the customer recognizes and asks for a Ford car or a Bosch alternator. But more, and in the case of Toyota or Nissan much more, than half the value of the product originates outside the factories of the firm which badges it.

Because 'cost is elsewhere', the price and quality of bought-in components is crucial to competitivity. For all car firms, especially those which are financially struggling, the most immediately obvious lever of cost reduction is always component prices: car manufacturers who want to take costs out quickly must access cheaper components or, if they can do it themselves more cheaply, bring component production in-house. Components are also a major determinant of end product quality; half or more of warranty claims on new cars are caused by component failure. Unrecovered warranty costs dent manufacturer's profit as well as consumer confidence; the 1991 edition Rover 800 was a large car with poor build quality whose first year warranty cost for the low specification base model were £325 per car which was probably three to four times as large as on comparable Japanese cars (Coffey, 1992). Purchases, of course, include services and materials (as well as components) but neither of these is a dynamic source of substantial competitive advantage. Most of the materials used in cars and components are internationally traded commodities whose prices are often denominated in dollars and effectively equalized through trade.

Value-added is, in additive terms, the sum which represents that which the firm adds to the value of bought-in components, materials and services. Or, alternatively, in subtractive terms, value-added represents the sum which remains in the firm after it has paid for bought-in components, materials and services. This value-added is appropriated by (or distributed to) labor and capital. Labor claims its share as wages and salaries whilst capital obtains its share as depreciation and retained profit (which covers the claims of physical capital) and distributed profit (which covers the claims of shareholders and those who have lent to the firm). Any analysis of value-added at the firm level brings out the significance of internally controlled labor costs whose importance is obscured as long as the analysis considers only cost composition where the main item is bought-in materials and components. The centrality of internally-controlled labor costs is then further obscured where accounting classification is practiced, making total costs equal to prime (direct costs) plus overheads (indirect costs).

Internal labor's share of total costs is never trivial if we add together all the wages paid to different kinds of internal labor (direct, indirect, supervisory and managerial). Management accounting claims that direct labor accounts for only 10-12 percent of total costs in modern manufacturing are misleading because they refer only to the cost of direct labor which accounts for only about one-third of total payroll costs. As has been argued elsewhere (Williams et al., 1989) in mechanical engineering the payroll costs of all internal labor add up to an average of 30-35 percent of total costs.

If labor's share of total costs is important the share of labor costs in value-added (net output) is overwhelming. This fact is illustrated in Table 2.2, which again removes the effects of cyclicality by presenting an average.

Table 2.2: Labor's Share of Value-added in Twelve Major Car
Companies, Average 1980–91.

Company	Labor's Share of Value-added (percent)
Toyota	42.2
Nissan	68.5
Honda	50.9
Mazda	64.9
GM	73.8
Ford	71.5
Chrysler	76.6
VAG	72.2
BMW	63.1
Fiat	64.3
PSA	71.9
Ford UK	66.6

Notes: 1. Value-added is calculated as labor costs including social charges, plus depreciation, plus net income or profits pre-tax. Labor's share of value-added is labor costs as a percentage of the value-added;

2. In all cases the period covered by the above calculation is 1980–1991 except as follows: Fiat 1987–1991, PSA 1984–1990, Ford UK 1982–1991, Mazda 1982–1991.

Source: Consolidated Company Reports and Accounts, various years.

The message of Table 2.2 is simple: in all major car firms (except Toyota and Honda) labor's share of value-added is in the range of 63 to 76 percent. Or, less exactly, in most years labor claims two-thirds of what the car firm adds as value. In this context it is clear that labor costs matter a great deal. If, at any time, and for any reason, labor's share of value-added rises above its 'norm' of around 70 percent, then labor very quickly squeezes what is available to capital for investment, depreciation and profit.

As Chapter 7 demonstrates, world leading manufacturers, like Ford (Highland Park) at the beginning of this century, and Toyota at the end, are distinguished by their ability to take labor out of the finished product. But even these heroic leaders find it difficult to hold labor's share of value-added below 40 percent; Ford's (Highland Park) labor share of value-added was rising to 39 percent in 1915-16 and labor's share of value-added at Toyota averages 42 percent over the period 1980-91. The problem of labor's relatively high share of value-added is eternal because labor still takes the better part of half of value-added even in firms which have spectacular success in continuously taking labor out. Labor's share does not fall below 40 percent because the benefits of taking labor out are either claimed by the workforce in the form of higher real wages or given away to consumers as a result of marketing strategy or competitive pressures in the product market. In such cases the long run result is a re-normalization of labor's share at absolutely lower cost levels.

If labor costs account for two-thirds of value-added in most car firms, that conclusion prompts a re-definition of the component cost problem which was identified in the earlier discussion of the composition of costs. 'Component' is the engineering or accounting term for the physical object that presents itself in the later stages of production in an assembler/manufacturer's factory; but the cost of that component mainly represents congealed labor from the earlier stages of adding value. When the car firm buys in components from outside, much of that cost is labor cost. At a sectoral level, taking physical labor hours out or accessing lower wages is the main determinant of competitivity. The obvious immediate problem of the car manufacturer may be component costs, but for the sector as a whole the fundamental problem is that, at whatever stage it appears, manufacturing conversion requires a substantial physical labor input, and adding value incurs substantial labor costs. The fundamental problem is simply disguised if the manufacture of components takes place at different stages and the work is performed by (legally) separate firms in a long value-adding chain.

At the firm level, the importance of labor's share of value-added is reinforced because management of labor's share of value-added is crucial to the maintenance of healthy cashflow and positive contribution to profit. This is a matter of simple arithmetic when cashflow = value added − payroll, and profit = value-added − (labor costs including social charges + depreciation). The problems of managing the residual are aggravated because depreciation usually takes a large part of that which remains when labor has been paid.

Table 2.3: Depreciation's Share of Value-added in Twelve Major Car Companies, Average of 1980–91.

Company	Depreciation's Share of Value-added (percent)
Toyota	25.3
Nissan	20.0
Honda	17.1
Mazda	25.7
GM	18.1
Ford	14.6

Table 2.3 (*continued*)

Company	Depreciation's Share of Value-added (percent)
Chrysler	13.2
VAG	19.1
BMW	17.4
Fiat	13.1
PSA	10.6
Ford UK	17.1

Notes: 1. The above calculation expresses depreciation as a share of value-added conversion costs. When companies make a loss, this is included in the value-added calculation;

2. In all cases the period covered by the above calculation is 1980–1991 except as follows: Fiat 1987–1991, PSA 1984–1990, Ford UK 1982–1991, Mazda 1982–1991.

Source: Consolidated Company Reports and Accounts, various years.

Each year car and component companies have to make a depreciation allowance for consumption of existing capital stock. Depreciation can be regarded as a semi-fixed item because all the major car manufacturers depreciate plant and machinery at the rate of 10 percent per annum. The resulting depreciation charge is substantial because all car companies have a large stock of capital equipment per worker. As will be demonstrated in the next chapter, most car manufacturers have around $50,000 of net fixed assets per employee and Japanese majors like Toyota have more than $140,000 per employee. As a result, depreciation claims an average of 11-25 percent of the firm's internal value-added fund.

After depreciation has claimed a large part of what remains when labor has been paid, the residual of the residual has to contribute to net new investment, tax and distributed profit. In these circumstances it is hardly surprising that profitability is precarious and, as we will argue in Chapter 5, highly vulnerable to market fluctuations.

The general pattern of value-added distribution is such that the mission of all car firms and national sectors must be to take labor out so as to improve absolute labor costs and relative value-added ratios. But many car companies and most national sectors do not succeed in this mission. As we shall see in the second half of this book, the German and American car sectors have no sustained record of taking hours out from 1969 to the late 1980s, and the reduction of hours in the Japanese sector was not sustained during the 1980s as the Japanese product became more complex when the industry moved up-market. To understand how and why the mission fails, it is necessary to understand more about the physical characteristics of the activity and about the external circumstances in which car firms operate.

Physical Characteristics

According to the dominant ideology of American management over the last generation, the physical does not matter or, at least, is of secondary importance. Management is asserted to be about strategic planning and financial control skills which can be transferred between activities; the operational detail of widgets, cars or fast food is secondary and irrelevant for top management. The most successful car companies and national sectors have not shared this ideology. Toyota, like Ford (Highland Park) in its glory days, is concerned with the physical detail of production; Toyota inverts the American ideology with its company slogan of *genbashugi* or 'production comes first'. In Germany, the national manufacturing culture puts considerable emphasis on *Technik* or the practical knowledge relevant to an activity, a knowledge which includes production. Within the Japanese or German frame of reference, productive improvement is an important lever for improving the financial ratios of the business.

As a result of the relative down-grading of operational detail in America for much of the post war period, many senior executives and business school academics have an inadequate understanding of the problems of production which are considered in this chapter and the possibilities of intervention which are analyzed in the next. Taichi Ohno, the Toyota production guru, observed that 'no one can understand manufacturing by just walking through the production area and looking at it' (Ohno, 1988, p.57). The writings of many academic commentators on the activity suggest that they are determined to prove Ohno right because they miss the activity's essential characteristic of pathway standardization and see imaginary characteristics such as standardization of the product or dedicated machinery.

There are important cross sectional differences in the size of supplier factories and the extent of vertical integration in different sectors. Equally, over time, there are important changes in available process technology with the advent of Automatic Transfer Machines (ATMs) in the 1950s or robot body lines in the 1970s. But in car manufacture the materials and work in progress always travel down the same standardized conversion pathway and car manufacturing is therefore an example of repetitive manufacturing which is the polar opposite of job shop manufacture where the conversion path is different with each new job. The conversion pathway has work stations for manual and machine operations and the machines along the pathways are commonly described as 'dedicated' meaning that they are only capable of performing a particular operation. This description is at best imprecise, if not downright misleading. The car and component industry today continues the pre-1916 American engineering practice of using mainly general purpose machines such as drills and presses which are fitted with special purpose, removable tools and fixtures that adapt them for particular productive tasks; the significance of this requirement for special purpose tools is explored in the discussion of investment in the next chapter. For the moment we need only observe that those who use the concept of 'mass production' are mistaken when they assume that any change in model or specification involves scrapping the machine.

Repetitive manufacture has broad possibilities and characteristic limitations. Within the constraint of the standardized pathway it is never easy (but usually possible) to accommodate variety such as cars with different bodies or alternators with different outputs. Variety is possible if the machines can be changed over so that they can work on pieces of different dimensions and if the assembly labor content is roughly similar. Thus many car and component factories operate on a multi-model or mixed model basis at different stages in the production process: multi-modeling means production of assemblies like axles in batches with tool changeover in between; mixed modeling means production of two or more models simultaneously as when cars of different, maybe unrelated, types run down the same final assembly lines. There are obvious limits to this kind of flexibility. Since, for example, the pathway and process requirements are different for alternators and starter motors it would be very difficult to shift between these product lines within the same production area.

The nature and shape of the pathway also needs careful consideration. This is all the more necessary since in popular culture the car factory is appropriated through the image of the final assembly line where the finished product takes shape. Thus there is a strong immediate tendency to construe pathway in terms of a straight line sequence of operations. From this point of view, the whole of the production system which produces a car can be conceived, in Woollard's metaphor (Woollard, 1954, p.48), as being like a complex river system; the final assembly line is an estuary leading to the sea of the market and the estuary is fed by an upstream network of tributaries and branches. While the river metaphor may be useful in putting the role of the final assembly line into perspective, it is also seriously misleading because it over emphasizes linearity and continuity. In particular it obscures the distinction between stages in the production process and activities within a particular process.

The basic sequence of major conversion stages along the pathway has to be linear and progressive; with pressed steel bodies, for example, it is necessary to press metal panels before they can be welded into bodies at the next stage, just as welding has to precede painting. But within major process stages, it is not necessary to organize production tasks on a linear basis because the work in progress can be diverted into U-shaped cells or processed in side bays. Thus the Japanese have developed cellular systems for manufacturing such assemblies as rear light clusters and German firms like Mercedes Benz, as well as the Japanese, are developing substitutes for the final assembly line which route car shells into bays where teams of workers can work on several fitting-out tasks.

The analogy of the river is also misleading because there cannot be continuous flow along the pathway when it is segmented into discrete (supplier) factories which are owned by independent firms. No one since Henry Ford has pursued the ideal of building all or most of the car under one roof in a factory where iron ore goes in at one end and finished cars roll out at the other. In the inter war period, Ford constructed three factories at Rouge, Cologne and Dagenham on the principle of integrated, single-site manufacture for each major national market. More recently the dominant tendency has been in the opposite direction so that we now have flows across national boundaries. From the late 1960s, Ford of Europe pioneered a new kind of multinational factory network so that its final assembly lines in one European country would be fed with gearboxes and engines that had been manufactured and assembled by Ford in other European countries; the Japanese do much the same across the Pacific when they feed their American transplants with Japanese components.

All this permits a wide variation both in the degree of integration and the means of its implementation. Despite the growing international trade in components and assemblies, national and regional peculiarities and differences remain important so that the pattern of segmentation is different in each of the major producing areas (Japan, America and Europe). To begin with there are important differences about the methods of control and ownership used to coordinate different factories in the supply chain. A firm like GM (US) which has traditionally been relatively vertically integrated, has used bureaucratic coordination of factories like those of Saginaw which is a wholly-owned subsidiary producing power steering mainly for GM. Most other Western car firms prefer arms-length market relations with independent suppliers who sell their expertise and product to several car firms. BMW and GM (Europe) both buy power steering from the German supplier firm ZF which also makes automatic gearboxes for many smaller European manufacturers. As for the Japanese, interlocking shareholdings are used to create networks of captive suppliers which feed most of their output to one major assembler.

There are also substantial national differences in the pattern of physical segmentation into establishments of different sizes. In final assembly plant size there is relatively little significant variation because all national industries have a strong preference for final assembly plants which integrate press, weld, paint and final assembly operations in modules of 200,000 or multiples thereof. Engines and gearboxes can normally be fitted into more than one model and need a larger output to pay back heavy development costs: they are thus often supplied from separate plants which feed more than one final assembly plant. As the next chapter demonstrates, this general preference for a minimum size of assembly plant reflects the technical requirements of the high speed automatic equipment which is generally used in pressing and welding. The largest final assembly plants in the world are VW Wolfsburg and Toyota Takaoka, both of which have capacity to assemble more than 700,000 cars per year. But these plants are less different than this suggests because they generally use industry standard equipment and techniques with the lines doubled up as necessary to meet the output requirement.

If there are no great national differences in size of final assembly plant, there are (Table 2.4) very large variations in average plant size over the motor vehicle sector as a whole. This reflects the very large differences in the average size of the component supplying plant in the various national industries. The table shows that the German industry is distinguished by a strong preference for large plants because the average size plant in the German motor vehicle sector as a whole employs more than 1,000. The United States and the UK have a much smaller average plant size with 120 to 140 employees, while the average size establishment in the Japanese motor vehicles sector employs just 73. Given that Japan's final assembly plants are comparable in size with those elsewhere, this means that there must be a substantial number of very small establishments in the Japanese motor vehicle sector.

Table 2.4: Average Size of Motor Vehicle Establishments in Five Car Producing Countries.

Country	Average number of employees per establishment	Year
Germany	1,036	1989
USA	143	1987
France	100	1990
Japan	73	1989
UK	124	1988

Source: Industrial Statistics Yearbook, various years.

Only the Germans have set up a national industry which conforms to the stereotype of car and car component production as a 'large-scale', big establishment activity. Japan shows that the production of many small and simple components, like window winders or throttle return springs, can be organized on a semi-workshop basis. It is equally possible to organize final assembly on a small scale basis where 'knocked down' kits of parts are supplied from a central facility; after 1912, Ford introduced a policy of regional 'branch assembly' in the United States and many manufacturers still use this system to supply small markets which restrict finished imports.

The physical segmentation of the pathway into different establishments establishes one kind of discontinuity in production. It is a discontinuity which is both embodied and symbolized by the racked components and assemblies in the containers which shuttle between the manufacturing and assembly factories. There may be differences about the number of components in the rack and the length of the journey but all national car industries have their container shuttles. Another kind of discontinuity is established by the nature of the process work undertaken within the factories. Any significant span is likely to include distinct and heterogeneous process operations with machines which run at different rates and take different times to complete their operations. It obviously becomes difficult to sustain continuity of production as soon as these conversion operations have to be repeated on a short cycle to meet high-volume demand.

In repetitive manufacturing, goods are fabricated or assembled as they pass through a series of work stations each of which consists of one or more machines and/or one or more workers. Car and component factories are loose systems of interconnected work stations which are either adjacent to, or connected by, handling systems such as slides, roller beds or powered conveyors. The work of the stations can be scheduled on a push or pull basis; in a push system the order to build is given to the first work station and in a pull system the order to build comes from the last station. In either case the system is fundamentally driven by the build requirement for regular delivery of one finished unit at a set-time interval: every major process stage which produces assemblies for the finished product must operate on this delivery cycle which is calculated by dividing the number of units required each day into the available operating time. In car or component factories the standard working day consists of two shifts of around eight hours (except in a few continuous or capital intensive processes) and operating time will always be shorter because the lines stop for meal breaks, machine changeover and breakdown.

The broad principles apply over a wide range of repetitive manufacture. But whereas in making super-tankers or railway rolling stock, the delivery cycle can be measured in weeks or days, volume car manufacture involves the high-speed repetition of the process and assembly tasks on a very short delivery cycle which is usually measured in seconds. Take, for example, a typical final-assembly plant producing 200,000 units a year, working a two-shift system and operating for 80 percent of the day. In this quite ordinary plant, the delivery cycle will be around one car every sixty seconds. There is an additional complication that, periodically, the plant must also changeover to produce a new model or mix of models at the same rate. Cars is a business which combines fashion with improvements in features and performance that necessarily require the occasional introduction of new models. Individual models now generally have lives of three to ten years before replacement. At that stage many components will be changed although some assemblies such as engines, gearboxes and floorpans may be carried over. Changeover, when much of the tooling has to be replaced and many of the process operations are modified, is at least only an occasional problem. The larger difficulty is the everyday one: coping with processes which are heterogeneous and where natural work rates are often very different from the required delivery cycle.

The resulting obstacles are best illustrated by considering the imbalance between work rates in pressing and final assembly, the first and last operations in a typical European final-assembly factory. A final assembly line will usually be 'balanced' by subdividing the assembly tasks into units each of which corresponds to the delivery cycle; but, given the nature of many assembly tasks and the limits of the human operative, it is practically very difficult to divide assembly tasks into units smaller than sixty seconds. Thus, where large outputs are required the final tracks must be doubled up; VW Wolfsburg, for example, had no less than five final-assembly tracks producing 3,700 cars per day in the 1980s. By way of contrast the traditional lines of four or five heavy presses, which work in tandem to form car panels in successive operations, operate at a rate of five to seven power strokes per minute (Ford UK communication, 26 May 1992). This work rate is so fast that presses must be regularly changed over to produce batches of different panels. Problems of balancing and synchronization are complicated by the need for variety when larger car factories typically produce a mix of models. Furthermore some irregularity is unavoidable because machines break down and have to be maintained as well as changed over; heavy press equipment will probably only be available for use for 80 percent of the working day.

Problems about differences in work rate and irregularity can be covered in a variety of ways so that downstream process operations are not continuously interrupted by upstream irregularity. Layout is relevant because if work stations are, for example, laid out in circle or bay arrangements, it is not necessary to synchronize the cycle speed of every work operation within the bay. It is not easy to implement such a response. Thus, the 'solution' of holding buffer stocks within and between different process stages remains the most common way of limiting downstream interruption. Some car firms manage to keep minimal buffers within process stages but all keep significant buffers between processes with large differences in work rate; when we visited Toyota Takaoka in 1988 they were pressing panels for stock in batches equal to the requirements of three shifts. Because most car and major component manufacturing operate with substantial buffer stocks, the work in progress typically spends much more time queuing between work stations than it spends being processed at the work stations. If we again take the example of the final assembly factory, process cycle times are measured in seconds, but the time taken to 'build' a car from cutting sheet metal to driving the car off the final line is measured in hours or even days. Ford at Dagenham estimate that if body building and final assembly times are added together it takes two days to build a Fiesta. (Ford UK communication, 18th August 1993).

This description of the physical problems of car manufacture raises the issue of what, if anything, is distinctive about this particular kind of manufacturing activity. Part of the answer is that the equipment and physical activity inside car and component factories is quite distinct from what goes on inside most (non-car) factories. For example, all car and major component factories use powered final assembly lines, but a recent general survey of British manufacturing found that only one-third of British factories use assembly lines and only half those lines were power driven or mechanically paced (New and Myers, 1986, p.6). This point must not be pressed too far because powered lines are by no means unique to cars and the problems of rapid/short cycle repetition, heterogeneous processes and occasional model changeover also occur, for example, in the production of electrical and electronic consumer goods like refrigerators or televisions.

Another part of the answer is that, in relation to these other kinds of consumer-good manufacturing, the cars business is distinctive because it manufactures a product which is heavier and more complex in its process requirement than any other consumer durable. These characteristics make for quite fundamental differences. Even modestly-sized cars like the VW Golf and the Fiat Tipo in the European medium hatchback class weigh around one ton and the slightly larger Honda Accord weighs four hundredweights more; the class leading 1993 VW Golf in standard 1.8 CL hatchback form had a kerb weight of 20.3 cwt. Furthermore, cars of this type and size incorporate a total of 12,000 to 15,000 separate parts, depending on design and specification of the individual model; in a Western car firm like Ford 2,500 to 4,500 of the parts for each model will originate in-house from the company's own factories (Ford UK communication, 21 May 1992). Generally in the cars business there thus seems to be a good correspondence between the proportion of value-adding work undertaken by the final assemblers and the proportion of parts originating in-house. One implication is that the Japanese final assembler's task is considerably less complicated than in the West.

Whatever the differences between national assemblers, the scale and complexity of the sector's requirement for parts differentiates cars from other kinds of consumer goods manufacturing. Many of the parts are mechanically engineered to a very high standard; many of the in-house and bought-in parts are pressed, cast, forged and cut from metal to high standards of precision and interchangeability. Precision is necessary for in-service reliability; interchangeability is internally necessary because final-assembly tracks are working to short delivery cycles which do not allow for extra 'fitting' time. Interchangeability is also externally desirable in the after-market which requires perfect pattern-replacement parts. As all good engineers know, weight, number of parts and close tolerances are generally good proxies for manufacturing expense and difficulty.

The composition of costs and the distribution of value-added in car manufacturing are much the same in many other kinds of mechanical engineering. As a manufacturing activity, car making is distinguished by an unusually acute difficulty with sustaining continuous operation and flow between the processes. Having established this point, the next chapter will explain how solving the physical problem can improve financial results.

✦ ✦ ✦

3

Investment and Productive
Intervention

———— ❖ ————

The argument so far has established that the physical conversion problem of the activity is to build cars with less labor in them; the corresponding financial objective is to reduce labor costs or, more exactly, to take labor costs out without unbalancing the precarious division between the shares of value-added going respectively to labor and capital. This chapter provides an analysis of the two main ways in which a car or component firm can realize these objectives at firm level by making productive changes inside the factory. These are firstly, by adding more investment which substitutes capital for labor; and secondly, by productive intervention to improve the utilization of the existing capital and labor stock. The concept of investment is of course a staple of social science and management discourse. This chapter aims to show the limitations of this established concept before introducing a fresh concept of productive intervention which covers a range of actions and activities that have traditionally been neglected in economics, accounting and management texts.

Investment

If the concept of investment is familiar, that reflects the pervasive influence of a general cultural stereotype of manufacturing and the widespread diffusion of the orthodox economic model of production. Both the stereotype and the model start from premises which are very different from those in our analysis of specific manufacturing activity; and on the basis of these assumptions, establish a misleading quasi-knowledge of manufacturing.

Since the Industrial Revolution, manufacturing has been culturally stereotyped as mechanization, power-driven machines and relatively large-scale production. According to its Latin root manufacture means to 'make by hand', but in popular accounts of manufacture, from Lancashire cotton spinning to Detroit car making, it is the machines, rather than the workers, which are the dramatic centre of attention. This licenses an historical assumption that manufacturing since the Industrial Revolution has involved the progressive substitution of power driven machines for human labor; as long ago as 1835, Andrew Ure argued that 'the most perfect manufacture is that which dispenses entirely with manual labor' (Ure, 1835). Hence the excitement in each generation about new forms of automation (such as automatic transfer or robotization) which promise to deliver that future; and also the surprised rediscovery in each generation of the old industrial district based on craft skills.

The cultural stereotype of manufacturing is reinforced by the economic concept of production as a generic activity which encompasses agriculture and services as well as all manufacturing. The economist's trick is to resolve the real disjuncture between these disparate activities into a theoretical continuity by hypothesizing an underlying identity of production inputs and fixed input/output relations. Thus the inputs to manufacturing, and all other kinds of production, consist of labor and (fixed) capital which are combined in a black-box production process whose nature and content is largely irrelevant. One result is that, as we have argued elsewhere, the textbooks in 'industrial economics' generally fail to discuss the complexities of multi-process production (Williams et al., 1991). The discourse of economics operates in a kind of input/output problematic where attention is focused on either side of a black-box production process rather than on what happens in the box in the course of production. As one economist put it in relation to the economic theory of innovation, 'the economics profession has adhered rather strictly to a self-imposed ordinance not to enquire too seriously into what transpires inside that box' (Rosenberg, 1982, p.vii). Technicalities inside production can be ignored because orthodox production function analysis explicitly assumes that a particular mix of labor and capital produces a fixed quantum of output.

This 'cake-mix' concept of production inevitably encourages the idea that semi-automatic benefits can be obtained by increasing output or changing the input mix by adjusting the quantity or quality of the production inputs. The economics literature canvasses a stereotyped and limited range of options for cost reduction which are defined by the framework. The two classic options are: first, increasing output volume which may allow the firm to realize technical economies of scale; and, second, increasing the quantity of fixed capital input at a given level of output which may allow a profitable substitution of capital for labor. More recently, it has been argued that capital may include human capital so that increasing the quality of the labor input by training may produce diffuse benefits. While these options have been created and exist within the economics framework, they have also been assimilated into a variety of other more recently developed discourses, especially those of management. The highly influential work of Porter, for example, serves as a conduit from economics to strategy because Porter takes an entirely orthodox view of the benefits of fixed capital investment (Porter, 1985).

These introductory points are pertinent because the cultural stereotype about manufacturing and the economic doxa about production have together created a concept of the capital input which is in many ways at odds with the realities of the cars business. To begin with, it should not be assumed that all or most of the car firm's investment goes into physical equipment; because of the irregularities of segmented multi-process production, many Western car firms have much money tied up as working capital in the form of stocks. For all the major car firms in 1991 (except Toyota) the value of working capital accounted for nearly one-quarter or more of the value of plant and equipment. In several Western firms (Chrysler, VAG and BMW) and one Japanese firm (Honda) the capital tied up in stocks approached one-half the value of fixed capital in the form of plant and machinery (Table 3.1).

Furthermore, it should not be assumed that all or most of the car firm's new investment in equipment goes into machinery whose function is to displace labor. Obviously all car firms do buy machines and equipment aimed at raising the rate at which the direct workforce converts the material. The nature of the resulting labor saving is most obvious in the case of auxiliary equipment at the worker's elbow which allows the worker to do more material conversion in each minute; for example, electric or pneumatic power tools allow the assembly worker who is fixing road wheels to run more nuts per unit of time. Automation goes one step further by removing the direct worker altogether; it is, for example, fairly easy to construct an 'iron hand' or robot which mounts the wheels and then tightens the nuts. With the introduction of automatic-transfer machines for metal cutting in the 1950s or robots for body welding in the 1970s, it became possible to buy a line which dispensed with all the direct workers in one process stage.

Table 3.1: Total Value of Stocks and Total Value of Plant and Equipment in 1991.

Company	Value of stocks (Millions)	Value of plant and equipment (Millions)	Ratio of stocks to plant and equipment
Toyota (yen)	404,663	2,999,363	13.5%
Nissan (yen)	713,388	2,488,637	28.7%
Honda (yen)	641,499	1,288,353	49.8%
Mazda (yen)	106,424	766,832	13.9%
GM (dollars)	10,066	43,922	22.9%
Ford (dollars)	6,215	27,650	22.5%
Chrysler (dollars)	3,571	7,174	49.8%
VAG (marks)	9,049	20,404	44.4%
BMW (marks)	2,998	6,532	45.9%
Fiat (lire)	10,921	n/a	n/a
PSA (francs)	24,128	99,227	24.3%
Ford UK (pounds)	836	2,162	38.7%

Note: Stocks include raw material, work-in-progress and finished goods.

Source: Consolidated Company Reports and Accounts, various years.

Nonetheless a substantial part of the car firm's expenditure on equipment does not involve new labor saving mechanization of this kind. As we have already noted, in cars and other repetitive manufacturing activities, fixtures and tools attached to the machines are as, or more, important than machines; for example, a pillar drill can be adapted for faster, more precise, hole drilling if it is fitted with a jig that holds a workpiece of specific dimensions and a stop that sets depth of cut. The fixture directly articulates the use of labor in the productive process thereby reducing the machine's productive cycle time and/or the unproductive service time that is wasted on loading and unloading. Fixtures also increase precision which saves out-of-process labor because it allows assembly without fitting or rectification. Because many of the machines in car and component factories are fitted with fixtures which must be scrapped when models are changed over, fixtures are also a renewal expense necessary to the maintenance of the efficiency of capital and labor.

It is largely because model changeover is part of the activity that expenditure on tools, dies, jigs and fixtures typically accounts for half or more of what the assembler spends on plant and machinery. The burden is particularly heavy for the final assembler firm which usually bears all the cost of the dies which are used to form the panel shapes in a pressed steel body. Thus in the case of Ford over the period 1979 to 1989, from cyclical peak to cyclical peak over the decade of the

1980s, expenditure on tools and fixtures accounted for 56 percent of total investment in plant and machinery. However it is measured, and whatever the firm, a major part of the firm's total investment over this period is absorbed by the need to convert existing capital equipment for new productive tasks. In Chrysler tools and fixtures accounted for 61 percent of investment in plant and machinery, and in GM for 57 percent.

Table 3.2: Cumulative Expenditure on Tools and Fixtures versus Plant and Equipment at Ford, GM and Chrysler 1979–1989, Million $US.

Company	Expenditure on tools, dies and fixtures	Amortization	Expenditure on plant and machinery	Depreciation
Ford	13,901	12,034	24,613	17,310
Chrysler	4,802	3,410	7,823	3,291
GM	35,211	28,507	62,066	36,633

Source: Consolidated Company Reports and Accounts, various years.

The burden of this renewal investment in the cars business is considerable because it is customary to write off or amortize all the expenditure on tools, dies, jigs and fixtures in the year in which it is incurred, whereas investment in plant and machinery will be recovered by depreciation over many years. Amortization payments are a major drain on cash flow; in Ford between 1979 and 1989, amortization absorbed a sum equal to 70 percent of the accumulated depreciation charges. In this activity, Parkinson's law might be reformulated as 'amortization expands to absorb the cash flow that is available'. This result is possible because expenditure on amortization is driven by the rate of new model introduction which is determined by management on a partly discretionary basis. Successful car companies, like Toyota and Nissan in the 1980s or BMC in the 1950s, reinvest a substantial proportion of the cash proceeds of success in renewing and extending their model range. The hope is that this expenditure will consolidate market advantage, especially against competitors who cannot afford to spend and spend.

It is important to understand the composition of investment and to establish the limits on what can be achieved by investment. Nonetheless, when all these qualifications have been registered, the fact is that mechanization and automation in the orthodox sense is important. All volume car manufacturers have a large amount of plant and machinery per employee.

Table 3.3: Gross and Net Stock of Plant and Equipment per Employee in Twelve Major Car Companies in 1991.

Company	Gross fixed assets per employee $US	Net fixed assets per employee $US
Toyota	329,643	144,189
Nissan	220,954	114,479
Honda	192,070	91,234
Mazda	313,645	134,559
GM	90,482	37,559
Ford	125,958	67,634
Chrysler	128,718	78,721
VAG	112,443	48,978
BMW	137,961	51,472
Fiat	52,922	21,149
PSA	88,926	58,800
Ford UK	118,659	80,455

Note: Gross fixed assets (plant and equipment) are valued at historic cost before depreciation. Net fixed assets equal gross fixed assets minus depreciation.

Source: Consolidated Company Reports and Accounts, various years.

The total can be calculated in two ways; firstly, as gross capital per worker which represents the cumulative total of all investment to date in plant and machinery; or, secondly as net capital per worker which represents the same investment after the deduction of depreciation. Table 3.3 shows that at the outset of the 1990s the major manufacturers had a gross stock of $110-330,000 per worker and a net stock of $50-$141,000.

World-leading companies like Toyota in our own time, or Ford in the early twentieth century, usually have more capital per worker than others, but that may be as much a luxury allowed by financial success as the cause of high labor productivity; if the causal relations to and from capital stock are uncertain it is certain that, as we shall see later in Chapter 7, these leaders are also distinguished by a variety of other characteristics and capabilities. In the case of other companies, the correlation between more capital and greater productive and financial success is weak, as we would expect given the multi-dimensional nature of the business; Volkswagen-Audi-Group (VAG), for example led the European volume cars business at this time although its investment per worker was modest by industry standards.

If most car companies in the early 1990s had much less capital per worker than Toyota that was because they could not afford grand investment strategies which deployed large amounts of new capital

equipment in an attempt to buy higher labor productivity. The immediate practical problem is always that any extra equipment has to be
paid for initially from accumulated cash flow, with the cost recovered
afterwards using depreciation as a source of funds. Western accounting textbooks construct investment in external financial terms; the firm
should proceed with investment projects whose discounted receipts in
future years meet a certain target rate of return which reflects the
opportunity cost of funds sourced outside the firm. In cars it is much
more realistic to construct investment in terms of internal labor saving; the firm should only consider investment projects which save
labor hours and costs and are effectively financed by a suppression of
labor's share in future years. Significantly many car companies proxy
this effect on labor's share of value-added when making investment
decisions by giving some weight to physical-engineering calculations
of labor saving. The preference of Japanese companies for simple pay-
back calculations rather than discounted cash flow is again quasi-ratio-
nal in this framework because any investment which saves a lot of
labor is likely to pay back quickly.

Practically, all this means is that if internal funds are available, the
most attractive investments for firms with substantial throughput
requirements, are investments in short-cycle/high-speed machines
which displace a large lump of labor in one process. Or to make the
same point in a slightly different way, the scope for labor saving
investment is limited by the scale of a company's operations. It may
be technically possible to extend the cycle time and run the machines
slowly as Rover did on its automatic welding lines when demand for
the Metro failed to materialize, but in that case the rationale for the
investment was negated because the equipment failed to displace a
large enough lump of labor.

This is the underlying reason why final assembly and manufacture
of the finished car, just like engine and gearbox production, is usually organized on a relatively large-scale basis. High-speed automatic
machines cannot be used continuously unless certain minimum
throughput requirements are met. This requirement is generally
known as the 'minimum efficient scale'; press machines and robot
body lines require throughput of around 200,000 per year, while the
automatic transfer machines used in engine and gearbox production
require throughput of 300,000-500,000 per year. The tyranny of scale
is eased because ingenuity and electronic control allows mixed modeling in smaller firms like BMW whose carousel welding gear is

designed and programmed to weld two or more different body shells while the company's transfer lines in the late 1980s were set up to machine a four cylinder and a V8 engine on the same tools.

If the limits of scale can be finessed, the benefits of labor-saving investment are limited because such investment frequently only displaces direct labor and may actually increase the requirement for indirect workers. This represents another limitation on the power of investment: capital substitution often buys modest labor-saving at the expense of increased depreciation. The general result of mechanization and automation within the car factory so far appears to be a shift in the composition of the workforce rather than the total elimination of labor. Machines, for example, take out direct workers who undertake process tasks, and multiply indirects who maintain the machines, write the software programs and so forth. In all car companies since Ford, the direct workforce is heavily outnumbered by indirects who are employed in maintenance, materials handling, supervision, general management and non-production functions. In the Ford Motor Company at Highland Park the ratio of indirect to direct wage payments was 1.5 to 1. In most modern motor companies the ratio is even more adverse, running at 4 to 1.

Nearly forty years ago in pioneering work on productivity, which was based on the British Standard car company, Seymour Melman argued that productivity depended on controlling the numbers of indirects (Melman, 1956). This point has still not been taken on board in much orthodox discussion; for example, even Lewchuk's well-received historical work on the Ford Motor Company assumes throughout that productivity is determined by the effort of the direct worker (Lewchuck, 1987). A full appreciation of what extra investment in machines can and cannot do, demands that attention is given to its effect on the labor force as a whole.

Productive Intervention

Management discourse does recognize that there is something wrong with the economist's preoccupation with investment and putting capital in to take labor cost out. The PIMS project long ago showed that more investment does not necessarily bring higher profits. More positively, the Boston concept of the experience curve raises the issue of productive intervention under the rubric of learning to use the existing stock of labor and capital more effectively. However, the question of whether and how this kind of cost reduction could be managed was never posed; the crucial analytic question was displaced by the generalized observation that costs did fall as volume cumulated. In our view the reticence of management discourse reflects the absence of what sociologists used to call 'theories of the middle range'. Management as a discipline leaps from the individual case to the universalistic frameworks of the strategy texts which consist of taxonomies that cover every business eventuality; the boxologist's discourse hides productive intervention just as the letter rack hid the purloined letter.

All discourses work by constructing an area of the visible which is shadowed by an area of the invisible; the problem with economics, accounting and management is that they leave productive intervention in the area of the invisible. Possibilities of intervention figure hardly at all. This section addresses the task of rectifying the absence by presenting an activity-based analysis of productive intervention in the cars business. There are two main phases to such activity: intervention can be made before production begins and/or during the production process. In the pre-production phase, design, development and marketing can be brought together to configure a new generation product which is cheaper to produce and/or requires less material and labor input than the old generation. In the production phase, the car firm's objective should be to improve material and labor flow as a way of continuously taking labor costs out.

In management accounting, economics and management discourse, the decisive point is the moment when funds are sunk in the purchase of fixed capital equipment. In cars, it is altogether more plausible to suppose that the decisive moment is the pre-production phase and design and development (D and D). As the discussion of Austin Rover in Chapter 8 shows, 'product-led recovery' is usually a chimera for firms which are disabled by other problems such as market limitations. But design is the activity which adds the non-price characteristics that influence model sales volume and factory utilization; companies like VAG and Toyota bet their main factory every time they introduce a new Golf or Corolla and the early 1990s underutilization of the Toyota plant at Takaoka shows what happens when a major gets it wrong. Toyota chose to introduce a new Corolla which offered a number of extra features, including a galvanized body and standard air conditioning, at a price which was 25 percent higher than the old Corolla. This turned out to be more than the Corolla's traditional buyers were prepared to pay, at least for a product which was badged as a Corolla. Such experiences and calculations explain the cautious incrementalism of most car firms who understandably prefer short odds bets which give the public look-alike products and slow evolutionary development; when Volkswagen (VW) came to replace the Golf 1, the company commissioned a series of competing designs and chose the most conservative design as Golf 2.

In more narrow productive terms, D and D is equally crucial. It determines the initial manufacturing cost platform for the next generation of product; materials cost is fixed when the specification is written and labor cost is influenced by the number and type of fabrication and assembly operations. Every new design is an opportunity for simplification through the incorporation of fewer components as well as for components which are easier to manufacture and assemble. The number of components and process operations is most easily reduced in electronic subassemblies; the control unit for first generation Bosch anti-lock brakes in 1972 incorporated one thousand parts while the comparable unit in 1989 incorporated just thirty parts. But even in the case of mechanical subassemblies there are very large differences in manufacturability between best and worst designs; Saab product engineers who selected doors from equivalent Saab and Honda models, found that (using the same methods and technology) Honda doors could be assembled in a quarter of the time (Berggren, 1993).

If number of parts is a significant predictor of manufacturing expense, so is total product weight. The market success of the Ford Model T in the 1910s or the first generation Ford Cortina in the 1960s was built on cost-reducing weight; both these cars were two-thirds the weight of their full size competitors. But it is generally difficult to remove weight without compromising other desiderata like structural safety, handling or durability; the light weight French cars of the 1970s and 1980s, like the Renault 9/11 and Citroen AX had a 'disposable' quality which was never reassuring. More recently, Europe's light class hatch backs, like the VW Golf 3 and Opel Kadett have been putting on weight because the new American safety regulations of 1994 require stronger passenger compartments and heavier cars; the Golf 3 1800 is 10 percent heavier than the Golf 2 1600 which it replaces.

It would be wrong to represent D and D as a simply technical matter of engineering decisions because specification has an important marketing dimension. As Coffey (1992) argues, if a car company builds to individual customer order and offers a range of line-fit options, cost of manufacture will be substantially higher than if the company offers a restricted range of trim and option packages; most of these higher costs will be hidden away as 'overhead' costs of ordering and handling at the assemblers and as costs of changeover in the suppliers. Even with basic build-components for relatively cheap cars, up to 100 variants of the component are required to accommodate market requirements and customer choice; Rover in the early 1990s bought eighty different wiring harnesses for the 200/400 (Coffey, pp.9-10) and Nissan complains that it buys ninety separate types of door mirrors for the Sunny. Traditionally the Japanese have trimmed costs and simplified build logistics by offering option packs; this philosophy is still applied to a Japanese luxury product like the Lexus which is sold on price in the American market. It should of course be remembered that choice extends the market for individual models and the ultimate question is whether the costs of building to individual order can be recovered from the customer; this is what BMW and Mercedes have traditionally succeeded in doing by predatory pricing of options which have a high uptake. To paraphrase Chapman, a marketeer is someone who can list a sunroof for three times what it costs to buy and fit.

If D and D is of instrumental importance, it is also an object of major significance in itself because development is a large expense that has to be paid for before production begins and then recovered over the model run. The whole subject of design and development has recently become fashionable in management literature but the approach of authors like Clark et al. (1982) to design and development in cars only illustrates the problems of the reductionist single-level analysis of the cars business which was criticized in the introduction to this book. In Clark et al. and Altshuler et al. design and development is presented as an independent source of advantage; the argument is that the Japanese do it quicker with fewer man-hours and therefore Japanese manufacturers can afford more new models and shorter model lives. This interpretation ignores many of the complexities about the composition of development costs and neglects the complex two-way relation between market success and failure which generates or cuts off the cash flow for new models. The simplest point is that firms which do not generate cash cannot afford new models, regardless of their ability to develop individual models more or less cheaply. The constraints imposed on GM by the failure of its cash flow in the early 1990s are a dramatic example of this point, as is Volvo's experience at much the same time (see Chapter 9). Issues

about the composition of D and D costs further complicate the calculations of individual firms. The in-house burden of development arises because it is a nearly-fixed staff cost which must be met regardless
of decisions about replacement cycles; firms with aggressive replacement strategies use their development staff more intensively and, in
this respect are more cost effective. The full costs of model replacement also include bought-in tools and fixtures which are usually
model-specific. The costs of tooling up for rapid model replacement
are very high and almost certainly outweigh the benefits of using
development staff more intensively. All this reinforces the basic point
that firms with healthy cash-flows always have a major advantage,
regardless of their ability to develop individual models more cheaply.

Development, including production tooling, is always hugely
expensive because modern cars are so complex and new models have
to meet a variety of regulations on safety and emissions; in 1990
money values, the Ford Sierra/VW Passat cost £500-£1,000 million
to develop. The Volvo 850 series incurred total development costs of
£1.5 billion of which £1.1 billion was plant and equipment and tooling costs and £420 million was internal staff research and development costs. Recovery of these costs over the production life of the
model is a major problem for manufacturers with low annual model
sales or high model-development costs; assuming that Volvo sells
100,000 units of the 850 series over the next ten years then each car
must recover £1,000 of development costs in the sales-price per unit.

Table 3.4: Average Profit per Vehicle as a percent of Average Sales
Revenue per Vehicle Sold, 1981–1990

Year	Nissan	VAG
1981	3.5	-0.7
1982	3.1	-0.5
1983	2.6	0.5
1984	1.7	1.1
1985	1.8	1.1
1986	0.6	1.1
1987	0.5	1.0
1988	1.5	1.2
1989	2.4	1.6
1990	2.0	1.4
Average	**1.97**	**0.78**

Note: Sales price per vehicle is calculated by dividing units sold into total net sales revenue.
Profit per vehicle is calculated by dividing units sold into net income or pre-tax profit.

Source: Consolidated Company Report and Accounts, various years.

Volvo is a marginal car producer but most car manufacturers have problems with covering development costs because the margin per vehicle is very low and a large development charge per unit can easily wipe out the profit; Table 3.4 shows that average profit as a percentage of average sales price per vehicle from 1981–90 was 1.97 percent for Nissan and 0.78 percent for VAG.

Design and development costs can possibly be recovered by extending model life but that is a risky strategy given the tendency of sales to fall off in later years. It may be equally risky, especially in a recession, to bank on recouping costs quickly by using rapid model change as a means of seizing competitive advantage.

Once the product is in production and running down the lines, margins can be improved and costs can be lowered by a second kind of productive intervention which improves the flow of materials and labor. Management and social science texts do not provide a satisfactory analysis of the nature and scope of this kind of intervention and the account which follows builds on our own analysis of physical characteristics which was presented in Chapter 2. At the same time it draws on the classic production-engineering texts of Woollard (1954) and Ohno (1988), whose level of analysis and understanding of production engineering is so far unsurpassed, although it neglects the market whose influence we analyze in later chapters.

In the texts of Woollard and Ohno the business of repetitive car and component manufacturing was described as 'flow manufacturing'. This description is perfectly adequate provided it is always remembered that flow, within and between the manufacturing processes, is an ever-receding complex ideal rather than an achieved reality. The presence of buffer stocks within and between processes is a visible sign of the failure to realize the ideal. Thus the first aim of productive intervention is to modify existing capital equipment so that it is used continuously and smoothly in a way that improves physical materials flow. The result of this intervention is improved labor utilization and less labor content per unit of throughput. Continuity improves the utilization of direct labor because it increases the ratio of productive-to-unproductive delivery cycles each day. It also reduces the indirect handling-labor requirement because it removes stocks which buffer irregular and unproductive cycles and require indirect labor to check, store and move the stock. For these reasons Woollard (1954, p.70) concluded that 'continuity is the secret of production'.

From this point of view, the irregularities and failures of synchronization so characteristic of repetitive manufacturing present themselves as a multiplicity of problems and points of intervention. There is no mystery about the principles of intervention. What is required is a close attention to layout, most simply via strict enforcement of machines in order of use; better cycle-synchronization of machines or subassembly process spans; and reduction of the downtime lost due to breakdown or changeover on high-speed machines. In pursuing these practical changes, however, it is easy to lose sight of the superordinate objective. It is thus necessary to stress that although these modifications will reduce stock levels, the dynamic is not destocking but the productive intervention that allows smooth production with low stocks. If buffers are removed without productive intervention, flow will be reduced because downstream production is interrupted when the early stages of production falter. The modifications also incidentally increase potential process throughput. This arises because any improvement in the productive-to-unproductive cycle ratio increases daily-throughput capability. The extra throughput capability can usually be turned into an output gain by busting a few bottleneck processes; at these points of obstruction it is usually necessary to add extra machines and workers.

On this basis it is possible to correct the popular and commonly-held academic misunderstanding which equates reduced labor content with 'speed-up' in the sense of running machines or lines faster. The idea of speed-up, incarnated in Chaplin's *Modern Times*, is central to the traditional iconography of mass manufacture and to the recent historiography on Ford whose achievement is reinterpreted in Chapter 7. But speed-up is fundamentally misleading because, as the Central Policy Review Staff (1975) noted in a 1970s comparison of German and British car assembly, productive machines and lines do not run faster but more steadily throughout the day. If speed is required for particular process tasks, very high-speed machines are usually available off the shelf; manufacturers can, for example, buy transfer presses which perform four or five press operations in the bed of one machine and deliver finished car panels at the rate of up to thirty per minute as well as offering easier die change through the open side of the machine (Ford Company communication, 27 May 1992). But within repetitive manufacturing this kind of equipment often creates more problems than it solves and, in any case, it is irrelevant to flow because as Ohno (1988, p.63) trenchantly observed 'speed is meaningless without continuity'.

At the same time continuous machine operation and materials processing is a dangerous principle because it simply wastes labor time and materials if the machines are producing defective or unsaleable output; in this case the firm incurs conversion cost without realizing value. Hence Ohno (1988, p.128) cautions against 'work forced to flow' and observes that 'a production line that does not stop is either a perfect line or a line with big problems'. Furthermore, the composition of costs is such that it is almost always better to suffer idle machines rather than idle workers. Henry Ford and Toyota's practice was 'machines rather than men must wait' and this position was endorsed by Woollard (1954, p.104) when he argued that 'the full employment of the operators should come before studying the balance of the machine capabilities'. Perfect materials flow does not guarantee 'full employment of the operators' because it is compatible with a large waste of labor within each process cycle. Consider, for example, a line of adjacent cutting machines, whose cycle times are perfectly synchronized so that there is no work in progress between the machines; the usage of labor will still be profligate if each machine has a 'minder' who performs a short unload and load operation and spends most of the cycle waiting for the machine to finish. The problem is that smooth physical conversion of materials is not the same as high value-added per minute of worker time and therefore it is necessary to intervene at another level by recomposing labor tasks so as to raise value-added per unit of worker time.

In most operations, every minute of purchased worker's time yields considerably less than sixty seconds of value adding. The direct worker's production time can be divided into three categories: working, servicing and idle time. Working time includes only the essential operations such as mounting and fixing a component in final assembly or pushing the start button on a press. Service time covers activities such as walking to pick up the component from a line-side bin or loading a machine; these tasks are necessary under present working conditions but do not add value. Idle time is time that is wasted such as wait to finish time for a machine minder when the worker stands and does nothing. Utilization of worker's time is improved by raising the ratio of working to service and idle time. If workers in various processes have different ratios of working to service and idle time, it is usually necessary to redivide the value-adding and service tasks amongst a group of workers. This third kind of productive intervention is again about flow but entails flowing individual workers between tasks rather than material between processes. The aim of labor flow is to obtain a higher ratio of working time for a collective group of workers engaged in a particular process stage or even the whole factory; thus Woollard's classic text explains that the technical desideratum is a better 'overall utilization of worker hours'. An industrial sociologist would add the point that too zealous a pursuit of this objective can put strains on workers which may be unacceptable, at least in the West (Garrahan and Stewart, 1992).

Economics since Adam Smith has recognized that the static division of labor is a source of once and for all 'productivity gain'. Effective repetitive manufacturing exploits continuous re-division of labor so as to realize incremental gains from eliminating the waste of time that is inherent in any complex division of labor. The aim is to fill each assembly or fabrication job cycle with appropriate productive sub-tasks and this requires more than a simple reassignment of existing tasks between the work group. If service and unproductive time is to be eliminated, it is also necessary to redesign machines, fixtures and layouts according to certain general principles which include abolition of work-to-finish time, reduction in time-consuming service operations such as loading, and the elimination of all walking which does not contribute to value adding. Virtuoso manufacturers like Ford (Highland Park) or Toyota are often remembered for layout innovations which raised the ratio of working time in particular process stages; thus Ford's moving line brought the work to the stationary worker in assembly while Toyota's cellular system used the walking worker as machine loader and starter in subassembly production. As Chapter 7 will show, the significance of such innovations can be easily overrated. Improved labor flow (like much else in repetitive manufacturing) requires infinite attention to detail; in a Toyota factory which we visited in 1988 the final assembly line had been fitted with component trays that reverse-tracked up the line to deliver components to workers so that it was unnecessary to walk to a line-side bin.

This chapter has distinguished between reducing costs through productive intervention which involves using existing stocks of capital and labor more effectively, and reducing costs through extra investment which involves adding capital as a substitute for labor. In conventional discourses, like economics, only the latter is visible. But whilst investment in this sense remains important, the composition of investment in the motor vehicle industry is such that both D and D expenditure and model-specific tooling expenditures are as, or more, important. Against this background the additional concept of productive intervention signals the possibility of cost reduction from realizing better materials flow to improve labor utilization as well as from flowing labor between tasks to improve the value-adding yield of worker time. The next chapter explains why it is difficult for most firms to capture these benefits and examines the alternatives available to firms unable to secure a high level of materials flow.

✦ ✦ ✦

4

Better Flow or Lower Wages

———— ❖ ————

The discussion in the last chapter suggests that productive intervention to improve flow is a very attractive option for car companies;
improved materials and labor flow takes labor hours and cost out of
the product without incurring the costs of new investment. Investment is in any case a very partial fix best used in those processes
where the scale preconditions are satisfied; if productive intervention
promises 'something for nothing' that does not translate into universal benefits for all companies; this will be demonstrated in this chapter. If all assemblers and major component manufacturers want
improved flow, few are able to realize it. Many firms thus have to
accommodate by adjusting their organization and objectives to the
non-attainability of flow. Furthermore, it will be argued that flow is
not the single privileged key to success because in terms of end product competitiveness, national conditions about hours and wages are as,
or more, important than flow superiority.

Flow

The introduction to this book briefly described the managerialist doxa
about world-class manufacturing through Japanese techniques: this
orthodoxy implies that any firm which chooses productionist goals
and instruments can become excellent and thereby close a competitivity gap. The analysis of flow in this section provides a critical antidote to this universalist doxa. Against this we argue that productive
intervention is only possible and successful under certain specific conditions inside and outside the firm. As most firms do not operate
under these conditions, productive intervention is thus a major source
of advantage for a few 'heroic exceptions', like Ford (Highland Park)
and Toyota. The achievements of these exceptional firms cannot be
widely emulated and do not therefore provide the basis for universal
systems of mass or lean production.

These points are not obvious because the limits of productive intervention are not as palpably immediate as in the case of investment. Nevertheless, we would argue that management commitment to, and understanding of, intervention will not generate significant cost reductions unless the firm meets certain internal conditions and operates in an appropriate external environment. The two main internal conditions of successful productive intervention are a high level of technical control over production and a high level of social control over the workforce. Beyond this there is also the external economic condition of brisk demand and sustained market pressure.

The technical prerequisite for improved materials flow is engineering control. It is practically difficult to intervene productively because each intervention requires a grasp of process detail plus effective remedial action to remove the cause of irregularity. For example, if the problem is machine breakdown, it is necessary to identify the cause and to change the appropriate variable such as maintenance schedules or machine cutting speeds. If the problem is die changeover time, it is necessary to separate external preparation work, standardize die height and fit quick-release fastenings. The problem is not that it is impossibly difficult to identify what needs to be done, but that execution is difficult because a significant improvement in overall factory flow will require hundreds or thousands of focused interventions and a commitment to continuous improvement. Firms like Ford (Highland Park) and Toyota which sustain improvement must create a culture that incorporates managers and supervisors and does not exclude ordinary workers. The Japanese have named this approach *kaizen* but they did not invent it because Henry Ford c. 1915 had the practice without the slogan.

The conditions for improved labor flow are more explicitly social. The problem is not the division of labor because division of labor creates relatively simple semi-skilled direct labor tasks whose training requirements are modest. When Toyota was developing cellular production of sub-assemblies in the 1970s, it experienced some problems in creating multi-skilled workers. Nonetheless when Ohno summarized the company's general achievements in the 1970s, he agreed with Henry Ford who believed that individual tasks could be designed so that any worker would be task proficient after three days training (Ohno, 1988, p.22). In a company that is changing layout and modifying machines, the problem is the redivision of labor which creates endlessly recomposed 'task bundles'. The basic prerequisite for success is thus a high level of social control over the workforce who must accept constant changes in job definition and content.

Management can exercise the necessary control in a variety of ways and Friedman's (1977) opposition between direct control and responsible autonomy is a useful way of thinking about management choice. The control regimes operated by different car firms usually combine variable elements of formal or informal direct control with responsible autonomy; engineers or foremen specify or show workers what to do, while individual workers or groups retain a measure of autonomy over the organization of their time and the extent of their commitment which may or may not include co-option in improvement efforts. Almost invariably management will control layout, basic time allowances and payment systems because these determine the structure within which effort is supplied. These control mechanisms and structures are not the secret of success and failure because their effects depend on external circumstance. This point is brought out in Chapter 8's analysis of BMC and its gang system of delegated control and group piecework. The BMC case shows the problem was not an inappropriate payment system but the company's failure in terms of capacity utilization and output growth after the early 1960s: incentive pay systems always work better in firms which are trying to get metal out the door.

Car firms which satisfy the technical control conditions necessary for materials flow may yet be frustrated because they operate in labor markets which deny them social control over the workforce; most forms of independent unionism to a greater or lesser degree provide a challenge to management's prerogative over the labor process and constrain management's ability to recompose labor tasks. As Chapter 7 will show, virtuoso firms like Ford (Highland Park) and Toyota operated in exceptional circumstances where management's prerogative was nearly unlimited and most other car firms have been denied this advantage. The ultimate technical limits on recomposition of the labor task are uncertain but it is clear that firms must consider the trade off between better labor utilization and increased capital expense. A nearly perfect system for utilization of worker time which eliminates waiting time is likely to be extravagant in its requirement for under-utilized capital equipment which, in such a system, must always be available so that the worker can rapidly initiate a sequence of value adding operations. These developments may create difficulties for particular companies which are financially unable to maintain high levels of capital investment provision out of cash flow.

The technical limits of productive intervention are ultimately unclear partly because the external economic constraints are pressing and prevent firms from reaching and exploring the technical limits of productive intervention. The benefits of internal flow in companies like Ford and Toyota are circumscribed by the ability of the company to sell product into limited markets; as we shall see in Chapter 7, flow against the market explains Ford's failure in the late 1920s and Toyota's uncertain prospects at the beginning of the 1990s. From this point of view, the necessary external condition for flow improvement is sustained demand pressure. As the previous chapter demonstrated, improved flow implies increased throughput capability because it increases the ratio of productive to unproductive cycles during the working day. Firms which can sell all that they make have a strong incentive to modify capital equipment and recompose labor tasks: if the bottlenecks can be busted, such firms can realize the throughput gain as saleable output which will improve their financial ratios. Firms with stagnant or declining sales must normally cope with an embarrassment of unsaleable output. Demand context is a theme which recurs again and again in the accounts of particular enterprises and sectors in the second half of this book.

The most fundamental point is that sustained failure of output growth (or fluctuations in demand) remove the incentive for productive intervention. If demand pressure is not sustained, the firm does not want the extra output or can most easily meet temporary demand by extending operating hours through overtime and extra shifts as the European manufacturers did in the cyclical upturn of the late 1980s. In many texts on manufacturing techniques, the Japanese are credited with a general commitment to productive intervention which is sometimes attributed to a difference in technical competence and/or social values. As we shall see in the next chapter, the most obvious difference is that the Japanese car firms have operated in very much more favorable demand circumstances so that the pressure and scope for productive intervention has been much stronger.

If achieving flow is difficult, measuring flow is no easier. The difficulties of measuring flow nicely illustrate the problems about the non-transparency of the activity which were discussed in the introduction. It is not possible to provide a general measure of labor flow which would allow us to compare flow in different processes, factories and companies. It is possible to construct general measures of materials flow based on stock levels which do allow comparison.

These stock-based measures can be used as indicators of the extent and success of productive intervention because, *ceteris paribus*, productive intervention which improves flow will reduce the level of stock cover required, in the form of raw materials, work in progress and finished product, to cover production irregularities. Unfortunately, the indicator remains ambiguous because lower stocks can reflect the vacuum effect of market demand as well as the smoothing effect of productive intervention. This ambiguity is to some extent inherent in any measure of flow: as long as market pressure is a necessary precondition of flow, the measure registers the joint variation in external circumstance and internal competence.

These problems can be palliated though not abolished by the choice of the most appropriate materials flow measure. Most existing flow measurements focus on the stock/sales turnover ratio which relates all stocks (including raw materials, work in progress [WIP] and finished goods) to the sales turnover of the company. For a variety of reasons we prefer flow measures based on WIP/value-added ratios or WIP and raw materials/value-added ratios. WIP is the best denominator because stocks of finished goods are for obvious reasons more sensitive to variations in final product demand than WIP or WIP plus raw materials; measurements which put stress on WIP provide a better measure of factory flow because WIP is primarily determined by the exigencies of productive irregularities. As for the numerator, value-added is preferable to sales turnover when the comparisons involve firms or sectors where there are differences in the amount of conversion work undertaken by the final assembler/ manufacturers. In cars, if turnover is used as the numerator the measure flatters the performance of the Japanese firms which, as was noted in Chapter 2, are substantially less vertically integrated than their American and European counterparts; much of what appears as WIP inside a firm like General Motors becomes raw materials and finished goods held outside a firm like Toyota. Value-added as numerator incorporates an automatic correction for the shorter span of operations in the vertically disintegrated firm.

A selection of the available evidence on major car manufacturers is summarized in Table 4.1 which gives WIP/value-added and WIP + raw materials/value-added ratios. What is presented is a snap shot picture of cross-sectional variation of flow in one recent year; the nature of both ratios is such that the higher the ratio the better the flow. On these performance measures, as on most others, the Japanese firms do not stand out as a group. Instead what emerges is that Toyota is in a class of its own on the first ratio, although it is dramatically surpassed by Honda on the second measure. The main point is that apart from Toyota, no other Japanese company is consistently good and Mazda and Nissan are generally worse than the Europeans. Nissan's poor performance is in line with its apparently limited capacity for productive intervention: this is a company which tried and failed to introduce a variant on the Toyota *kanban* system. The American majors turn in a very creditable performance which has not been greatly compromised by their difficulties with their domestic market which are analyzed in the next chapter. It may be that the Americans may have insulated themselves from the effects of demand deficiency by their practice of shutting down plants for whole weeks or months to adjust output; the alternative practice is to extend cycle times as Rover did on the Metro lines in the mid-1980s.

Table 4.1: WIP/Value-added and WIP + Raw Materials/Value-added Ratios for Twelve Major Car Manufacturers in 1991

Company	WIP + raw materials/ value-added	WIP/value-added
Nissan	5.7	13.9
Toyota	14.1	24.1
Honda	7.0	46.5
Mazda	8.1	10.0
Ford	9.8	n/a
GM	9.3	n/a
Chrysler	8.9	n/a
BMW	7.5	15.2
VAG	6.1	12.0
Fiat	n/a	7.4
Ford UK	11.1	14.0
PSA	8.4	17.5

Note: Value-added is calculated as labor costs (inc. social charges), plus depreciation, net income or pre-tax profit. WIP = work in progress.

Source: Consolidated Company Report and Accounts, various years.

European performance is very variable but, if the two flow measures are averaged, it is quite creditable: companies as diverse as BMW, Ford UK and PSA all beat Nissan and Mazda on both flow measures. This result suggests that productive incompetence was not the major cause of the acute difficulties facing the European car industry in the 1990s. Other factors, and especially the importance of the social settlement, will be explained in Chapter 9.

The overall message is that most car firms do not meet the internal and external conditions so that their flow performance is mediocre at any moment of time and we believe that in most cases time series analysis would not show sustained improvement in flow. This is accommodated by a displacement of goals and organizational forms in non-flow car companies. Non-flow companies can compete through superior marketing, better design, or different ways of organizing the company.

If all car companies could realize flow and if cars were simple undifferentiated commodities then 'unproductive' activities which did not contribute to conversion would be competitively eliminated or minimized as unnecessary expenses. But cars are differentiated consumer goods where many unproductive activities can contribute to conversion efficiency. Downstream marketing, like upstream design and development, plays an obvious major role in adding the non-price characteristics which make the product desirable. These activities are especially important for car firms which cannot realize flow because they must compete in other ways. Thus GM in the 1920s used model change, consumer finance and trade-ins as a way of competing against Ford; and in the 1980s Nissan relied on design against Toyota. When in 1990 we asked a senior Nissan manager how his company competed against Toyota, he replied immediately 'through faster, cheaper design and development'.

Furthermore many car firms choose organizational forms which may deliver various benefits but are ill-adapted for sustaining productive intervention. As Chandler's history showed (Chandler, 1962), GM was one of the pioneers of M-form organization in the interwar period and this form of divisional structure has since been adopted by virtually every Western car company, including Ford which was not divisionalized in its productionist glory-days at Highland Park. Toyota always tells its visitors that it is not divisionalized and other Japanese companies such as Honda are only now introducing M-form. The organizational innovation of M-form, with its vertical formal hierarchy and functional specialisms, promises benefits of financial control and strategic planning. It could be represented as the response of the productively unsuccessful because the few successful productionists, like Ford (Highland Park) or Toyota, prefer flat, informal, task-oriented organizations which focus the efforts of generalists on practical problems.

The benefits of M-form may often be illusory because many advantages can be accessed by productionists with simpler organizational structures. Just like Toyota, the early Ford enterprise was adept at finding a supplementary financial advantage. In the Ford company of the 1910s purchasing and management of creditors was ruthlessly organized by Couzens who levered up profitability and improved cash flow by building, selling and collecting the money for Model Ts out of materials which the company had not paid for. However, the difficulty of maintaining flow is such that the balance of advantage between differently organized companies with different sets of priorities is always uncertain. History does not license the conclusion that non-flow companies, with non-productionist priorities and complex internal hierarchies are doomed to fail in competition. All we can say is that when an M-form company, like GM in recent times, gets into difficulty, changing direction is never easy because of the cumbersome management super-structure which meanwhile imposes a large indirect cost burden on the firm.

Finally, it should be emphasized that the few firms which have successfully practiced productive intervention are not unambiguous examples of virtue. Or, to make the same point another way, the diversion of so many car companies from productionist goals is by no means an unalloyed disaster from a broad social perspective in which the gains in consumer welfare are weighed against losses in producer welfare. In the activity of car manufacturing, success through productive intervention may pay off in lower costs and cheaper cars for the consumer, but it has its own cost in terms of producer welfare. The gurus of the car factory always claim to have revolutionized work and to have rescued workers from the back-breaking toil which was a feature of heavy industrial work and earlier car factories. Henry Ford and Ohno's claims on this point do have content. Henry Ford's battery of devices for transferring materials between processes (see Chapter 7) undoubtedly reduced much heavy manual handling, and, more recently, it was demonstrated that Fiat workers who had performed difficult and awkward spot-welding tasks with manual guns preferred the clean and light supervisory tasks of the replacement robot line (Bonazzi, 1992, p.18). Nonetheless the general logic of effective intervention is greater intensity of worker effort as waiting time and unproductive cycles are eliminated, whether under a regime of Taylorist short cycles or Toyota style perambulation round the cell. As the price of accepting this kind of work in car factories, organized labor usually demands and obtains a package of higher wages and/or shorter hours which has traditionally made car assembly workers a blue collar elite *within* each national economy. But, as will now be shown, *between* national economies differences in wages and hours can be an important source of competitive advantage.

Wages and Hours

In the first phase of volume car production, the relation between competitivity, wages and hours was straightforward. Ford (Highland Park) was a master of physical flow which realized better financial ratios and lower absolute-cost levels than any competitor. The benefits were initially appropriated in the form of high profits for Ford, dramatic price cuts for the consumer, and a better deal for the semi-skilled workforce; in 1913 Ford offered an unprecedented $5 per day at the same time as he cut the standard shift to eight hours. There was a strong element of self-interest in the policy because Ford faced a serious problem about high rates of labor turnover which reached a phenomenal 70 percent in 1913 (Meyer, 1981, p.162). But the outcome was that the world's leading car company offered both the highest wages and the shortest hours in the business and Ford became a social ideal as well as a manufacturer of motor cars.

The position now is considerably more complicated. As will be shown below the world's leading car firm, Toyota, like the rest of the Japanese industry, has ceded raising real wages (but does not pay wages which are the highest internationally), while, in the period before the current downturn, Toyota's workforce put in longer hours than in any other advanced country. The producer welfare prize for highest wages and shortest hours c.1990 went to the German industry whose competitive position was regionally strong within Western Europe but globally much weaker because its wages and hours are a social burden, the implications of which are discussed in Chapter 9. To make the same point in a more abstract and formal way, the effects of productive intervention and investment are now mediated by the national settlement on wage levels and hours worked and also by the wage gradient between assemblers and suppliers. Within the activity, 'taking labor out' is the general objective and improved flow can be an important instrument, but the car and component companies which play this game do not do so on a level field.

We can begin by considering the range of variation in hours worked and wage levels between major producer countries. Although capital-intensive press, foundry and metal cutting departments typically work three shifts, most car plants around 1990 still operated their weld, paint, trim and assembly shops on the basis of two shifts of about eight hours for five days each week. So the standard car assembly plant week was a nominal forty hours (less meal breaks and stoppages). The exception was Germany where the length of the standard working week had been increasingly curtailed by IG Metall's insistence on a shorter working week. Since the mid-1980s, the collective agreements for the German metal working and electrical industries have steadily reduced the working week per employee from forty to thirty-seven hours and a further reduction to thirty-five hours was scheduled for autumn 1995.

All definitions of the standard working week exclude overtime which adds further complications. All plants can, and most do, work a sixth day on Saturday when demand is brisk. Furthermore, if the plant operates a day and night shift system, of the kind which is traditional in most British and Japanese car factories, there is always a gap between the end of one shift and the start of another when up to two hours of overtime can be worked; until the early 1990s, Toyota workers routinely worked sixty to ninety minutes overtime in this slot. Overtime is much more difficult in car factories, like those of VW in Germany or Honda in Japan, which work a 'Continental shift' system of early and late day shifts which change over at 1400 or 1500 hours. Partly for this reason, when demand was brisk in the late 1980s, there was considerable European interest in new shift patterns which did not increase hours worked by the individual but did extend plant operating hours and thus increase capacity; in 1988 GM Antwerp introduced a system of three crews working 11 shifts of ten hours (Lehndorff, 1991).

Thus, although the standard week was nearly the same everywhere, there were substantial differences in hours actually worked per year in different national industries. Table 4.2 summarizes Bosch's study of hours worked in the four major Japanese car companies and Lehndorff's study of hours worked in the European body and assembly shops of VW, GM and Ford. The European totals exclude shut down days and forty to sixty minutes of meal breaks whereas the Japanese totals exclude holidays and include meal breaks. In our view this does not create a serious comparability problem because meal breaks in Japan are often taken up with company business such as Quality Circle meetings; these obligations are more than formal when in Toyota the Quality Circles generated thirty-two suggestions per worker in 1988. To complete the picture, we obtained data from the United Automobile Workers (UAW), the dominant motor industry labor union in the US, on hours worked in the American factories of the Big Three assemblers.

Table 4.2: Hours Worked in Japanese Companies, European and American Plants, 1990.

Company	Blue collar hours worked
Toyota	2,268
Nissan	2,296
Honda	2,036
Mazda	2,229

Source: G. Bosch (1991).

Company	Average hours worked in body and assembly
VW	1,626
GM Europe	1,657
Ford Europe	1,710

Source: S. Lehndorff (1991).

Company	Hours worked per year
GM US	2,059
Ford US	2,251
Chrysler	2,141

Source: UAW, 1991.

With the exception of Honda, all the Japanese companies obtained many more hours per worker each year than did European firms. The margin of difference between the three European companies working 1,600–1,700 hours and the high hours Japanese companies which work more than 2,200 hours is of the order of 25 percent. Or, to make the same point more graphically, the Japanese car worker in 1990 supplied in twelve months the number of hours which his/her European counterpart supplied in fifteen months. The hours worked in the United States seem nearer the Japanese, although those reported probably do not make full allowance for absenteeism and sickness: in contrast 'in Japan absenteeism due to illness is virtually unknown' (International Metalworkers Federation, 1992, p.32).

The pattern established by national variation in hours worked is complicated by a second set of national variations in employment costs per hour. The VDA, the German Society of Motor Manufacturers, evidence summarizes national trends over the past decade in 'employer costs' which include social security and pension contributions as well as gross hourly earnings. The gap between earnings and costs is usually of the order of 25 percent, although in France and Germany it is significantly larger; in Germany the social charges per employee in the early 1990s accounted for more than $10 out of the total employment costs of $27 per hour.

Table 4.3: Employer Labor Cost per Employee Hour for Major National Motor Industries, 1980–91 in US$.

Country	1980	1985	1990	1991
Japan	7.40	11.15	18.03	20.52
USA	12.67	22.65	20.22	21.24
France	10.03	10.20	15.57	16.42
Germany	13.70	13.72	26.03	26.95
Italy	9.05	10.40	16.94	19.13
UK	7.63	8.70	15.48	16.15
Spain	6.95	6.76	16.31	17.91
Sweden	15.70	12.33	26.40	27.52

Source: VDA, (fax communication), 1992.

Table 4.3 shows that all the established producing countries are relatively high wage producers compared with newly industrializing countries, but some have much higher employment costs per hour and others have recently changed position in the wages league table. Throughout the 1980s, German labor costs, currently around $27 per hour, were exceeded only by those of Sweden. Against this background, it is hardly surprising that, within the European industry, the Swedes have long specialized in middle-size, middle-class cars from Saab and Volvo; nor is it surprising that companies, like VW, Ford and GM, with factories inside and outside Germany, produced their smallest cheapest models of the 1980s (Polo, Fiesta and Corsa/Nova) elsewhere, and especially in Spanish and British factories where labor costs are not much more than half those in Germany. As for the Japanese, they have changed their relative position in a way which moves them from the bottom to the middle of the league table. As recently as 1980 the Japanese were low-wage competitors in the United States which was then, and has remained, their main export market; by 1991 Japanese hourly labor costs were 97 percent of American hourly costs, but in 1980 Japanese costs had been only 58 percent of American costs.

The discussion so far has concentrated on hours worked in major assemblers and wages in national industries. The picture is further complicated by the wage gradient between major assemblers and the component suppliers which, as we have noted, determine most of the

cost in each motor car. The VDA employment costs series does not
capture all or most of the effects of this wage gradient in different
national industries. As a qualification and supplement, the basic evidence on wage differentials and distribution of value-added for four of
the major car-producing countries is summarized in Table 4.4.

Much recent academic discussion of Japanese success has argued
that the Japanese assemblers have different and permanent relations of
mutuality and trust with their suppliers and implies that these intangi-
bles are a powerful source of advantage. Whatever the truth of that,
Table 4.4 shows that the vertically disintegrated Japanese industry also
has the unique practical advantage of a steep wage gradient combined
with an unusually large proportion of employment and value-added
conversion undertaken in the smaller firms which pay lower wages.

Table 4.4: Wage Gradient by Size of Firm in the Japanese, US,
British and French Motor Industries

Japanese motor industry, 1989:

Firm size	Wage gradient top to bottom 1000 + = 100	Share of value added (%)	Share of employed (%)	VA/ purchases ratio by size of firm (%)	Purchases /sales ratio by size of firm (%)
1-99	56.4	15.1	26.5	68.3	58.0
100-499	72.4	15.4	20.3	44.1	67.2
500-999	86.2	11.1	12.6	45.5	66.8
1000+	100.0	58.4	40.6	33.1	70.4

Source: Japan Statistical Yearbook, Ministry of Management and Co-Ordination.

US motor industry, 1987:

Firm size	Wage gradient top to bottom 1000 + = 100	Share of value added (%)	Share of employed (%)	VA/ purchases ratio by size of firm (%)	Purchases /sales ratio by size of firm (%)
1-99	51.5	4.0	7.9	76.4	51.5
100-499	59.3	11.1	18.0	80.0	55.1
500-999	68.3	6.8	9.7	77.1	56.4
1000+	100.0	78.1	64.0	42.9	77.6

Source: US Department of Commerce, Bureau of the Census.

Table 4.4 (*continued*)

British motor industry, 1989:

Firm size	Wage gradient top to bottom 1000 + = 100	Share of value added (%)	Share of employed (%)	VA/ purchases ratio by size of firm (%)	Purchases /sales ratio by size of firm (%)
1-99	78.3	5.6	9.2	66.9	59.9
100-199	74.7	3.2	4.9	72.8	57.8
200-499	79.5	6.1	8.6	57.9	63.3
500-999	79.6	6.3	8.8	68.5	59.3
1000+	100.0	78.7	68.5	44.6	77.1

Source: UK Census of Production, PA1002, HMSO.

French motor industry, 1989:

Firm size	Wage gradient top to bottom 1000 + = 100	Share of value added (%)	Share of employed (%)	VA/ purchases ratio by size of firm (%)	Purchases /sales ratio by size of firm (%)
1-99	86.0	3.6	5.9	60.0	62.4
100-499	86.2	8.3	10.1	52.4	65.5
500+	100.0	87.8	83.9	35.0	74.1

Source: Ministere l'industrie, Paris, 1991.

As a recent report put it: 'Being able to pay the highest wages and benefits to a much smaller population of workers is one of the key advantages of Japanese assemblers' (International Metalworkers Federation, 1992, p.9). Thus in 1989, Japanese motor industry firms employing less than a hundred workers paid wages little more than half those in the large assemblers and in addition accounted for 26.5 percent of motor-industry employment. All the other major national industries are denied one or both of these advantages. In Britain and France the wage gradient is much less steep and, although the United States has a steep Japanese-style wage gradient, firms employing less than a hundred account for less than 8 percent of total American motor-industry employment.

Differences in wages and hours worked would not be decisive if the Japanese motor industry really could always build a vehicle in half the hours as the MIT 2 study (Womack et al., 1990) implies. If this was so, we would expect the Japanese industry, just like Henry Ford in an earlier era, to devastate all competitors almost regardless of relative wages and hours worked (unless and until its advance was halted by trade barriers). In this case, Japan's long hours, moderate wages and steep wage gradient would be a supplementary social reinforcement of competitive success which was more fundamentally guaranteed by technical/economic differences. In fact the evidence shows that, within a multi-dimensional frame, the social differences are considerably more important because the hours and wages have historically tilted the balance of advantage to Japan in the case of the otherwise fairly evenly matched Japanese and American industries and constitute an additional crushing burden for the lower-productivity German industry. The nature of the competitive gap and its implications for the future of different national industries will be analyzed in the second half of this book. At this stage in the argument, the object is simply to vindicate the importance of wages and hours.

Table 4.5 presents the results of a calculation of the sectoral hours to build a vehicle for a range of different countries over a span of twenty years. These results are based on the output and employment in the motor vehicle sector as a whole (not just the final-assembly firms), and they are obtained by dividing the number of vehicles built per employee, in each country in each year, into the available worked hours per employee. Although vehicles includes trucks as well as cars, that complication is offset by the fact that roughly two-thirds of the sales value of each industry's output consists of cars; in 1989 cars accounted for 69 percent of the value of the American industry's output and 62 percent of the value of the Japanese industry's output (*Automotive News*, 1990). If the hours worked are reasonably accurate,the result is a much more significant measure of competitive status than that offered in M.I.T.'s *The Machine that Changed the World* (Womack et al., 1990) where the claim that the Japanese can build vehicles in half the time is based on engineering comparisons of assembly-plant operations which only account for 15 percent of the value of each car.

Table 4.5: Build Hours per Vehicle in the US, German, Japanese and Korean vehicle industries

	USA	Germany	France	Japan	Korea
1969	173	269	n/a	280	n/a
1970	189	278	267	254	n/a
1971	162	270	257	224	n/a
1972	169	268	241	217	3033
1973	167	266	238	203	2244
1974	182	308	248	200	2378
1975	174	279	292	176	1475

Table 4.5 (*continued*)

	USA	Germany	France	Japan	Korea
1976	163	246	254	173	1360
1977	165	258	251	158	1270
1978	170	278	253	146	1006
1979	179	294	241	147	917
1980	202	318	252	139	1255
1981	204	271	260	138	1118
1982	204	267	243	140	839
1983	163	262	225	139	725
1984	165	266	237	141	670
1985	155	258	220	139	572
1986	154	266	199	133	453
1987	173	255	175	132	348
1988	174	256	162	132	352
1989	170	286	n/a	132	n/a

Note: Build hours per vehicle are derived by dividing annual vehicle production by sectoral hours (employees multiplied by hours worked).

Sources: Industrial Statistics Year Book, United Nations, various years; *Yearbook of Labor Statistics,* International Labor Office, various years, *Automotive News Market Databook.*

From 1979 onwards, the Japanese did manage to build a vehicle with fewer labor hours than the Americans. But the gap is always relatively narrow; over the period from 1979 to 1988, the Japanese take an average of 137 hours to build a vehicle against an American average of 176 hours which is some 27 percent worse over the period covered. But throughout the earlier period of the 1970s when the Japanese car industry was establishing itself as the leading exporter to the United States, the Japanese motor sector had a higher build-hour requirement than indigenous American firms and the Japanese covered that requirement by paying much lower wages and working much longer hours. The German industry is nowhere near competitive on build hours with either the Americans or the Japanese and in recent years has taken almost twice as many build hours per vehicle. This kind of physical–productivity differential is not new; the classic productivity studies of the 1940s and 1950s showed that American manufacturing productivity was often twice as high as European. But in a new era of direct global competition, the build hours gap means that the German industry is peculiarly ill-placed to pay the highest wages and work the shortest hours.

The other point which emerges from Table 4.5 is the difference of trajectory between the American and German industries whose build hours simply fluctuated, and the Japanese and Korean car industries,

which have taken labor out progressively. The Asian recipe for successful new entry into the international cars business is to take labor
hours out from an initially very high level as the Japanese did in the
1960s and the Koreans did in the late 1980s; competitivity is achieved
when the new industry has reached something like the German level
of build hours which is covered socially by paying much lower wage
rates and working much longer hours: in 1988, the Korean employment cost was $6.44 per hour and the number of hours worked in the
Korean motor industry was officially reported as 2,605 hours
(International Labor Organization, 1992). Equally interesting is the
fact that, in the 1980s, the Japanese failed to sustain build-hours reductions which would have opened up a large gap against the Americans
who have been around 170 hours for more than thirty years. This
observation suggests that, with anything like present production techniques, there is an irreducible minimum labor content in each car,
particularly if the complexity and value-added of each unit is increasing as it was for the Japanese over the 1980s. The American and
German fluctuations around a static norm are interesting in themselves
and the background to these fluctuations is explained in the next
chapter which examines the external market characteristics facing the
sectors and enterprises. Cyclical variations in the level of demand are
important because in a good year at the top of a cycle American sector
build hours per vehicle closes to a gap of just 15 percent against Japan.

❖ ❖ ❖

5

Market Characteristics and Volume Fluctuations

❖

The activity of car manufacture has so far been mostly represented in a static universalistic way: all assemblers and major-component manufacturers struggle with the same physical and financial problems although the internal and external constraints on management action are variable. In this chapter, we begin to differentiate the problems and opportunities facing different manufacturers in terms of the market environment in which they operate. Half or more of each major assembler's output is usually sold in one of three major national or regional 'home markets' (North America, the EC or Japan) which have very different characteristics. Thus the first half of this chapter describes the characteristics of different home markets and the variable commitment of different manufacturers to those markets; while the second half of the chapter analyzes the consequences of market-driven fluctuations in volume and capacity utilization which are a particular problem for the American and European manufacturers.

Market Characteristics

Since Adam Smith, economists have understood that the extent of the market is important because it limits the division of labor and the scope for substituting capital. Size is not everything because it does not determine the scope for the redivision of labor but the extent of the 'home market' is important. The car firm's home market is defined in supply and demand terms by three criteria: first, the absence of trade barriers constraining the advance of more successful companies; second, broad similarity of price structures so that a given product can be similarly positioned within the market; and third, homogeneity of consumer tastes so that volume products will claim a substantial share right across the market.

In an earlier period the home market was always a national market because until the 1960s national markets were effectively divided by trade barriers and differences in consumer tastes. Henry Ford had the great advantage of a national market with Continental dimensions in a period when the European producers all supplied much smaller national demands. But the world has changed since the 1960s, let alone the 1910s, so that the EC as well as North America now constitute regional home markets which are unified by formal free trade agreements. Within Europe, the initial Common Market phase of EC development was the crucial development: it created opportunities for large scale intra-regional trade between the six, and later twelve, member countries. The four established producing countries (Germany, France, Italy and Britain) came to export 25 to 45 percent of their output to near-European markets, whilst the more recently developed Spanish production base exports nearly two-thirds of its output to other EC countries. Japan thus survives as the last and only major case where national borders still align with those of a home market: Japan includes in one country an affluent population of 130 million, roughly half that of the EC or North America.

Most of the world's leading assemblers are still centered on one home market which serves as the main outlet for their finished product as well as the main production site for meeting home demand plus any export demand for finished products and components from outside the home market. These generalizations about market presence and productive concentration are illustrated, developed and qualified in Tables 5.1 and 5.2 together with the accompanying commentary. The first table (5.1), on market share, shows that at the end of the 1980s even the strongest European firms were part of a fragmented industry where no firm claimed more than 17 percent of the EC home market and all the volume firms were effectively confined to that one market; only the German luxury producers (BMW and Mercedes) have had a credible niche presence outside their European home market. The Japanese firms were building shares in America and Europe but, in the case of the two largest Japanese majors (Toyota and Nissan), there was still a marked disparity between their market share in Japan and in the other two markets; Toyota dominated its home market with a 40 percent plus market share but was a minor player elsewhere with 7.0 percent of the American market and just 3.0 percent of the European market. If Honda and Mazda did relatively better in America that was small consolation because their home-market presence was so weak. Only the American big two (GM and Ford) have had a long established double presence with more than 10 percent of two home markets; Ford balanced 22.1 percent of the American market against 11.9 percent of the European market.

Table 5.1: Major Company Shares of 1989 Passenger Car
Registrations by Regional Blocs.

Company	Share of EC registrations (%)	Share of Japanese registrations (%)	Share of North American registrations (%)
VW	15.0	1.1	1.6
BMW	2.8	0.7	0.6
Fiat	15.6	negligible	negligible
Peugeot	13.2	negligible	negligible
GM	10.9	negligible	34.8
Ford	11.9	negligible	22.1
Toyota	2.0	43.9	7.3 (including transplant 1.5)
Nissan	2.6	23.1	5.2 (including transplant 1.1)
Honda	1.0	10.8	7.9 (including transplant 3.6)
Mazda	1.4	5.9	2.7 (including transplant 2.1)

Sources: Annual Report on the Motor Industry, VDA; *Japanese Motor Industry Statistics*, JAMA.

The second table (5.2) gives exports by destination from national
production bases and this immediately puts market presence into productive perspective. If Ford and to a lesser extent GM are decentered
anomalies in terms of market presence, in productive terms they are
firms with split centers which have a history of independent manufacture on either side of the Atlantic that dates back to the interwar
period of national manufacturing autarchy.

Table 5.2: National Car Production and Exports by Destination in 1990.

Producing country	National production (000 units)	Destination		
		Western Europe	Japan	North America
Germany	4,661	2,064,000	132,000	290,000
France	3,295	1,646,000	14,000	2,000
Italy	1,875	698,000	5,000	8,000
UK	1,296	345,000	19,000	30,000
Spain	1,679	1,113,000	0	0
USA	6,077	49	39,000	–
Japan	9,948	1,483,000	-2	2,154,000

Source: VDA Annual Report on the Motor Industry.

Because GM and Ford as companies have had independent production bases in two home markets, and an interest in the third via minority stakes in Mazda and Isuzu, their American factories have traditionally supplied only the American market: these factories serve their home market just as exclusively as those of European companies. Despite all the media hype about exports from American transplants like the Honda Accord, much the same is true of the recently opened Japanese transplant factories. The European assemblers do export on a large scale from their still largely national production bases but mostly the exports remain within their European home market. The Japanese are unique in that they have developed a substantial volume of exports from their Japanese national base to the other two home markets; 36 percent of Japanese car production in 1990 was sold in North America or West Europe.

This general pattern of centering on one market is significant because, while the three major home markets may share some basic similarities, they are also separated by important differences. The difference of size is the most obvious. In 1990 the Japanese market reached a cyclical peak of 5 million new cars a year but for most of that decade the sales total was nearer 3 million cars and the average of the decade (1980-1989) was 3.3 million. By way of contrast US and EC markets are three-times larger with annual sales over the same decade averaging 9.7 million for the US and 10.0 million for the EC. There is also an important difference in terms of 'maturity' which has major consequences for the different manufacturers.

In the cars business there is a basic distinction between markets in the process of 'motorization' when car ownership per capita is increasing rapidly, and mature markets where replacement demand dominates because most consumers have one car and are replacing it with another. Mature markets are distinguished by the two characteristics of slow overall growth and cyclical variation in demand. Slow growth is determined by the durability of the product when each new car has a long and useful life. Modern cars are extraordinarily durable; the German industry now makes cars with a useful mechanical and body life of ten years and 200,000 kilometers. Cyclical variation is largely determined by the fact that statistically each new car will change hands three or four times during its life; at each stage in the ownership cycle replacement can be delayed or brought forward.

The three major home markets are differentiated in relation to these crucial characteristics of growth and cyclicality. They can usefully be seen as ranging across a continuum: the American market is closest to the stereotype of maturity and the pattern of no growth with violent fluctuations; the European market has occupied an intermediate position with growth and less-severe cyclical problems; while the Japanese market is probably best classified as a maturing market whose problems regarding cyclicality and saturation were only emerging in the early 1990s. The basic data on new car registrations in each home market is summarized in Table 5.3.

Table 5.3 shows that the first oil crisis around 1973 marks a major divide. All three home markets showed substantial growth before 1973. The American and European markets both more or less doubled in size between 1961 and 1973, while the Japanese market was then in the earlier phase of motorization and showed a twelve-fold increase during these years. Since 1973, the experiences of the different home markets have diverged around generally less favorable growth trends. The American market shows no sustained growth since 1973; the peak sales in the two best years since 1973 (1978 and 1986) fall short of the 1973 total. The European market shows ratchet-type growth with each major cyclical peak higher than the last; thus the peak sales of 1979 were 11 percent up on 1973 and the peak sales of 1990 were 32 percent up on 1979.

Table 5.3: New Car Registrations in the EC, Japan and USA 1961–1992, 000s units.

	EC	Japan	USA
1961	3,346	229	5,855
1962	3,895	259	6,939
1963	4,523	371	7,557
1964	5,234	494	8,085
1965	5,368	586	9,314
1966	5,524	740	9,009
1967	5,670	1,131	8,357
1968	6,019	1,569	9,404
1969	6,597	2,037	9,447
1970	7,049	2,379	8,388
1971	7,596	2,403	9,729
1972	8,361	2,627	9,834
1973	8,503	2,934	11,351
1974	7,423	2,287	8,701
1975	7,668	2,738	8,262
1976	8,331	2,449	9,752
1977	8,853	2,500	10,826
1978	9,295	2,857	10,946
1979	9,426	3,037	10,357
1980	8,888	2,854	8,761
1981	8,722	2,867	8,444

Table 5.3 (*continued*)

	EC	Japan	USA
1982	9,208	3,038	7,754
1983	9,772	3,136	8,924
1984	9,166	3,096	10,129
1985	9,495	3,104	10,889
1986	9,737	3,146	11,140
1987	11,211	3,275	10,166
1988	11,819	3,717	10,480
1989	12,204	4,404	9,853
1990	12,400	5,103	9,160
1991	11,822	4,868	8,175
1992	12,607	4,454	8,214

Source: Motor Industry Statistics Yearbook, SMMT; *Japanese Automobile Statistics Yearbook,* JAMA, various years.

After 1973, as before, the Japanese had the most favorable growth rates because 1990 registrations were 45 percent up on 1973. Nevertheless the Japanese did not enjoy steady year-on-year growth in the 1970s and 1980s; during the period 1978-1987 the Japanese market fluctuated around 3 million and only a late spurt took the market over 5 million in 1990. Even more striking was the effect of the recession of the early 1990s when all three regions experienced a sharp downturn in sales. This indicates the severity of the current slump and signals the onset of maturity in Japan.

Much the same pattern of difference shows up if we examine the number and severity of fluctuations in each home market. Table 5.4 summarizes the history of major downturns in each market since 1961. The cyclical downturns in America start in the 1960s and are subsequently more severe than in other home markets; the three major downturns since 1973 all show peak-to-trough falls of more than 25 percent. If Europe occupies a gentler position in terms of fluctuation this is largely because fluctuations in the various national markets have tended to average out over Europe as a whole. As we shall see in Chapter 8 individual national markets like the UK had severe fluctuations in the 1950s and 1960s, the creation of a Europe-wide single market eased the position by bringing together Northern European markets with different cycles as well as providing growing South European markets where the use of cars was still spreading. The EC market suffered just three downturns between 1973 and 1991 which brought an average demand fall of 8.3 percent. The Japanese market had more downturns but four of its five downturns were very brief. The average fall in demand was 8.9 percent, mostly because of the two sharp but short falls of the early 1970s and 1990s.

Table 5.4: Down-swings in US, EC and Japanese New Car Markets Since 1961.

USA:

	Peak sales 000s units	Trough sales 000s units	Percentage fall
1965-67	9,313	8,357	-10.3
1969-70	9,447	8,390	-11.2
1973-75	11,351	8,261	-27.3
1978-82	10,947	7,754	-29.2
1986-91	11,140	8,175	-26.6

EC:

	Peak sales 000s units	Trough sales 000s units	Percentage fall
1973-4	8,503	7,424	-12.7
1979-81	9,426	8,722	-7.5
1990-91	12,400	11,822	-4.7

Japan:

	Peak sales 000s units	Trough sales 000s units	Percentage fall
1973-4	2,934	2,287	-22.1
1979-80	3,037	2,854	-6.1
1983-4	3,136	3,100	-1.2
1990-92	5,103	4,454	-12.7

Sources: *Motor Industry Statistics Yearbook, SMMT;* 1992 EC and USA figures direct from SMMT; 1992 Japanese figures from *Monthly Report* June 1993 no.261, Industrial Bank of Japan.

Slow growth and unstable demand create a less favorable environment for firms which are centered in markets with these characteristics. The American operations of GM and Ford are clearly most disadvantaged on this count. Any firm with a large-volume exposure to the American market over the last twenty-five years would have suffered from demand fluctuation and bouts of capacity underutilization which in this case would be, not so much the just reward of an uncompetitive and unsuccessful minority of firms, but the arbitrary punishment for majors operating in an adverse and unstable environment. Over the same period the Japanese firms enjoyed the advantage of a much more favorable home-market environment which absorbed roughly half their total output. This advantage was reinforced because most of the rest was sold in European and American markets where the Japanese were minor players who had been gently increasing their share and were thus, at least temporarily, immunized against the worst effects of downturn. Whether the Japanese can retain this market advantage over the next twenty years is very doubtful. Their exposure in the US market (exports plus transplant production) has now become significant, whilst at the same time the Japanese home market is maturing and becoming more like the American market. Japanese firms in the early 1990s were enduring their first serious sustained downturn in home passenger-car demand since the first oil crisis some twenty years previously; the demand for cars was 13 percent down for the year ended April 1993 compared with the year ended April 1990.

The next section of this chapter looks at the consequences of market instability for financial ratios, but before turning to examine this problem it is necessary to consider distribution expenses. The rationale for this is that distribution is another major item of expense in the cars business which (like design and development) can easily wipe out the profits that would otherwise be made. Furthermore, although all the Japanese firms operate in a much more favorable home-market demand environment, the Japanese majors incur large distribution expenses which absorb a significant part of the surplus that would otherwise be generated as profit. It is difficult to prove these points because no car firm adds up all the costs of distribution and marketing which are incurred or subsidized by the assembler.

The available fragments of information on distribution cost allow us to make an upper and lower bound estimate of the distribution cost which is incurred on European luxury cars. The lower-bound estimate can be derived from the allocated distribution-cost allowance made in Rover's conventional costing system for the 800 series car; the 800's distribution costs are modest here because this model is effectively sold only in the company's home market alongside a range of volume cars. Rover allocates a distribution cost of £530 (or $1,000) to each car and that amounts to some 5 percent of the wholesale price of an entry level 800 (Coffey, 1992). An upper-bound estimate can be derived from the Bureau of Commerce data on import/sales ratios for the German car wholesalers in the United States who sell mainly luxury imported cars, especially BMW and Mercedes, in small volume at very high distribution cost. The German wholesalers in 1990 had an import-sales ratio of 68 percent (US Bureau of Commerce, 1991) which implies that, after profit, maybe $5,000 or more than 20 percent of the wholesale price was absorbed by transport, advertising, sales and marketing staff, parts back-up and dealer support. If this is an extreme case, the *Autocar* study of 1990 shows that end-market distribution costs are substantial on the most mundane European family hatch backs.

Against this background the fundamental point is that distribution costs are very high on all cars sold in the Japanese home market. Like much else in the Japanese car industry distribution expense has been driven by Toyota which has more than 40 percent of the home market. Market-leading firms with a large market share (like Toyota in Japan, GM in America or BMC in Britain in the 1960s) often pursue multiple-outlet distribution strategies which make their product, like Coca Cola, available everywhere. Such firms may also attempt to defend and increase their market share by selling different models or differently-badged and kitted versions of the same model through systems of parallel outlets. Thus GM had its divisions, BMC had its badge-engineered marques and Toyota maintains no less than five chains of dealers which sell variegated selections from the Toyota range: in 1992, the 310 Toyota dealers within Japan maintained 5,200 sales outlets which were divided into Toyota, Toyopet, Corolla, Auto and Vista chains, (Toyota corporate profile, 1992).

If that much is familiar for Westerners, the unexpected element in Japanese distribution is the labor-intensive methods of door to door car selling which Toyota and its major competitor Nissan have traditionally used to sell their cars and block home-market advance by the minor Japanese firms. The IMVP study argued that the Toyota style of distribution was also functional because it gave the Japanese majors a mass of useful information about home-market consumer tastes and preferences (Womack et al., 1990, pp.188–90). For a variety of reasons this argument is implausible. The Japanese majors sell well in export markets where they rely on orthodox Western-style market research rather than Japanese distribution. Moreover the volume of information on home-market consumers does not prevent occasional major mistakes with new model introductions.

Japanese-style distribution is certainly labor intensive and imposes substantial extra costs on dealers and assemblers. All comparisons show that the productivity of the dealer workforce or of the dealer salesforce is much lower in Japan than in either Europe or America; IMVP claims that the 'average sales representative' sells ten cars per month in the US against four in Japan (Womack et al., 1990, p.187). Japanese-style distribution also adds a massive burden to the car assembler's payroll. On average over the decade of the 1980s, 25 percent of Toyota's Japanese employees were employed in its 'motor sales' subsidiary. In

Nissan, which maintains a comparable sales operation on half of Toyota's market share, no less than 50 percent of the Japanese workforce is in the 'motor sales' subsidiary. This direct employment of a huge sales staff is unprecedented in Western car manufacturing. If we take GM, for example, that company employed 383,000 in 1991 and, of its 98,000 white collar workers, only 2,000 were officially classified as sales workers (GM Communication, 14th August 1992).

All this is a useful antidote to the 'different and in every way better' message about lean production, and to the mirror image of that Japanolatory which takes the form of a critical reaction against American M-form organization. Against these positions we would argue that the diverse national capitalisms of the late twentieth century generate different rather than better forms of managerial hierarchy. All capitalist managerial hierarchies have their armies of supernumaries in suits who are (well) paid out of what an old-fashioned Marxist would call the surplus value generated in production. In America and Japan the supernumaries perform different but equally ambiguous functions. American car firms employ armies of middle managers in functions like financial control, and senior managers in strategic planning. Japanese car firms open a sales subsidiary which employs an army of door knockers and their supervisors.

Volume Effects

Volume fluctuations, especially cyclical up-swings and down-swings, have significant consequences for build hours per car and for financial ratios. The general problem is that most modern car firms are, for technical or social reasons, unable to take labor out in line with falling output in a cyclical down-swing; the usual combination of short-time working and lay offs simply does not take out sufficient labor quickly enough. Conversely, when the up-swing comes, the typical modern car company starts with considerable underutilization of labor as well as capacity so that the company does not have to take on extra labor to meet the increase in demand.

If these generalizations express a cyclical truth they should not be represented as a universal hypothesis which is simply testable. Any observation of cyclical relations between output and employment is complicated by secular upsizing and downsizing in successful and unsuccessful firms which produces lumpy changes in workforce size. Furthermore, the orthodox cyclical pattern is recent, relative and no doubt reversible. The inhibition on hiring and firing was consolidated in successful national industries operating in full employment economies like Japan or Germany in the 1970s where employers could guarantee employment and/or unions could obtain generous deals on lay offs. But it is necessary to register that this kind of concession had been won by organized labor for the first time in Detroit after 1945; major national industries, like the British industry between the wars, had previously operated with a casualised workforce that was hired and fired according to seasonal and cyclical fluctuations. If Henry Ford paid the highest wages, he did not offer continuity of employment; Ford's factories were closed for months in the slump after World War One, and again when the company changed over from the Model T to A.

The modern cyclical relation between output and employment has physical and financial consequences which complicate the analysis presented in our earlier analysis chapters. The discussion in those chapters offered a simplified, static representation of the cars business; subject to prerequisites and limits, any productionist firm which intervenes productively should be able to produce next year's car with fewer labor hours and less labor cost. In fact the dynamics of the business are considerably more complex; if capacity utilization falls, next year's car will probably have more labor hours in it. Car firms are often caught in a kind of parallelogram of opposed short-run forces where the labor-saving effects of productive intervention are cancelled by the labor-wasting effects of capacity underutilization. And this point is of more than academic relevance because changes in the physical labor input per car will shift key financial ratios.

Financially, when firms operating in cyclical markets cannot adjust labor-hours input in line with output fluctuations, they must endure fluctuations in labor's share of value-added above and below the normal 65 to 70 percent level. This point emerges fairly clearly if we average labor's share of value-added in the Western car firms that operate in cyclical car markets. Table 5.5 presents the results of that exercise for a sample of five to eight Western car companies. The labor share of value-added for these firms averaged 69 percent over the decade 1979–1989. But this average obscures the wide range of performance within the cycle. In the bad years of 1980–2 when an annual average of 17.3 million cars were sold in the American and EC markets, labor's share of value-added rose to an average of almost 79 percent. By way of contrast in the good years 1988-9 when an annual average of 22.2 million cars were sold in the American and EC markets, labor's share of value-added averaged 62 percent.

At a company level, the relation between overall market cyclicality and labor's share of value-added breaks down because individual companies are winning and losing shares of the markets in which they compete and making secular adjustments to long-term market success and failure. Nevertheless, the company-level analysis presented in Table 5.6 is illuminating because it shows that at the level of the individual firm the high to low range of variation in labor's share is typically much larger than in the group; if we take GM, Ford and Chrysler, the three American-owned manufacturers, their highs over the years between 1980 and 1990 range between 88 and 126 percent while their lows range between 58 and 64 percent.

Table 5.5: Year by Year Variation in Labor's Share of Value-added in Eight Western Car Companies, 1979–91.

	Average labor share of value added (%)	Number of companies covered
1979	71.2	5
1980	85.7	5
1981	76.9	6
1982	73.6	6
1983	66.8	6
1984	72.2	7
1985	67.4	7
1986	68.6	7
1987	65.4	8
1988	61.9	8
1989	62.5	8
1990	70.7	8
1991	81.3	7

Note: For each year the unweighted average of labor's share of value-added is calculated for major Western car makers: GM, Ford, Chrysler, BMW, VAG, PSA, Fiat and Ford UK.

Source: Consolidated Company Report and Accounts, various years.

As might be expected, the Japanese companies (with the exception of Toyota) show damped and slightly less extreme fluctuations: in Nissan, the range from high to low is 75 to 60 percent. In this respect, as in so many others, Toyota is in a class of its own with a labor share that is fluctuating at much lower levels in the range 47 to 38 percent over the decade of the 1980s. Western car companies, even undistinguished ones like Ford UK, can approach this level of labor's share of value-added in good years but their problem is that they cannot sustain a low labor share of value-added when demand drops sharply from peak to trough in the cycle.

Table 5.6: High and Low Labor Share of Value-added in Twelve Major Car Companies, 1980–91.

	High year	High (%)	Low Year	Low (%)
Toyota	1982	46.9	1985	37.5
Nissan	1987	75.2	1981	60.4
Honda	1991	62.0	1985	40.1
Mazda	1989	80.5	1985	60.0
Ford	1980	91.0	1988	58.3
GM	1991	88.2	1983	63.9
Chrysler	1980	126.1	1985	58.6
PSA	1985	86.7	1990	53.2
Fiat	1991	69.9	1990	60.8
VAG	1982	78.6	1985	64.6
BMW	1991	69.7	1983	58.3
Ford UK	1991	110.0	1988	38.1

Note: The high year is the year in which labor's share of value-added is highest and for ease of comparison the high is expressed as a percent of value-added. Where the percentage exceeds 100 percent payments to labor exceed the value-added recovered from market sales. The low year is the year in which labor's share is at its lowest.

Source: Consolidated Company Report and Accounts, various years

We now turn to consider the impact of cyclical variation in demand on the residual of profit which remains after both labor costs and depreciation charges are deducted from the value-added fund. The depreciation charge is relatively fixed, and so if labor's share is high and rising because of cyclical and other pressures, net income (retained and distributed profit) becomes a precarious residual. Net income is a source of cash, the existence of which is always threatened by the prior claims of labor and depreciation. Table 5.7 illustrates this point by presenting data on the variation in profits after tax as a percentage of sales revenue in good and bad years. The basic point is that the surplus in the form of profits pre-tax or net income may be substantial in good years but in a number of cases negative or nonexistent in bad years.

Table 5.7: High and Low Profits to Sales 1980–1991 for Twelve Major Car Manufacturers.

	Profit as a percent of sales in a good year		Profit as a percent of sales in a bad year	
	Year	Profit to sales percent	Year	Profit to sales percent
Toyota	1985	6.0	1982	3.7
Nissan	1981	3.5	1987	0.5
Honda	1981	10.2	1991	3.1
Mazda	1985	1.9	1989	1.2
GM	1983	7.2	1991	-3.2
Ford	1988	11.1	1980	-2.1
Chrysler	1985	12.9	1980	-11.1
VAG	1985	8.0	1982	0.6
BMW	1984	9.6	1991	3.1
Fiat	1987	9.0	1991	5.5
PSA	1990	12.9	1986	0.8
Ford UK	1987	10.1	1991	-8.9

Source: Consolidated Company Reports and Accounts, various years.

Toyota, where labor's share is uniquely low and steady, is able to maintain net income's share of value-added consistently above 25 percent and so maintain a good profit to sales ratio. Elsewhere the mainly cyclical fluctuations in the other components of value-added are buffered by the variation in retained profits between zero or negative in a bad year. Retained profits are usually applied to smoothing fluctuations because surplus in a good year is accumulated in the balance-sheet revenue reserve. Even so Table 5.7 implies that most car companies (including most of the Japanese car companies) are just as vulnerable to cyclical market fluctuations which damage the residual profit margin.

At the end of the queue of claimants stand the shareholders who make a modest claim on the value-added fund. But the difficulties of the business are such that it is not possible to protect the shareholders from the consequences of cyclicality; the shareholders in most car companies can expect 3 to 6 percent of value-added in a good year and little or nothing in a bad year. In the general theory of capitalism, the claims of the rentier can never be abrogated without throwing the firm into crisis: if any firm regularly failed to pay dividends to ordinary shareholders, the firm should not long survive. In specific capitalist national economies, expectations of profit and rules about the consequences of unprofitability vary considerably: Japanese shareholders do not expect rising payouts whereas American shareholders do; hostile takeover of the unprofitable is unusual outside Britain and

America where large size still affords some protection. This is indeed good news for most of the world's car companies who must regularly disappoint shareholders.

Break-even analysis provides another insight into the problem of the precarious residual. We are fairly sceptical about orthodox economic or accounting analysis of break-even which allocates costs into a universal fixed and variable cost schema; the status of labor costs depends on the historical and social inhibitions on hiring and firing. So we have constructed our own simple alternative which assumes that the wages bill stays the same as output falls and then measures the percent by which output can fall before the firm is covering only its basic operating costs of pay and depreciation from internally-generated value-added. The assumption that the wages bill stays the same is not realistic but puts all the companies on an equal worse case footing. For obvious reasons, the calculation is also based on the most recent cyclical-peak year in the relevant home market which is 1986 for the USA and 1990 for the EC and Japan.

Table 5.8 conveys two essential messages. The first message is that a majority of the world's car companies, including the leading European assembler VW and Japanese firms such as Nissan and Mazda are ill placed to meet cyclical turn down and other pressures because in cyclical-peak years they are only 10 to 15 percent above break-even. The second message is that it is possible to create robust firms able to withstand cyclical downturns in a variety of ways, with or without productive excellence; there is more than one way to skin a cat. Thus the minority of robust firms includes an intriguing variety: Toyota (of course) which maintains a very low labor share of value-added, Fiat which relies on a moderate labor share and much lower depreciation charges; as well as Ford US and Chrysler which had responded to market difficulty by downsizing their firms which then gushed cash on the upswing and temporarily became very robust.

Table 5.8: Percentage above Operational Break-Even for Twelve Major Car Companies in the Last Cyclical Peak Year.

Company	Year	Percent above break even
Toyota	1990	48.5
Nissan	1990	11.4
Honda	1990	24.1
Mazda	1990	11.5
GM	1986	7.8

Table 5.8 (*continued*)

Company	Year	Percent above break even
Ford	1986	27.3
Chrysler	1986	48.5
BMW	1990	17.9
VAG	1990	10.3
PSA	1990	56.1
Fiat	1990	35.8
Ford UK	1988	113.5

Note: Operation above break-even calculated as profit (net income) as a percent of value-added minus net income.

Source: Consolidated Company Reports and Accounts, various years.

The strategy of downsizing is difficult to execute, as will be shown in the Chapter 8 discussion of Rover under Edwardes. More immediately to the point, if the market pressures persist and overcapacity recurs at lower levels of output on the next downswing, it only brings temporary relief. This is what seems to have happened to the big American-owned firms: by 1992 *Automotive News* reported a utilization rate for the Big Three of 65 percent for car production (*Automotive News*, Market Databook 1993). It was unsurprizingly the American Big Three firms that fell below break-even and registered large losses in 1991. In the American case, the effects of home-market cyclicality are exacerbated by international trade in cars which is considered in the next chapter.

✦ ✦ ✦

6
Unbalanced International Trade

—— ❖ ——

Although most of the world's assemblers are still centered on one home market, their problems and opportunities cannot simply be discussed in terms of home-market characteristics. Unbalanced trade within and between home markets is a lever for obtaining extra volume and capacity utilization at the expense of losses for competitors. The first section of this chapter therefore analyzes the emergence of the present pattern of unbalanced trade which is both an intensifier of market pressures on the unsuccessful and a release from national constraints for the successful. The second section establishes the point that unbalanced trade is likely to persist and argues that this pattern is a cause for concern and should be an object of regulation because of its adverse macroeconomic consequences for the unsuccessful.

The Development of Large Scale Unbalanced Trade

Thirty years ago, international trade between car-producing countries was a small-scale business involving mainly niche speciality products; in Britain at this time drivers of imported cars flashed their headlights when they met another car of the same marque. Manufacturing autarchy had been conditioned by trade barriers and differences in size and packaging. This had long been the case; the Model T was put together in branch assembly plants within the United States, but UK and Canadian demand had to be met by setting up full manufacturing operations in those countries. Furthermore, because European demand for the American type of large, cheap car was limited, GM and Ford developed parallel and independent manufacturing operations in Britain and Germany.

The result was that at the beginning of the 1960s, domestically-produced cars held a 90 percent or larger share of sales in all the major car-producing countries. Trade was initially stimulated by the differences in the type of car produced and especially by the absence of domestically-produced small cars in the ranges of the American Big

Three; the most important development of the late 1950s was the growing American import of small European cars which owed much to the clever marketing of the VW Beetle as a low-cost alternative car. The prospects of further rapid growth of imports into the United States then seemed rapidly to fade: when the European share of the American market climbed towards 10 percent in 1959, the American manufacturers successfully introduced their own range of 'compacts' (Altshuler et al., 1984, p.25). They used their cost advantage to offer more car for the money and drove all the European volume car importers (except for VW) back into the sea.

Nevertheless, manufacturing autarchy was rapidly eroded over the next fifteen years as trade barriers were lowered and differences in product size and packaging were greatly reduced. As a general rule of thumb industrial leaders become free-trade missionaries. Thus the United States had the lowest tariff levels in the early post-war period and led the way to free trade in cars. By 1950, the US tariff on imported cars was only 10 percent and there was a gradual reduction to 3 percent by the early 1970s. Other countries started from much higher levels - usually around 35 percent in Europe - and these only fell significantly with the EC's move to a common external tariff from the mid-1960s. The EC external tariff was substantially lower but nevertheless remained significant at a level of almost 11 percent in 1980. For Europe the more decisive change was the removal of all tariffs on trade between Community members, and the predictable effect of this change was the expansion of intra-European trade in cars. In Japan an initial 40 percent tariff on imported cars had only dropped to 30 percent by the late sixties: a decade later, when the Japanese were being obliged to restrain export volumes to the United States and Europe, the Japanese tariff on imported cars had been totally removed. The Japanese had followed (though more rapidly than usual) the classic path from being determined protectionists to free-trade missionaries.

The reduction in tariff levels was a permissive condition whose effects were activated by a convergence of product types and a new pattern of full line direct competition between all the major manufacturers. Thus the Americans had through the 1950s and 1960s specialized in the very large, V8 engine, automatic-transmission 'turnpike cruiser'. Partly as a result of the 1970s oil shocks, North American demand shifted dramatically: in the early 1970s the very large cars still took about 60 percent of the market; a decade later this had fallen to 30 percent (Altshuler et al., 1984, p.130, fig 6.1). At the same time the main producers in Europe and Japan were all extending their ranges to produce a full line of models which competed directly against similarly packaged offerings from the rest. Thus, within Europe after 1976, GM, Ford and VW entered the small 'super mini' class which had hitherto been the preserve of BMC, Fiat and Renault. The Japanese moved inexorably up-market from their initial position as producers of small, cheap cars and utility taxis; by the late 1980s Honda, Nissan and Toyota had entered the luxury-car market with products that were, in the United States, priced to sell against Mercedes Benz and BMW.

From the mid-1960s to the end of the 1970s, autarchy collapsed and import penetration rose rapidly and unsteadily everywhere except in Japan. As Table 6.1 shows by the late 1980s, imports accounted for one-third or more of new car sales in all the major producing countries except for Japan. The weakness of the British industry must partly explain the rise to 50 percent plus, levels of import penetration which have not been reached in any other major producing country. But, more generally, the rise of imports to take one-third of the market is a secular development which reflects the demand-side influence of the consumer taste for diversity rather than the supply-side strength or weakness of the indigenous industry. In its prime the VW Beetle took 30 percent of the West German market; however good the VW Golf is as a product, it is no longer possible to persuade so many Germans to buy the same car.

Table 6.1: Percentage Import Shares of New Car Registrations in Major Car Producing Countries, 1965–90.

	USA	Japan	Germany	UK
1965	6	n/a	11	5
1970	15	1	23	14
1975	18	2	25	33
1980	23	2	26	55
1985	26	2	27	60
1990	32	4	33	56
1991	33	5	35	40

Sources: Survey of World Automotive Industry, SMMT; Motor Vehicle Statistics of Japan, JAMA; Automotive News Market Data Book, Crain Publications; Statistical Yearbook, VDA, various years.

As the volume of international trade in cars increased, what separated the national winners from the losers was not their ability to defend home market share but their ability to find export sales which would, in volume terms, compensate for the erosion of home market share. This point emerges very clearly from Table 6.2 which shows the share of output exported by the major producing countries. The two losers were the USA, which was always a non-exporting country, and the UK, which became one. As we have already noted, the Big Three had never used their American factories to serve non-American markets and this policy was not changed as import penetration of the US market increased. The British story is even more interesting because in the later 1970s the British industry exported 38 percent of output, a performance which was quite respectable if we take French and Italian performance as the yardstick. But, by the end of the 1980s, British exports had collapsed into insignificance.

Table 6.2: Percentage Export Shares of Domestic Production in Major Car Producing Countries, 1979-90.

Country	1979	1985	1990
USA	9.4	8.6	13.1
Japan	50.2	57.9	45.1
Germany	55.5	67.2	57.3
France	47.7	48.9	43.3
Italy	43.7	32.4	39.6
UK	38.3	22.9	7.4

Sources: Survey of World Automotive Industry, SMMT; Motor Vehicle Statistics of Japan, JAMA; Automotive News Market Data Book, Crain Publications; Statistical Yearbook, VDA, various years.

By way of contrast, the two winners were Japan and Germany which escaped the limits of their national markets and managed to export more than half their output. Table 6.3 puts these achievements into perspective by presenting basic data on the growth of overall export volumes and on export destinations. The Japanese export achievement after 1960 is phenomenal by any standard but the spectacular success is all the more extraordinary since the Japanese were in 1960 starting from nothing as entirely new entrants into the export business. Their national industry, which exported 7,000 cars in 1960 had expanded exports to 4.5 million in 1990. Japanese export success is based on volume penetration of the American and EC home markets; the USA, which was a consistently much larger market for the Japanese, absorbed more than 2 million Japanese units per year in the 1980s while the EC market had grown to more than a million units by the end of that decade.

Table 6.3: Japanese and German Export Volume and Destination Since 1979

Japanese car exports

	1979	1985	1990
Total exports	3,102,000	4,427,000	4,487,000
Exports to EC	630,000	792,000	1,086,000
Exports to N. America	1,608,000	2,413,000	2,154,000

German car exports

	1979	1985	1990
Total exports	2,183,000	2,801,000	2,670,000
Exports to EC	1,348,000	1,637,000	1,805,000
Exports to N. America	374,000	483,000	290,000

Sources: World Automotive Statistics Yearbook, SMMT, various years.

By way of contrast, the Germans were established exporters who already in 1960 exported 841,169 units or 46.3 percent of domestic output and in the next thirty years consolidated their success so that they exported 2.7 million cars or 57.3 percent of domestic car output in 1990. The German producers consolidated their position as major exporters by switching between the American and European markets. When the US compacts in the 1960s and the Japanese small-car imports of the 1970s shut the door on German volume-car sales in the United States, the German producers had, and cultivated, a highly-profitable luxury niche in the United States. Although this never amounted to more than 500,000 cars a year, they were mostly high-value cars. They also developed a similar position in Japan where the German industry exported 132,000 cars in 1991. More fundamentally the creation of an EC-wide home market was the salvation of the German industry because it offered a way of escaping the limits of the German national market where one-third of sales were claimed by imports. By 1979, other EC markets took 1.4 million German cars or over 60 percent of German car exports and by 1990 the number of cars taken by these markets was much the same at 1.8 million or 68 percent of all German car exports.

The consequences of these various changes in the international market was that the volume of cars entering into world trade increased spectacularly in the thirty year period after 1960. Whereas just under one-fifth (19.2 percent) of the cars produced by the nine major producing nations entered into international trade in 1960, by 1990 the proportion of a much larger output had increased to one-third. If that was the prime fact about international trade in cars, the second fact was that the gains were unequally divided so that almost all the volume increase was captured by the two winning countries, Japan and Germany. Between the years 1960 and 1990, there was a total increase of 7.9 million in the number of exported cars entering into international trade; during these same years German and Japanese car exports accounted for 6.3 million extra units, leaving a residual-trade growth of just 1.6 million units for the other seven major producing countries to squabble over.

The volume of cars traded internationally was large enough to influence not only capacity utilization but also installed capacity and thus change rankings in the international league table of volume-car producers. In 1960 America still bestrode the world of cars like a colossus. But by 1990, after thirty years of slow home-market growth and trade failure, the US share of world production had fallen from 55 percent to 20 percent. Moreover, although the path taken by American car output was jagged and irregular, there was no upward trend in the absolute number of cars produced; if anything the trend was downward although the 34 percent fall suggested by the difference between a 1990 output of 6.1 million against an output of 9.3 million a quarter of a century earlier exaggerates the change since the 1965 level of production was unusually high. The chief beneficiary was Japan where home-market growth and export success raised output from an insignificant 165,000 in 1960 to a level of 9.9 million, more than 50 percent greater than the US in 1990. In the case of Germany, the developing intra-European trade allowed the Germans to retain in 1990 the 15 percent share of world car production which they had captured by 1960. Thanks to trade, Japan has joined Germany and the USA to make up the dominating triumvirate in world motor production.

The unequal division of the spoils of the car trade between a couple of national winners (Japan and Germany) and a couple of national losers has resulted in a pattern of severely unbalanced trade. It is possible to find balanced flows between moderately successful second-division producers who have volume positions in each other's markets. The trade in cars between France and Italy would be an example of this kind of relative balance, France sent 244,463 cars to Italy in 1990 and took in return 166,338 (SMMT, 1991, Table 84). But the more general pattern is that the three major producing countries and home markets are connected by bilateral flows which are highly unequal in volume and value terms. It should also be noted that none of the major flows offset each other so that there is no realistic prospect of a balanced and equilibrating series of multilateral flows. The question of values, deficits and surpluses is discussed in the next section of this chapter and at this point we will only illustrate the physical imbalance in terms of units imported and exported. The matrix table 6.4 shows, for one recent year, the pattern of physical deficits and surpluses in terms of cars traded between the major markets and producing countries.

Table 6.4: Surplus and Deficit in Units (Cars and Commercial Vehicles) Traded Between Major Producers and Markets in 1991.

	Japanese producers	Exports by German producers	Exports by US producers
American market	+2,475,398	+125,184	—
EC market	+1,139,049	+724,050	-102,200
Japanese market	—	-458,488	-2,475,398

Source: World Automotive Statistics Yearbook, 1992, SMMT.

One important qualification must be registered before considering the consequences and future of unbalanced trade in the next section of this chapter. So far what has been discussed has been national success and failure because trade statistics are available in this form and because the nation state remains an important decision making agent whose actions influence the volume and direction of trade. At the same time it must be recognized that 'national success and failure' is a mercantilist abstraction which covers up important issues about the behavior and strategy of multinational companies; it is an over-simplification to assert that the American and British car industries failed in trade without giving some consideration to the effects of the sourcing decisions of GM and Ford.

The British industry was undoubtedly weakened by the failure of BLMC/Rover which once held a 40 percent plus share of the British market and in the late 1960s exported 400,000 cars a year. There were strong company-specific explanations for part of this decline: for example, the response of the company to a high pound in the early 1980s was to pull out of export markets, thereby compounding the general fatuity of the Edwardes plan for 'product-led recovery' which failed to address the problem of where the product was to be sold (Williams et al., 1987a). But the industry was also severely affected by the decisions of Ford UK and GM/Vauxhall to source tied imports and kits of components from their Continental European factories; as Jones demonstrated, between 1974 and 1984 Ford brought in 230,000 tied imports and was simultaneously UK market leader and Britain's largest importer (Jones, 1985, p.30). By omission rather than commission, the same two American multinationals play an equally crucial role in American trade failure; as import volumes increased the big American companies did not attempt to shift their American factories to export products but opportunistically participated in the import boom by bringing in tied imports from Asian affiliates. The message of all this is simply that the national and corporate interest do not always coincide and that message will be reasserted in the next section of this chapter on the consequences and future of unbalanced trade.

The Consequences and Future of Unbalanced Trade

Economic discourse constructs an account of the gains of trade within an *a priori* which focuses selectively on micro benefits rather than micro and macro costs. The primary emphasis is on gains in consumer welfare through trade which offers the consumer a choice of higher quality and cheaper goods. The costs in terms of producer welfare are covered up with the anodyne assumption that displaced resources (especially labor) will smoothly flow into alternative uses. This assumption was classically legitimized by the theory of comparative advantage which provided an assurance that, even if one trade partner was absolutely less efficient in all tradeable goods production, production of tradeable goods will not be monopolized by the more efficient partner; according to the theory of comparative advantage the more efficient partner should concentrate on those activities where its relative advantage is greatest and leave the rest to the less efficient partner. The conclusions derived from this two-country, two-commodity model, have been confirmed by subsequent economic analysis. This orthodoxy continues to focus on the microeconomic consequences of trade; macroeconomic consequences such as trade constraints on a country running persistent deficits, are largely excluded from the field of the visible.

This discursive preconstruction of the benefits of trade is reinforced by the political shift which has constructed a post-modern politics of consumerism. In the inter-war and early post-war period, national welfare was intellectually and politically defined so that the interest of domestic manufacturing firms and their workforce was usually privileged. Thus Keynes, in the early 1930s, endorsed free trade but argued that tariffs were necessary if, as a result of free trade, British production of steel or cars was threatened. Calculations of this kind were the principle of policy in countries like Italy which prevented Ford from opening an Italian plant because that would damage Fiat. There has been a sharp change in recent years: across Western Europe and America, Galbraith's 'comfortable classes' have (and vote for) a choice of the world's finest consumer goods and hang the consequences for national firms and their workforces (Galbraith, 1992). Self interest acquires a higher moral purpose within the demonology of radical-right politics where producer interest groups always figure as reactionary obstructions which prevent competition and the market from delivering their benefits.

Against this background, we would insist that free trade is a dubious generalization which covers up the specifics of unbalanced trade in the three 'home' markets. There is legitimate cause for concern about the structural consequences in countries which lose. In these countries the micro gains in consumer welfare may not be large, there may be offsetting losses in producer welfare and, in the case of cars, those countries which lose must suffer macro trade constraint. These points demand serious consideration.

The gains in consumer welfare from trade in cars are modest. If we consider non-price characteristics, by the early 1990s, the packaging, quality and reliability differences between national products are much smaller than they were twenty years ago; Ford, GM and Chrysler models now figure prominently in the JD Power survey of customer satisfaction. Second-hand buyers, who make up the majority of car buyers, often prefer the home manufactured product; the devil you know (by Ford or Chevrolet) is often easier and cheaper to repair. Within the American and European home markets, local manufacturers in any case offer a large choice; it is a gross distortion to suggest that the alternatives are limited to a choice between accepting either free trade or the old East European model of the same car for everybody. Furthermore, as we argued in Chapter 4, the differences in price reflect differences in social settlement (wages, wage gradient and hours worked) as much as technical efficiency. In the EC market where prices are higher than in America or Japan, the Japanese firms appropriate the surplus as profit by selling at nearly local prices; in Britain in the early 1990s a Lexus cost more than a BMW 735 and only 12 percent less than an entry level version of the new and larger Mercedes Benz S class.

Any losses in producer welfare should be balanced against these modest gains in consumer welfare. The micro questions about producer welfare are pertinent because we know that 'deindustrialization' or a general run down of manufacturing has serious consequences both for the volume and the composition of employment in an advanced country. In Britain, for example, where manufacturing output shows no sustained increase since 1973 the total number employed in manufacturing has declined from 7 million in the late 1960s to 4.5 million in the early 1990s. In what Keynes called a 'jammed economy' disemployed manufacturing labor flows into the pool of unemployment or finds its way, through a segmented labor market into low-wage service employment. These structural considerations take on more significance when it is realized that, in all the advanced economies, manufacturing is an important generator of relatively high paid blue-collar jobs.

Nonetheless this observation needs to be set in perspective. The motor vehicle industry is only one sector of manufacturing and the hyperbole about cars being 'the industry of industries' obscures the basic fact that cars account for a relatively small proportion of manufacturing value-added and employment in all the advanced economies. National motor vehicle sectors (cars, trucks and components) account for 4 to 12 percent of manufacturing employment in the major producing countries (Table 6.5) and these shares of employment would roughly double if we were to include employment which lies outside of the motor vehicle sector. Excluding Germany where mechanical engineering in general and vehicles in particular are important, the vehicles manufacturing sector accounts for just 4 to 7 percent of manufacturing employment. The micro consequences of car-trade failure are catastrophic for individuals and communities. Disemployed older car workers stand little chance of reemployment at comparable wages in an economy like the UK where only one-third of men over the age of fifty-five are economically active. Similarly, in Detroit a generation of youth is working in fast food joints at $5 per hour because they cannot get a start at Ford or Kelsey Brake which pay $15 an hour. But in the aggregate, the direct economic consequences of trade failure in cars are necessarily bounded by the comparatively small size of the sector relative to the economy as a whole.

Cars are not the direct initiator and sustainer of national economic development in the twentieth century, no more than railways were in the nineteenth century. However, it does not follow that a declining national car industry and trade failure does not matter. Declining car industries do not directly account for the rising unemployment in all the advanced countries (except Japan) over the past twenty years. But in Britain and America, declining car industries have contributed to macro-economic trade constraints which prevent or discourage the adoption of reflationary domestic policies which would reduce unemployment.

Table 6.5: Motor Vehicles Sector Share of Manufacturing Value-added and Employment in Four Major Car Producing Countries, 1963–1989.

Percentage share of manufacturing value-added

	1963	1969	1975	1981	1989
USA	6.3	6.3	5.5	4.7	6.6
Japan	6.2	6.9	6.6	7.8	8.8
Germany	n/a	n/a	n/a	11.1	11.7
UK	6.8	6.2	5.8	5.3	5.5

Percentage share of manufacturing employment

	1963	1969	1975	1981	1989
USA	4.1	4.6	4.7	4.2	5.1
Japan	4.0	4.9	5.3	6.5	6.8
Germany	n/a	n/a	n/a	9.4	11.2
UK	5.0	6.1	6.5	6.4	5.4

Source: Industrial Statistics Yearbook, various years, United Nations.

Cars are unique amongst all the consumer and producer goods entering into international trade because they are the only high price-ticket item which is traded internationally in millions of units. Thus, when trade in cars is unbalanced, cars have a very important role in generating overall payment surpluses and deficits. In recent years cars and car parts have generated 40 percent of the German and Japanese surplus on manufactured trade and almost exactly 40 percent of the comparable American and British deficits (Table 6.6). The coincidence of these percentages is no more than an accident; what the table also shows is that the cars deficit played an initially much more important role in turning the UK and USA from manufacturing surplus to deficit. Only fifteen years ago the UK car industry was a major generator of surplus.

The overall deterioration in US and UK trade performance over the 1970s and 1980s was such that both economies were clearly balance of payments constrained around the peak of their last business cycle. In 1989, the UK balance of payments current account deficit peaked at 4.98 percent of Gross Domestic product (GDP), while the comparable US deficit peaked at 3.60 percent of GDP in 1987. Recession has since reduced the large US trade deficit, but the fact that British deficit was still running at £1 billion per month, or more than 1 percent of GDP, in 1992 in the depths of recession was a fundamental weakness that contributed to sterling crisis and devaluation in the autumn of 1992. In both these losing economies, it was not possible to reflate so as to bring unemployment towards tolerable levels of 3 percent or less without incurring an unsustainable payments deficit and around 40 percent of this deficit would be accounted for by increased imports of cars and car parts. This would be much less of a problem if the winners made reflationary adjustments that stimulated their demand for a range of imports. This would diminish their surpluses which are normally 40 percent generated by their trade in cars and components. Unfortunately, the well-attested reality of the international payments system is that surplus-running countries are never compelled to reflate. The early 1990s turnaround in the German payments position was the accidental result of a temporary reunification boom.

Table 6.6: Trade Balance on Cars and Car Parts as Percent of Overall Manufacturing Trade Balance (Standard Industrial Classification 5 to 8) 1976-90.

	Germany % of surplus	Japan % of surplus	UK % of surplus or deficit	US % of surplus or deficit
1976	28.3	23.0		-17.8 (s)
1977	29.5	25.0	29.0 (s)	-131.4 (s)
1978	29.8	28.3	17.6 (s)	90.4 (d)
1979	35.7	30.9	-1.2 (s)	-2318.4 (s)
1980	37.4	32.1	13.8 (s)	-69.3 (s)
1981	37.2	30.5	14.6 (s)	-123.0 (d)
1982	35.0	31.0	-540.3 (s)	614.1 (d)
1983	39.9	31.9	50.0 (d)	61.0 (d)
1984	38.8	31.9	36.1 (d)	34.8 (d)
1985	39.0	34.6	46.1 (d)	36.5 (d)
1986	39.1	37.7	47.7 (d)	37.5 (d)
1987	41.5	40.6	42.6 (d)	38.6 (d)
1988	40.7	38.1	39.6 (d)	42.4 (d)
1989	41.6	39.3	42.7 (d)	42.8 (d)
1990	35.4	34.7	39.0 (d)	66.6 (d)

Note: (s)=surplus or (d)=deficit on trade balance.

Source: Annual Trade Statistics Yearbook, various years, United Nations.

The power of the economic and political *a priori* is such that most academics and businessmen are reluctant to accept the bad news about unbalanced trade. Instead, even when the unbalance is noted, there is a determined and unreal attempt to find reasons to be cheerful. As a result we have the old industry doxa that unbalanced trade problems could be solved by reciprocal access and the new argument in *The*

Machine that Changed the World, that unbalanced trade problems are being solved by Japanese transplants in America and Europe (Womack et al., 1990, Ch.10).

The British car magazine *Autocar* runs a feature called 'open to question' where each week different industry figures answer the same list of questions. One of the more leading questions is 'should Japan be restricted in the number of cars it sells in the UK?' and until recently the stock answer has been 'not if Japan allows unimpeded reciprocal access to its own market'. The demand for reciprocal access was encouraged by the fact that when Japanese tariff barriers came down they were replaced in the 1980s by a series of informal barriers to car imports which were based on import and type approval formalities and limited distribution facilities. In addition Western component manufacturers came up against the Japanese assemblers' preference for purchasing from its own *keiretsu* suppliers.

But is was always a fantasy to imagine that reciprocal access could solve trade imbalance with Japan, especially for the Europeans who were accustomed to much higher prices for volume cars within their home market. It was always hard to see how the European industry could sell profitably in Japan outside the imported luxury niche. The American industry may be competitive on price but the disparity of home market sizes between Japan, America and Europe makes the exchange of equal volumes extraordinarily unlikely. The American and European markets are two-and-a-half to three times larger so that the Americans and Europeans could only balance Japanese imports unit for unit by claiming very high shares of the Japanese market. If, counter factually, the Americans were to cover their 1990 import of 1.8 million cars from Japan by exporting an equal number to Japan, the Americans would need to take a 36 percent share of the Japanese market. If the Americans were to cover both Japanese imports to America and transplant production in America, then the American producers would need to take a 62 percent share of the Japanese car market.

As the fantasy of reciprocal access has dissipated over the past few years so the element of wish fulfillment has been renewed by *The Machine That Changed the World* vision of how large-scale unbalanced trade will be superseded as Japanese transplant manufacturing inaugurates a return to dispersed production for local national and regional markets. According to *The Machine that Changed the World* the logic of 'lean production' is to do as much as possible close to the market because this system 'achieves its highest efficiency, quality and flexibility when all activities from design to assembly occur in the same place . . . [and] for this reason lean producers in the 1990s will need to create top-to-bottom paper concepts to finished manufacturing systems, in the three great markets of the world – North America, Europe and East Asia [centered on Japan]' (Womack et al., 1990, p.200). Thus, 'in North America the full implementation of lean production can eliminate the massive trade deficit in motor vehicles' whilst 'it can balance Europe's motor vehicle trade as well' (Ibid, pp.255-6). After this transformation, 'post-national' manufacturers will have autonomous design and production operations in all three regions, with trade in niche and speciality products flowing between regions in quantities which a diagram in the text insinuates will be fully balanced and the text itself then asserts will be 'reasonably balanced' (Ibid, pp.206-7, 221).

If this scenario appeared plausible, that was partly because IMVP provided no figures on the extent and nature of the current imbalance at the same time as it repeated the unsubstantiated claim that local content was rapidly increasing in Japan's American transplants. We have elsewhere produced a detailed critique of this influential and misguided text (Williams et al., 1992b) and also analyzed the available evidence on the transplants in cars and electronics (Williams et al., 1992a). All we need do here is briefly counter the *Machine that Changed the World* claim that transplants will solve the problem of unbalanced trade by considering the evidence on the United States where transplant production is much more developed than in Europe.

The rapid growth of transplant production has created a substantial new sector in the United States. Transplant production was insignificant in 1983, exceeded 500,000 in 1986 and 1 million in 1989, before reaching 1.4 million in 1991 and was planned to grow to more than 2 million in 1994 (Table 6.7). But the table also shows that the Japanese transplant sector in the United States is fragmented with no fewer than six Japanese assemblers operating stand-alone plants which are typically dedicated to producing one or two models at the rate of 150,000 to 200,000 per annum. Operations of this sort cannot easily sustain design and development or indeed full manufacture, including engines and gearboxes. It is not therefore surprising to find that the import content of American transplant production is much higher than the 20 percent which the companies claim and MIT accepts. The University of Michigan's Transportation Research Institute's (UMTRI) study of a 1989 Honda Accord cast doubt on this claim because 38 percent of the car came directly from Honda in Japan and a further 46 percent from transplant component suppliers in the United States who were importing as well as manufacturing: only 16 percent came from traditional domestic sources in the US (McAlinden et al., 1991). If the UMTRI analysis considers only one specific product, the Bureau of Commerce evidence shows that the import/sales ratio for the Japanese transplant car and component sector as a whole in 1989 was 48.6 percent.

The operations of the transplants and the growing park of ageing Japanese cars are together not abolishing imbalance but changing its form. What is happening is that, as the deficit on cars is stabilized, the deficit on parts increases. This point emerges from Table 6.8 which presents evidence on recent trends in the American trade balance with Japan in finished vehicles and in vehicle parts; in both cases 'vehicles' effectively means cars and car-based light trucks because the Americans do not import heavy Japanese trucks.

Table 6.7: Japanese Transplant Production in the USA 1983 to 1991.

	1983	1984	1985	1986	1987
Honda	55,335	138,572	145,337	238,159	324,064
Nissan	—	—	43,810	65,147	117,334
NUMMI	—	—	64,610	191,549	143,652
Toyota	—	—	—	14,264	43,726
Mazda	—	—	—	—	4,200
Diamond Star	—	—	—	—	—
SIA	—	—	—	—	—
Total cars	55,335	138,572	253,757	509,119	632,976

	1988	1989	1990	1991	Est 1994
Honda	366,335	361,670	435,437	451,199	510,000
Nissan	109,897	115,584	95,884	133,507	310,000
NUMMI	129,978	192,355	205,287	206,434	205,000
Toyota	18,527	151,150	218,195	190,453	480,000
Mazda	167,205	216,200	184,428	165,573	245,000
Diamond Star	2,409	90,741	148,379	153,931	240,000
SIA	—	2,600	32,461	57,945	60,000
Total cars	794,351	1,130,300	1,320,071	1,359,042	2,050,000

Source: The Motor Industry of Japan, 1992, JAMA.

Between 1985 and 1990, the American bill for imported Japanese vehicles levelled off at more than $20 billion, whereas the American bill for imported Japanese parts increased from $4.6 to $11 billion. The University of Michigan's Transport Research Institute's (UMTRI) 'most likely' scenario forecasts a bilateral vehicles and parts deficit of $38.1 billion in constant dollars by 1994, and this would represent a real deficit increase of 23 percent in just five years. (McAlinden et al., 1991, p.iii).

Table 6.8: United States Imports of Vehicles and Parts from Japan 1985–1990.

	Vehicle imports from Japan $US bill	Parts imports from Japan $US bill	Total automotive imports $US bill	Vehicle imports as percentage of total
1985	19.7	4.6	24.3	81.1
1986	26.0	6.4	32.4	80.3
1987	25.6	7.8	33.3	76.7
1988	23.1	9.4	32.5	71.1
1989	22.7	11.6	34.3	66.3
1990	21.2	11.4	32.6	65.0

Source: McAlinden et al., 1991, p.87.

Behind *The Machine that Changed the World* slogan about lean production is a managerialist political message: provided governments do not interfere and organized workers do not obstruct, the car companies can solve not only the problem of unbalanced trade but also the problems of congestion and environmental damage. We will consider the environmental issues in Chapter 9: on trade we would argue that balance is unlikely. *The Machine that Changed the World* prediction does not confront the awkward facts about the scale of the actual imbalance and the divergence between corporate and national interests. On current evidence, the discrepancy between US national interests and the corporate interests of Toyota and Nissan in the 1990s is as large as the discrepancy between UK national interests and the corporate interests of Ford and GM in the 1970s and 1980s. Where corporate and national interests diverge there is always a case for political regulation. The EC and the United States do have some regulation of finished imports from Japan, the relevant political question is whether and how regulation can now be re-focused onto component imports.

✢ ✢ ✢

7
Ford and Toyota:
Myth, Romance and Illusion

———— ❖ ————

The history of the cars business is increasingly appropriated through the stereotype of mass production and its opposite, which is lean production in Womack, Jones and Roos (1990), or flexible specialization in Piore and Sabel (1984). Ford and Toyota are important because they figure as system prototypes in this schema which goes on to provide an interpretation of history based on diffusion. The basic antithesis provides the justification for a description and classification of car firms and national sectors; thus mass production covers Ford and the Americans up to the 1980s while lean production covers Toyota and its imitators within, and now beyond, Japan. At the same time the schema provides a prescriptive model and an historical explanation of success and failure. All companies can realize large gains by adopting the appropriate system and the success and failure of companies and sectors is explained in terms of diffusion and incomplete adoption of production systems.

Our own analysis for explaining success and failure is different as the earlier chapters have explained and the aim of this chapter is to vindicate our analysis by demonstrating that the schema of production systems is unsustainable because Ford and Toyota were not prototypes of systems which subsequently diffused. The evidence and argument on these points is organized into three sections. A first section disproves the mythic identification of Ford with mass production. At Highland Park, Ford did not combine semi-skilled workers and dedicated equipment to produce a standardized product, but manufactured a stretchable product in a flexible factory. In this factory Ford metaphorically wrote the book on high-volume repetitive car manufacturing and, because the activity was afterwards recognizably the same, Ford's successors have done no more than add a chapter or two to Henry's book. All of Ford's successors owe him the homage of talent to genius because none can match Ford's facility and fecundity in product and process innovation.

The second section registers the ambiguity of Toyota's achievement. Cusumano's (1985) history accepts the romance of Toyota as a company which discovered different and better production-engineering principles under Taichi Ohno. Against this we will argue that the account of the 'Toyota Production System' in Ohno (1988) and Monden (1983) raises more questions than it answers about production practice and completely ignores the contribution of Toyota Motor Sales' American-style marketing under Kamiya. Comparisons between Ford and Toyota are difficult not least because Toyota directly manages a much shorter span of operations. But Toyota has never achieved an unprecedented level of technical efficiency; crucially stock levels, which are an index of manufacturing flow are no lower in Toyota in the 1980s than they were in Ford in 1915. Furthermore social comparisons suggest the superiority of Ford's practice; whereas Ford offered the highest wages and the shortest hours, Toyota offered long hours inside its own factories and exploited a steep wage gradient into its supplier network which produced most of each car.

The third section of this chapter reinstates historical complexity against illusions about the diffusion of imaginary systems. It may be possible to imitate techniques but it is not possible for all firms to replicate Ford and Toyota's results. These two firms moved along high performance trajectories because they operated in exceptional conditions which included rapidly-increasing demand and complete control of their workforces. The market dominance of the leaders on their high performance trajectory prevents their domestic competitors from realizing the same results; in this respect the cars business is like an airplane where there are a limited number of comfortable seats up at the front of the plane. Thus Ford and Toyota are not system prototypes but heroic exceptions whose very success ensures the failure of competitors unless, like GM in the 1920s, they can find the market space which spoils the leader's capacity utilization or until general market conditions reduce all firms to a level of mundane ordinariness. The history of car manufacture is the struggle of productive flow against market restriction, and in the last instance restriction always triumphs against flow.

The Myth of Ford

The Ford family which ran the company for seventy-five years could never decide whether they valued history or preferred myth. Thus old Henry said that 'history is bunk' and Henry II sold off his grandfather's first great factory at Highland Park. But the family also endowed a marvellous company archive at Henry Ford Museum, in Greenfield Village, and the firm commissioned the monumental Nevins history of the Fords and their company. Posterity's preference for myth is regrettably clear; the Nevins history languishes largely unread and unsurpassed while contemporaries like Womack et al. cite more recent accounts by Hounshell (1984) and Lewchuk (1987) which are the current academic authority for the myth of mass production.

The myth of Ford as mass production feeds off Ford's heroic achievements in production of the Model T at Highland Park between 1909 and 1916. The generally accepted basics of Ford's policy and its results are summarized in Tables 7.1 and 7.2.

Table 7.1: Ford Model T Prices and Profits 1909-16.

	Profit 000s $US	Cars shipped '000 units	Profit per car $US	Price of Touring T $US	Profit as % of selling price
1909	3,062	14	218.7	850	25.7
1910	4,163	21	198.2	950	20.9
1911	7,339	54	135.9	780	17.4
1912	13,543	83	163.2	690	23.7
1913	27,089	199	136.1	600	22.7
1914	24,698	188	131.4	550	23.9
1915	25,532	247	103.4	440	23.5
1916	57,157	506	113.0	360	31.4

Notes: Col.2, cars shipped during the period 1909 to 1913 are calendar year; for 1914 profit is measured over 9 months and in 1915 over ten months as the accounting period changes. Col.3, column one divided by column two. Col.4, car prices for the Touring T (rag top, four seat). Col.5, margin on selling price calculated approximately as column three into column four.

Sources: Col.1, Ford Motor Company, *Annual Report and Accounts*, various years; Ford Archive, Accession 463 Box. 1 and Accession 157.

As Table 7.1 shows, Ford got into volume production by cutting the price of the Model T. A fully equipped Touring T initially cost $950 and by 1916 Ford had cut the price to $360 and was shipping more than half a million cars a year. All this was achieved without reducing profitability because Ford's margin on sales increased to an all time high of 31 percent in 1916.

Table 7.2: Ford Cars per Employee and Labor Hours per Car.

	Cars shipped units	Employees	Cars per employee per year	Labor hours per car
1909	14,000	1,655	8.5	357
1910	21,000	2,773	7.6	400
1911	54,000	3,976	13.6	222
1912	83,000	6,867	12.1	250
1913	199,000	14,366	13.9	216
1914	250,000	12,880	19.4	127
1915	369,000	18,892	19.5	123
1916	585,000	32,702	17.9	134

Notes: Col.3, cars per employee per year calculated by dividing total number of cars shipped by the number of employees at Highland Park and Branch factories; Col.4, labor hours per car calculated on the assumption that up to and including 1913 a factory worker worked 6 ten hour days for fifty weeks. From early 1914, with the introduction of the 8 hour day, we assume 2,400 hours, and a 6 day, eight hour shift for fifty weeks.

Sources: Col. 1, Ford Motor Company *Report and Accounts*, various years; Col.2, A.Nevins (1954) *Ford: The Times, the Man, the Company*, p.648.

In the myth this result is attributed to internal productivity gains which were remarkable because, as Table 7.2 shows, between 1910 and 1916 Ford took two-thirds of the labor hours out of the T. The productivity gains are in turn attributed to the introduction of a mass-production system which combined three key elements: a standardized product, dedicated equipment and semi-skilled workers. All this is condensed into the image of the moving assembly line of 1913–4 which is generally presented as Ford's central productive innovation. The implication is that the dynamic of Ford's cost reduction was a kind of process task simplification and its cost was rigidity and inflexibility.

The identification of Ford with mass production is now so well established that, through the term 'Fordism', Ford has become the eponymous essence of mass production. Nevertheless, it is fairly easy to disprove the identification by contrasting the stereotyped assumptions and Ford's practice on the three key elements of product standardization, process equipment and workforce. These points are dealt with in greater detail in our article (Williams et al., 1992d and 1993c) which describes how Henry built the T at Highland Park and we will here only summarize our main conclusions.

In the myth of Ford, the aphorism about 'any colour so long as it's black' serves as a metaphor for a company policy of restricting consumer choice. Those who use the metaphor misunderstand the significance of black paint and misrepresent Ford's policy; Ford chose black for productionist reasons because it dried more quickly. The company's general policy was to win sales by extending consumer choice. In the early stages of Western motorization it was possible to persuade one-third or more of consumers to buy the national people's car, and small cheap cars tend to have model lives of ten years or more. But the T was a phenomenon amongst people's cars; only the VW Beetle stands comparison. In the eighteen years up to 1927, Ford produced 13.9 million Model Ts and at its post-war peak in 1921 the Model T accounted for 61 percent of all cars sold in America. Exactly for this reason, the Model T could not be one model but had to become a changing family of models. Right from the start, Ford extended demand by offering a range of different roadster, touring and closed body types. And the secret of Ford's subsequent success was his ability to stretch a robust basic design so as to accommodate rapid changes in market requirements.

Unlike later producers of long life people's cars, Ford faced the problem that the car was not a mature product when the Model T was introduced in 1908. When the T went into volume production American cars were open, gas lit, crank started and artillery wheeled; when the T ran out, American cars were closed, electrically lit, self started and balloon tyred on demountable rims. Ford maintained its position in the market by continuously developing the mechanics and restyling the body. Like Beetles, all T's had a 'once driven, never forgotten' design identity based on a few idiosyncratic design features; the T's thermo-syphon cooling, two-speed planetary transmission and exiguous rear-wheel brakes were the equivalent of the Beetle's air-cooled flat four. But early and late Ts which shared the same identity were part for part more or less completely different; when the ignition and electrics were completely redesigned no less than five times in the course of the model run, the T was the automotive equivalent of George Washington's axe. Regular styling changes successfully updated the appearance of the car by seating the passengers in, not on, the chassis. The limit of design stretch was reached when closed bodies became a standard market requirement because they imposed a weight penalty which required lower gearing which spoilt the car.

In the myth of Ford, the factory and its equipment are even more blurred than the product. Thus the most reproduced photo of Highland Park shows the 'body drop' scene outside the W building in 1914 as bodies slide down an improvised wooden ramp onto finished chassis which are coming off the end of the line. Those who reproduce the photo do not understand that it nicely represents Ford's escape from inflexibility. Before the T went into production, Ford's architect Albert Kahn had designed concrete decked multi-story buildings with inadequate provision for transfer of work between levels. Fortunately Kahn's proto-modernist design also included glass curtain walls which Ford engineers knocked out so that they could hoist and drop down the side of the building. As for the dedicated equipment, it is necessary to distinguish between one off special-purpose machines and series-built machines adapted for 'single purpose' use by the addition of tools and fixtures. Ford did use some special-purpose equipment like the machine which automatically painted rear axles. But most of Ford's metal working was done on bought-in series built lathes, drills, millers and presses which were adapted for single purpose use. The advantage of these machines was that they were cheap to buy and easy to re-use by changing the fixtures and the drive sprockets which set operating speed.

The implication is that the factory was not inflexible but reusable. And, if Ford never exploited this potential in peace time, the flexibility of Highland Park was triumphantly vindicated in the eighteen months of the First World War when 'practically all Ford machinery was dismantled and rearranged to produce war material'; the factory's war output included 825,000 steel helmets, 5,000 Liberty V12 aero engines, around 25 sets of 2,500 hp marine boilers, steam turbines and reduction gear and a two-and-a-half ton tank powered by two model T engines (Bryan, 1990). While all this was going on, in late 1917 Henry approached the US military with an offer to build 150,000 fighter aircraft for the Allies at a price of 25 cents per pound weight. The offer was rejected because the military believed it was impossible to build aircraft at such a low price. The proposed fighter was only a flying T with more engine and less body and Henry was already building the T for 33 cents per pound weight (including Ford's profit and dealer margin). The rejected offer signified Henry's personal belief that Highland Park could change over from the T and build with equal efficiency any mechanical engineering product which shared the conversion parameters defined by the size, weight, materials and process requirements of the old Model T.

In the myth of Ford, the semi-skilled line worker figures as Ford's invention. Of all the mass production elements, this is the most immediately plausible because most of Ford's direct workers were semi-skilled machine minders and assembly hands working on short cycles. But we should add the qualification that the coarser secondary accounts are wrong when they elide Ford with 'Taylorism'; Ford never practiced formal time-and-motion study. Furthermore, the pre-occupation with direct labor misunderstands the nature and sources of Ford's cost reduction. As Table 7.2 shows, Ford was spectacularly successful at taking labor hours out of the T whose total labor content was 400 hours in 1910 and 125-135 hours in 1914-16. But half or more of the hours taken out were indirect labor hours supplied by truckers, craftsmen and supervisors and mangers; this is the implication of the Model T cost book which applies a multiplicand of 1.33 or 1.5 to absorb overhead which was mostly indirect labor. The question is not only how did Ford take labor out, but also how did he manage with an unusually favorable ratio of indirect-to-direct workers. More fundamentally, internal labor costs were never the obstacle which prevented Ford from selling the Model T more cheaply.

As Table 7.3 shows, even if we add all the direct and indirect labor in the T, internal labor costs usually accounted for no more than $50-100 in each car. The reason why early Ts could not be sold cheaply was simply that they contained too many expensive bought-in components; when the T cost the consumer $950 in 1910, bought-in materials accounted for no less than $644 of the purchase price. As Table 7.3 also shows, the price cuts in the later years coincide with a significant reduction in the amount of each T that was bought-in; the purchase to sales ratio declines from a peak of 74 percent in 1911 to 50 percent in 1916. At the same time the value-added to sales ratio rises indicating that Ford is building more of each car in-house. The real question therefore is how was Ford able to build more of each car while taking out direct labor and maintaining an extraordinarily favorable ratio of indirect-to-direct labor.

Table 7.3: Labor and Material Costs in the Model T 1909-16.

	Sales price per unit $US	Labor cost per unit $US	Material cost per unit $US	Purchases as percent of selling price	Value added as percent of Gross output
1909	850	84.6	547	64.4	35.6
1910	950	100.4	644	67.8	32.2
1911	780	55.0	577	74.0	26.0
1912	690	65.0	465	67.4	32.6
1913	600	60.5	408	68.0	32.0

Table 7.3 (continued)

	Sales price per unit $US	Labor cost per unit $US	Material cost per unit $US	Purchases as percent of selling price	Value added as percent of Gross output
1914	550	70.0	341	62.0	38.0
1915	440	68.0	229	52.1	47.9
1916	360	74.0	180	50.0	50.0

Notes: Col.2, price of the Touring T in dollars; Col.3, calculated by dividing cars shipped into total payroll costs; Col.4, calculated as sales price per unit minus value-added per unit; Col.5, column four as a percentage of column one; Col.6, value-added (calculated as labor costs plus depreciation and profit per unit) as a percentage of sales price per unit.

Sources: List prices from Ford Archive, Accession 157; Sales from Ford Archive, Accession 463 Box 1. Payroll from Ford Archive, Accession 843; Ford Motor Company Report and Accounts, various years.

If we wish to provide an historical answer to that question, we must try to understand Ford's problems and achievements at the new Highland Park factory which came on stream around 1911 and was continuously extended up to 1916. Ford could only achieve cost reduction by substituting cheap in-house components for expensive bought-in components; the option of improving suppliers was never considered because Ford's suppliers were independent firms which could take cost reductions as profit for themselves and/or pass the benefits on to other assemblers thereby dissipating Ford's advantage. At Highland Park, Ford addressed the problem by creating a long-span conversion apparatus which could bring component work in-house; as Ford Times (July 1908) announced 'in this factory everything from screws to upholstery that enters into Ford will be manufactured'. The task was to create new repetitive-manufacturing techniques for a product that was heavier, more complex and more awkwardly shaped than previous products of repetitive manufacturing like sewing machines, bicycles and clocks. The Touring T was a relatively light-weight car but each finished product weighed 1,200 pounds and contained around 10,000 individually-numbered parts of which around half were eventually manufactured in-house in several hundred-thousand separate process operations. Ford's market place success increased the problems because as volume increased, even with doubling up of machines and lines, cycle times came tumbling down; by early 1914 when the Ford company was producing 1,000 cars a day and most of the factory was working two shifts of eight hours, the cycle time for the completion of finished cars and subassemblies like the engines and axles was already under one minute.

Ford had demonstrated his manufacturing flair in the product design of the T which combined the benefits of low weight and high strength through extensive use of alloy steels and heat treatment; the design allowed Ford healthy margins on a product which had the consumer benefit of lower running costs than its 30 hp rivals as well as unique easy-driving attributes. Ford's lieutenants then proved their creativity by improvising and inventing a variety of process improvements which involved productive interventions of different kinds at a multiplicity of points across a long conversion span. The three heterogeneous sources of cost reduction were machine modification, layout change and labor-task recomposition all of which were designed to improve materials flow and/or reorganize the labor process so that less direct and indirect labor stuck to each T component. Certain explicit Ford-company principles were consistently applied to these interventions. As Bornholt explained, in layout the basic principle was to arrange machines, regardless of function, close together and 'in sequence of use' (Bornholt, 1913). In labor utilization the corresponding principle was the elimination of unnecessary 'walking and waiting'; thus in all processes the workpiece was to be delivered to the stationary direct worker by belt, roller or gravity slide while these transfer devices plus the close-together layouts would eliminate unproductive indirect-trucking labor.

Ford's principles were focused successively on different sections of the conversion span in a series of overlapping phases that began with attention to engine, gearbox and axle production in the Highland Park machine shop which cut, pressed and assembled the metal that went into these components. The Model T could not be sold cheaply as long as these key high-value-added components were expensive to buy in or make. Thus in 1909 a 117,000 square-foot machine shop was part of the first phase of construction at Highland Park and by 1915 the single-story machine shop covered ten acres and contained 5,500 machine tools. The principle of machines in order of use was continuously developed so that, for example, the distance which the engine block casting travelled between finishing operations was reduced from 4,000 to 334 feet (Arnold and Faurote, 1915, p.38). As cycle times came down, so reduced cycle set-up time became a major issue because an increasing part of the diminishing cycle was being wasted on clamping the workpieces at each process stage. As Colvin explained in his 1913-15 articles, Ford attacked this problem with a variety of expedients which included what the Japanese now call 'one touch' quick acting clamps, gravity drop in location and multiple tooling so that a variety of cuts could be made at one clamping. These interventions were spectacularly successful because by 1914 Ford was casting, heat treating, cutting and assembling a complete engine and gearbox for a total cost of $61 in labor materials and overhead; by way of contrast Ford's body suppliers were then charging $55 for a bare open-touring body minus soft top and screens.

In the second phase of process improvement, which did not begin before about 1911, the main object was process improvement in the many component production operations which were undertaken mainly on the upper floors of the multi-story buildings at Highland Park before moving downwards and eastwards into the final-assembly shops. In this phase Ford discovered that it could extend and develop the principles of its low-cost machine shop to the production of any kind of mechanical component that went into the T. The layouts in component production were much more striking because of the heterogeneity of adjacent processes. Thus in distributor production on the third floor in building X, the line began with an aluminum foundry which fed cast bodies into an in-sequence machine line from which machined distributor bodies went directly into assembly which added the fixed and moving parts (Arnold and Faurote, 1915, p.71-95). The development of in-house component production cannot be measured precisely; Table 7.3 shows that purchases as a percent of gross output fell from a peak of 74 percent in 1911 to 50 percent, but this financial measure undoubtedly understates the extent of the physical substitution because Ford was invariably successful at producing more cheaply than his suppliers and this cost reduction damps the movement of the financial ratio. As a general rule, Ford could produce a component at a cost which was half the price that his component suppliers charged. For example, the top iron, (soft) top, hood and coil set were all brought in-house between 1914 and 1916 and in the Model T cost books their 1916 cost of production was estimated at just 54 percent of the 1914 purchase price. By way of contrast, the wheel set, carburetor and springs which were still out-sourced in 1916 show a purchase price reduction of just under 20 percent over the same two years.

In a final phase of improvement attention turned to assembly of components and final assembly of finished cars. The effect of earlier process improvement had been to reduce costs and raise throughput so that by 1913, as Klann observed, 'we were making parts a hell of a lot faster than they could put them together on cars' (Klann, 1955, p. 55). The problem was addressed by a variety of expedients. In the autumn of 1912 the company announced a new policy of decentralizing final assembly so that Highland Park could concentrate on the vital work of component production; by spring 1915, most of Highland Park's output was shipped in kit form for assembly in branch plants located in 24 'principal cities' (*Ford Times*, April 1915). The process of assembly itself was tackled by the introduction of moving assembly lines first used in flywheel magneto assembly in the spring of 1913 and then applied to a variety of subassembly tasks as well as final chassis assembly between spring 1913 and the summer of 1914. The moving assembly line (MAL) is central to the popular iconography of mass production and to the historiography of Ford which presents the moving assembly line as Ford's central process innovation. As we have argued elsewhere (Williams et al., 1993c) this interpretation is unjustified. The moving assembly line was only the culmination of a whole series of improvements in assembly techniques (Colvin, 1913) which reinforced the effects of the improvements in earlier processes; Table 7.2 shows that, of the total 250 hour reduction in internal labor hours between 1910 and 1916, 150 hours were taken out in 1910-11 when Highland Park came on stream. The role of the MAL in the further substantial hours reduction around 1913-14 is unclear partly because the chronology of other intra-process transfer devices, such as gravity slides is unclear. As an inter process transfer device moving lines only complemented other transfer systems such as craneways and an overhead monorail which were equally important in the earlier stages of production.

The aim and result of Ford's intervention was a high-flow, low-stocks factory and the literary and statistical evidence both show that Highland Park did achieve continuous reductions in stock levels. The factory had originally been designed to run with thirty-days stock cover but by 1915 it was running with a stock cover of three to five days for major components like chassis frames or engines (Arnold and Faurote, 1915, p.63). As early as 1913, buffer stocks between individual departments were down to a 'few hours' with zero stocks inside departments (Ford Times, January 1913). This impression is confirmed by Table 7.4 which presents a calculation of Ford's value-added to stocks ratio; the value-added to WIP ratio would of course give a better measure of factory flow but the Ford company did not disaggregate stocks into subcategories and so value-added/stocks is the best that we can do.

Table 7.4: Ford Value-added to Stocks Ratio.

	Value-added $ m.	Average stocks $ m.	Value-added to stocks ratio
1909	4.2	2.2	1.91
1910	6.4	3.0	2.13
1911	10.9	4.2	2.60
1912	18.7	7.3	2.56
1913	38.2	12.6	3.03
1914	39.2	12.3	3.19
1915	52.0	15.3	3.40
1916	91.0	24.3	3.74

Notes: Col.1, value-added calculated as payroll plus depreciation and profits pre tax; Col.3, stock turnover is calculated by dividing value-added by the average stocks for each year.

Source: Payroll, depreciation and profit per car calculated from Ford Archive, Accession 843; Stocks, from Ford Archive, Accession 96, Box 10;

The value-added to stocks ratio shows a sustained and continuous improvement from 2.13 in 1910 to 3.74 in 1915. The implication is that Highland Park was quite unlike the stereotype of a congested, high-stocks mass-production factory and in terms of the orthodox stereotypes it is much more like the low-stocks Japanese factory.

This sense of anticipation and recurrence is reinforced by the fact that many of the interventions and practices used at Highland Park were subsequently used not only in the Japanese factories of Toyota, but also in other productionist car factories like BMC Longbridge which we will consider in the next chapter. For example, because lay-out change was always important as a way of improving materials flow, Ford like BMC and Toyota recommended that, wherever possible, machines should not be fixed to the factory floor. Equally, because labor costs were always much more important than machine costs, Ford's successors at BMC and Toyota continued Ford's operating practice of shutting down machines and lines rather than running them slow; Toyota formulated the principle as 'machines rather than men must wait'. In our view, this recurrence is hardly surprising because the activity of high-volume repetitive manufacturing remains essentially the same and because Ford (like BMC or Toyota) was, as Sorensen argued, an organization that was continuously experimenting to get better production or 'progressive manufacture' (Sorensen, 1956). But where we see recurrence, most other social scientists and historians see difference and we must now confront their assertion that Toyota found a different and better way to make cars.

The Romance of Toyota

Success came late for Henry Ford who was forty-six when the Model T went into production. So it did for the Toyoda family's attempt to enter the cars business which began with the creation of Toyota Motor Company in 1937. Like Henry the Toyoda's had very little to show for their first twenty-five years of effort: as Table 7.5 shows, after twenty-five years the cumulative output of their firm was just over 1 million; for most of this period the company's main product line was a utility light truck; their company survived on domestic sales behind protective barriers and its first attempt to export to the United States in 1958 ended in failure because their cars were inferior. Toyota's next 25 years were years of spectacular success: as Table 7.5 shows, by 1992 the company had made 78 million vehicles and an annual output of 4.5 million made Toyota the world's third-largest car company; the company's product range was broad and its main-volume product, the Corolla, was often the world's best-selling model after the mid-1970s; as home-market leader and Japan's leading exporter, Toyota was the most feared competitor for other car companies inside and outside Japan.

Table 7.5: Toyota Vehicle Production, Home and Export Sales 1936-92.

	Average annual output	Cumulative output	Average home sales	Average home market share	Average export sales
1936-40	7,308	36,538	6,814	23.5	494
1941-45	11,347	93,273	10,760	44.1	587
1946-50	7,795	132,249	7,623	37.9	172
1951-55	18,066	222,578	17,777	33.0	289
1956-60	76,797	683,342	72,189	37.5	4,608
1961-65	332,638	2,346,531	301,934	25.0	30,704
1966-70	1,119,495	7,944,006	835,673	27.4	283,822
1971-75	2,160,259	18,745,303	1,369,040	31.8	791,219
1976-80	2,885,467	33,172,638	1,490,388	32.2	1,395,079
1981-85	3,346,436	49,904,819	1,686,362	31.5	1,660,074
1986-90	3,891,084	69,360,237	2,263,643	33.8	1,627,441
1991-92	4,525,170	78,410,577	2,475,886	34.5	2,049,284

Source: Motor Vehicle Statistics of Japan, various years, JAMA and M.Cusomano (1985), The Japanese Automobile Industry.

The story of Toyota is thus a romance of (delayed) success and like all romances it needs a hero. The Toyoda family cannot play this role because its dynasts are much more grey and colorless than the Fords and because Sakichi Toyoda, who took the family into the cars business, died in disgrace in 1952 after taking responsibility for the 1950 labor dispute and before the company achieved any real success. Posterity has therefore promoted Taichi Ohno, a company engineer whose place in the romance is much larger than his role in the company or his importance in Toyota City or Tokyo, where the company's leading fixer was Shotaro Kamiya who ran Toyota Motor Sales as a personal fiefdom for nearly thirty years. Ohno's main claim to fame is the book on *The Toyota Production System* which he wrote in 1978 after retiring from the company; this book, together with Monden's more academic account of the *Toyota Production System*, is the main source for Westerners interested in the company. The worm's eye engineering view of the company has not been challenged partly because it is sanctioned by Cusumano's history of the Japanese car industry which presents Toyota as the company which beat Nissan because it eschewed direct technology transfer under license deals; Toyota instead developed its own indigenous systems based on 'a tradition of independent experimentation, combined with the careful analysis of foreign auto makers' (Cusumano, 1985, p.376).

This section aims to challenge the romance of Toyota. To begin with, it provides an analytic summary of the character and development of the Toyota Production System according to Monden and Ohno. It then proceeds to register a series of ambiguities about the sphere and conditions of application of the Toyota Production System. The critique is extended and deepened by changing the point of view so as to record the contribution of Toyota Motor Sales to results which are then deconstructed so as to show that Toyota's margin of superiority has been greatly exaggerated.

Ohno was an autodidact with an odd, marginal background. He had worked in the Toyoda's textile factories until 1943 and, on his first visit to the United States in 1956, appears to have been more impressed by the supermarkets than the factories (Ohno, pp.26-7). He combined an exaggerated respect for Henry Ford with profound ignorance about American practice; Ohno, for example, represented the old Ford principle of machines in order of use as a Toyota discovery (Ohno, 1988, p.95). Nevertheless, Ohno had a very sound understanding of the basics of repetitive manufacturing. He understood the crucial importance of labor costs (Ibid, p.55) and realized that flow was the way to get cost out of the product; 'the basic achievement of the Toyota Production System is setting up the manufacturing flow' (Ibid, p.130). Like most autodidacts, Ohno exaggerated his own originality and it is unfortunate that he has been accepted at his own estimation by Westerners who know little about the history of Western production engineering. As our next chapter shows, Frank Woollard of BMC had a broadly similar understanding of manufacturing as flow; and Woollard, like Ohno, pursued the two objectives of developing the self-regulating pull through assembly factory and reorganizing machine and subassembly tasks to reduce labor content. If Ohno's approach to realizing these objectives was different, that was partly because his cultural resources and material circumstances were different.

As Barthes observed, Japan is 'the empire of signs' and within this cultural frame of reference Toyota did for car manufacturing what the Japanese have long done for calligraphy, gift packaging, food and everything else. The Toyota Production System is the most intensely visual of all repetitive-manufacturing systems. The *andon* lights above the assembly tracks like the *kanban* cards on the reorder bins are signifiers of production which render the state and requirements of flow immediately visible and at the same time provide the stimulus to appropriate action. Ohno's ideal was self-regulating pull through production and the most important formal instrument for realizing that ideal was the *kanban* card: within a two-bin reordering system the *kanban* travels backwards with the empty bin and provides the signal for work to begin on the ordered quantity which will then move forwards. The number of bins and cards is often larger than two but always fixed so that *kanban* is a system for limiting WIP levels. In practice, this kind of restriction will only work in a specific productive context where production flow has already been established as a 'basic condition' (Ibid, p.32). Thus *kanban* requires 'production levelling' or smoothing of final assembly output so that there is ideally 'zero fluctuation' in total throughput with demand fluctuation for variants accommodated by mixed modeling on the final lines (Ibid, p.37). At the opposite end of the assembly factory, *kanban* requires relatively small lot production in early processes like pressing and this requires productive intervention to reduce die change over time so that dies can be changed frequently to produce small lots without a large penalty in terms of downtime.

Because flow is difficult to establish, *kanban* spread slowly through Toyota and its suppliers after it was first introduced in the machine shop around 1953 (Ibid,p.26). *Kanban* was not applied to all Toyota's internal factory operations until 1962 (Ohno, pp.34–6) when Toyota began to extend the system into its supplier network. If *kanban* cards were an exotic Japanese invention, there was of course nothing new or unique about the principle of pull-through production; as we shall see in the next chapter, BMC Longbridge was regulated by pull through from the final-assembly lines so was Ford Highland Park which used human 'progress chasers' as a substitute for the *kanban* card. *Kanban* did add a new element of automatic self-regulation. But *kanban* did allow Toyota to eliminate forward planning at all stages except final assembly; in all other stages reverse action via the backward movement of *kanban* cards governed the production and forward movement of the necessary components and sub-assemblies in the appropriate quantity. Ohno's ideal was 'autonomic production' where *kanbans* regulated flow just as the human autonomic nervous system regulates metabolic functions without conscious control or planning (Ibid, p.45).

If culture was important in specifying the *kanban* form, material circumstances were crucial in shaping the cellular-layout systems which Toyota popularized. As we have already observed Toyota was, for more than twenty-five years, an unsuccessful low-volume car manufacturer. The company's first industry standard plant, with capacity for 250,000 vehicles, was Takaoka which opened in 1966 (Toyota 1985, p.188). Toyota's total car production was 25,000 in 1957 and under 100,000 in 1962; when this output was spread over several different model lines, cycle times of five minutes or more must have been common in many operations. From Ford onwards most successful Western car manufacturers were preoccupied with how little the worker could do by way of assembling or loading within cycles of one minute or less, Toyota's problem was the waiting time within much longer cycles. Thus Woollard at BMC developed the automatic-transfer machine to eliminate the manual-loading constraint and Ohno at Toyota developed cellular layouts which are in effect manual-transfer lines served by a walking worker.

Ohno's layout experiments began in 1947 with tests in the Number Two machine shop where one worker tended three or four machines laid out in parallel or C shaped lines (Ohno, 1988 p.4). In a second stage, during and after the 1950s, Toyota developed U-shaped cells with teams of workers engaged in machining and subassembly tasks; a third stage began in 1977 when Toyota began to experiment with interconnected cells in honeycomb layouts where multi-function workers could transfer between as well as within cells (Monden, 1983, p.108). Cellular layouts had been previously applied to manufacturing in the Soviet Union but they did represent a real break with ortho-dox Western practice which, as in Ford Highland Park, took the moving workpiece past a stationary worker. Cellular removes the linear requirement for equalized operation and cycle times at the different work stations (Ibid, p. 86) and more importantly, it opens up a new form of labor utilization; whereas the stationary machine minder must wait unproductively for the machine to finish, the cellular worker continuously initiates value-adding by loading and starting machines as (s)he moves around the cell. In the more sophisticated interconnected cellular layouts, the concern is not with the efficiency of the individual worker but with the team and the ideal is *shojinka*, which means varying the walkpaths within and between adjacent cells, so that it is possible to add or subtract individual workers in line with increases or decreases in demand (Ibid, p.45). The theoretical advantage is that in this kind of layout it becomes possible to reduce the work team in line with reduced demand as well as increase it when demand increases; by way of contrast, in a Ford-type factory labor content is governed by line speed and interruptions and there is no way of demanning when demand declines.

Logically, the universalization of *kanban* makes sophisticated cellular layouts necessary or at least desirable because if *kanban* fixes the internal stock levels then all the burden of adjustment to demand must fall on cycle time. If the cellular layout was invented for low-volume repetitive manufacturing, it can be adapted to the requirements of high volume by replicating cells. The cost of volume cellular production is a much higher requirement for fixed-capital equipment than in linear factories where it is possible to get extra output by doubling up on single machines and stations at the bottleneck; when capital is such a small proportion of total costs for most manufacturers, this is not a major disadvantage. Those who read Ohno and Monden will therefore derive the impression that *kanban* and cellular layouts are at the heart of Toyota's manufacturing practice and jointly deliver superior results which others can obtain by adopting the techniques; thus Ohno (p. xiii) writes that the 'Toyota production system has been studied and introduced into workplaces regardless of industrial type, scale and even national boundary.' Western firms have taken Ohno at his word so that just in time, cellular and team working have become the central terms in the rhetoric of Western manufacturing improvement. It is therefore important to register a first series of ambiguities about the sphere of operation and conditions of application of

Toyota's techniques before registering a second series of ambiguities about the results which they achieve.

Around 1970 the Toyota Motor Company itself started to use the term 'Toyota Production System' (Toyota, 1985, p.144), a label which has greatly encouraged the essentialist systems thinking which comes all too easily to most social scientists and some historians. But the label conceals more than it illuminates because the nature and extent of the 'system' remains unclear. As our chronology has demonstrated, *kanban* and cellular are not one system but a series of evolving techniques and there is no answer to the basic question about what proportion of the process span inside the factories of Toyota, and of Toyota suppliers, is operating cellular and *kanban* of varying degrees of sophistication. In the case of Ford, which we discussed in the last section, it is possible to measure innovation and outcomes fairly precisely and thereby establish that the moving assembly line was much less important than most commentators would have us believe (Williams et al., 1993c). In the absence of such measures all we can say is that everything we know about Toyota suggests caution about the sphere of *kanban* and cellular.

The first and most important point is that Toyota Motor Company long ago chose vertical disintegration and the company operates a relatively short conversion span in its own factories. As Table 7.6 shows, Toyota's short-span manufacturing operation accounts for less than 14 percent of the sales value of each car and no less than 85 percent of the car is bought in; by way of contrast Table 7.3 shows that by 1915 Ford's long-span manufacturing operation accounted for 48 percent of the value of each Model T. Toyota buys in more components and built-up subassemblies than any Western car manufacturer so its system might be better termed the Toyota Assembly System. But that again is inexact because since the mid-1960s Toyota has subcontracted the assembly of at least 30-40 percent of its output (Cusumano, 1985, p.192); by the 1990s this percentage was rising towards 50 percent. At that time Toyota used 'a network of eight subcontractors, which in 1991 produced 1.8 million vehicles, or 45 percent of Toyota's total output for the year' (International Metalworkers Federation, 1992, p.8). Thus, Toyota is a firm which manufactures some engines and gearboxes and undertakes the standard final-assembly operations of press, weld, paint and final assembly on half its output. It is at the very least paradoxical that so many academics and consultants should take as their model a firm which does so little manufacturing.

Table 7.6: Toyota Value-added to Sales and Purchases to Sales Ratio.

	Sales Yen m.	Purchases Yen m.	Value Added Yen m.	Value Added /sales %	Purchases /sales %
1980	3,310,181	2,857,911	452,270	13.7	86.3
1981	3,506,412	3,055,552	450,860	12.9	87.1
1982	3,849,544	3,329,435	520,109	13.5	86.5
1983	5,323,665	4,601,777	721,888	13.6	86.4
1984	5,908,973	5,094,452	814,521	13.8	86.2
1985	6,770,250	5,815,243	955,007	14.1	85.9
1986	6,646,244	5,708,102	938,142	14.1	85.9
1987	6,675,411	5,784,439	890,972	13.4	86.6
1988	7,215,798	6,233,274	982,524	13.6	86.4
1989	8,021,042	6,916,198	1,104,844	13.8	86.2
1990	9,192,838	7,841,683	1,351,155	14.7	85.3
1991	9,855,132	8,408,397	1,446,735	14.7	85.3

Source: Consolidated Annual Report and Accounts, various years.

If we then ask: where and how is cellular and *kanban* applied, the mystery deepens because much of what Toyota does do across its short span is fairly orthodox. Thus, despite Ohno's well-known scepticism about high-speed machines (Ohno, 1988, pp.54, 172), Toyota has, since 1956, operated transfer lines for engine and gearbox machining (Toyota, 1985 p.491); Toyota's automatic transfer machines are apparently orthodox apart from some attention to work-station position (Monden, 1983, p.124). Equally, the company has at various times at least experimented with Western-style high-tech production control and linear materials transfer; the company's first all-new car plant at Motomachi in 1958, which was laid out by Shoichiro Toyoda as an 'ideal plant' to build 60,000 cars per annum, featured a centralized production-line control system using TV cameras and no less than four kilometers of conveyors. As for the company's current assembly plants, the sections of Takaoka which we toured in 1988 and 1990 were different in detail but similar in principle to Western factories; thus the final-assembly track at Takaoka featured the 'Fordist' refinement of reverse-tracking component trays to eliminate 'walking to pick up' as well as *andons* above the track but was in every other way an orthodox line. By implication cellular and *kanban* must jointly find their major sphere of application in component and subassembly production inside the factories of Toyota's suppliers; and the 'system' becomes a way of reorganizing somebody else's factories at a distance. The extent of this reorganization is uncertain because Toyota's suppliers have always operated a more primitive version of the Toyota production system; in 1982, twenty years after the introduction of *kanban* into the supplier network, 98 percent of suppliers were delivering to Toyota on a *kanban* basis but only 50 percent were using process or production ordering *kanban* inside their factories (Monden, 1983, p.35). The paradox of subcontracting work to technically less competent suppliers is of course explained by the steep wage gradient which exists between Toyota's large assembly plants and its smaller suppliers.

Bessie Smith complained that a good man is hard to find; so is the Toyota Production System (TPS). This must be so partly because the system's conditions of operation are very restrictive on the side of both supply and demand. Many companies have been unable to operate key parts of the Toyota Production System presumably because the conditions are not satisfied outside Toyota; Nissan, for example, failed to introduce *kanban* which it called the 'action plate system'. Technically, on the supply side, TPS requires considerable capacity for productive interventions such as machine modification to allow rapid changeover. This capability cannot abolish basic technical constraints; thus, Toyota has been able to reduce its die-change time on heavy-press lines to ten minutes or less by performing most of the work in a preparatory phase outside the machines, but in 1988, when we visited Takaoka, the press shop was still running on lot sizes of 1.5 shifts because the constraint on minimum lot size is the total amount of time spent on die change inside and outside the machines. The more sophisticated versions of cellular also require a committed workforce because the variation in walkpath requires multi-tasked workers who have mastered a variety of semiskilled tasks which they perform in endlessly variable permutations. Significantly, even Toyota failed to meet its initial targets for creating fully multi-functional workers in the Tsutsumi plant by 1979 (Monden, 1983, p.108). Ohno, like Henry Ford, believed that it should take three days to train a semi-skilled worker in a single task (Ohno, p.22); but with the multiplication of tasks in complex cellular layouts, Toyota approached the limit of what could be expected from such workers even with the benefit of much longer periods of training.

The demand side conditions for Toyota Production System are equally restrictive. Interconnected cellular systems were introduced by Toyota after the first oil crisis in anticipation of a 'low growth period' (Ohno, 1988, p.124) where any system which could progressively downscale labor input in response to demand decline would have been obviously valuable. But their potential was never tested because there was no significant downturn in the Japanese car market for eighteen years after 1973. In any case it is fairly clear that the 'system's' capacity to absorb demand fluctuations is fairly limited because, as we have already noted, *kanban* requires stable, level demand for the factory's total output, if not for every product line. For Ohno, autonomic production was about creating a 'fine tuning mechanism' which could respond to 'small changes in the plan' (Ibid, p.46). These demand-side conditions are clearly stated in the original texts on Toyota Production System but they have been widely ignored by engineers who wish to represent Toyota production system as a universal set of techniques which could be beneficially applied in any and every set of conditions; one of the more bizarre manifestations of this tendency is John Hartley's (1981) book which recommends the Toyota Production System as a technical fix for Western firms facing conditions of low and fluctuating demand.

Beyond the ambiguities about the sphere of application and conditions of operation of Toyota Production System, there are a further series of ambiguities about the results which such techniques achieve. The first issue here is one about attribution and causal connections; insofar as Toyota achieves superior results, can these results be attributed solely or mainly to the influence of Toyota's productive techniques? The second issue concerns the results themselves and the taken for granted premise of superior results; do the available performance measures show that Toyota has a huge advantage over other firms?

One of Toyota's many slogans is *genbashugi* which asserts the primacy of production sites and Toyota has always presented itself as a production-led company. If that is true of Toyota Motor Company (TMC), that is only because for thirty years from 1950-83 Toyota's home and overseas marketing and distribution was handled by Toyota Motor Sales (TMS), an independent company created at the insistence of the banks whose rescue loans saved Toyota during the 1950 crisis of overproduction. TMS was independently capitalized from outside sources including the Mitsui group and given the modest target of a 1 percent return on assets because its mission was to cover the rescue loans both by restraining TMC's productionism and by finding an outlet for TMC product. TMS was headed by the cosmopolitan and shrewdly self-promoting Shotaro Kamiya who combined ability with unusual facility and timing in the choosing and changing of masters. As a young man, after working for Mitsui in Seattle and London, he went into business on his own account as a commodity trader; he joined the motor industry via GM-Japan where he rose to the number two position before transferring to Toyota in 1935 when the nationalist government was closing down the American firms; after serving the Japanese military during World War Two he re-emerged as an advisor to the American occupiers and managing director of TMC; he held that post for six years, resigning nineteen days before the start of the labor dispute which ended in the disgrace of the TMC board. With the creation of TMS, Kamiya became his own master; in the 1960s Shoichiro Toyoda wanted to merge TMS and TMC but that was not possible in Kamiya's lifetime (Cusumano, 1985, p.136).

Just as Kamiya's existence qualifies the general idea of the Japanese executive as a loyal company man, so his activity refutes the particular claim that Toyota was a company that preferred self development to technology transference. Kamiya was the principal in both the 1938 and 1950 negotiations when Toyota sought to acquire American manufacturing know-how from Ford; the 1950 negotiations were accidentally derailed when the American government blocked technology transfer at the outbreak of the Korean War (Kamiya, 1976, p.115). No such obstacle prevented Toyota (and then TMS) from using American marketing know-how, because Kamiya brought 'American sales methods' with him when he quit GM after taking key GM employees and guides such as the GM manual on dealer management (Ibid, p.51). The story of Toyota and TMS is therefore one of the adoption and adaption of these American methods.

Before the Second World War, Kamiya had already introduced the American basics of independently-owned local dealers and easy payment by instalment (Ibid, p.42). After TMS was established Kamiya more specifically borrowed the American GM system of parallel dealer networks selling overlapping but distinct ranges of product-planned models. The creation of the 'multiple marketing channels system' began in 1956 with the creation of a separate Toyopet chain and by 1970 Toyota had 251 dealers divided into five chains (Toyota, Toyopet, Corolla, Diesel and Sprinter) (Ibid, p.125). Toyota's first planned product was the cab over SKB/Toyoace truck of 1954 which succeeded in its objective of poaching three-wheel light-goods vehicles sales (Ibid, p. 66, 119). Later product-planning successes included the 1964 Corona RT40 with which the company re-entered the American market and the 1966 Corolla which became the company's best seller at home and abroad; the Corona offered air conditioning and automatic transmission options when most imports did not and the Corolla was sold against Nissan with the excruciating slogan 'the extra 100cc gives extra comfort' (Toyota, 1985, pp.190-1). While

TMS adopted the American techniques of distribution and marketing, it obtained further leverage by adapting these techniques to Japanese circumstances. Kamiya introduced a variety of methods for unlocking the 'latent demand' for cars in a relatively poor society. Because fewer than 10 percent of Japanese could drive, after 1957 TMS invested in driving schools (Kamiya, 1976, p.119). Because dealers could not pay cash for the cars, TMS invented a system of promissory notes which Toyota could exchange for cash (Ibid, p.117). Because Japanese customers expected home sales, Kamiya accepted their preference and played to it after 1953 by the recruitment of young graduate salesmen whose freshness and class would rub off on the product (Ibid, p.119).

It was this combination of adopted and adapted American sales methods (rather than factory techniques) which made Toyota such a devastating competitor for all the other Japanese companies after it had established clear market leadership. As Table 7.7 shows Nissan lost out to Toyota after 1975 when the output trends of the two companies start to diverge. The combination of door-step selling and multiple market channels had the double effect of shifting the metal for Toyota and increasing the expense of domestic distribution to the point where only Toyota with the market leader's volume could carry it. The minor Japanese firms could not hope to win against Toyota's distribution and historically have mainly succeeded by taking share off each other; as this cannibalism could not generate large sales volumes, the smaller firms like Honda and Mazda have been forced into export and transplant activity. These smaller Japanese firms export a larger percentage of their output and thereby acquire a higher exposure to the mature markets of Europe and North America which are more prone to cyclical fluctuation than the Japanese market.

Table 7.7: Toyota and Nissan Passenger Car Market Shares 1950-90.

	Toyota output units	Toyota % share of domestic passenger car market	Toyota exports as % of total output	Nissan output units	Nissan % share of domestic passenger car market	Nissan exports as % of total output
1950	463	29.0	neg	860	54.3	neg
1955	7,403	36.5	neg	6,595	32.5	neg
1960	42,118	25.5	4.3	55,076	33.3	8.4
1965	236,151	33.9	14.1	169,821	24.4	23.2
1970	1,068,186	29.8	32.4	898,610	24.7	29.7
1975	1,730,767	39.2	35.4	1,533,156	31.3	42.3
1980	2,303,284	39.7	50.0	1,940,734	29.0	53.6

Table 7.7 (*continued*)

	Toyota output units	Toyota % share of domestic passenger car market	Toyota exports as % of total output	Nissan output units	Nissan % share of domestic passenger car market	Nissan exports as % of total output
1985	2,569,284	45.0	46.7	1,864,701	25.2	55.3
1990	3,345,885	44.0	36.3	1,574,086	20.7	52.2

Source: Motor Vehicle Statistics of Japan, various years, JAMA and M.Cusomano (1985), Japanese Automobile Industry.

It is of course easy to win against weak opponents, but Kamiya proved his ability by the way in which he dealt with the much stronger Japanese number-two firm, Nissan, which was beaten on its home ground in the Tokyo market by the directly-owned Tokyo Toyopet dealer chain. As a result, Nissan was burdened with much the same level of distribution expense as Toyota on a market share which was half the size; as our final chapter comparisons show, Nissan currently compares quite favorably with Toyota in productive terms but is sinking financially under the burden of a directly-owned Japanese dealer network whose capacity to generate sales against Toyota has long been inferior. The fact of the matter is that, after Nissan had been beaten in the market place, its fate was sealed and its productive (in)ability was irrelevant. Thus Kamiya's attacking-market chess obtained a result which was beyond Ohno's game of endless productive improvement.

Any analysis of Toyota's results must be set in this context. As the analysis chapters showed and as Table 7.8 demonstrates, Toyota is financially like Ford Highland Park and unlike all other modern car companies because it operates with a consistently low labor-share of value-added and gushes cash; but as the analysis chapters also showed, Western car firms can achieve Toyota-style financial results at the peak of the cycle.

Table 7.8: Toyota Labor's Share of Value-added and Cash Flow.

	Labor's share of value added (%)	Cash flow share of value added (%)
1984	41.1	58.9
1985	37.5	62.5
1986	39.8	60.2
1987	43.2	56.8
1988	42.1	57.9
1989	42.0	58.0
1990	42.2	57.8
1991	43.7	56.3

Source: Consolidated Annual Report and Accounts, various years and company communication.

What Toyota has done is to manoeuvre itself into a market position where these results are quasi-permanent. The productive superiority of Toyota over all others is endlessly asserted and assumed but relevant measures are hard to come by and difficult to interpret because they partly reflect the knock-through effects of market success. We have elsewhere (Williams et al., 1992c) criticized the IMVP comparison of assembly plants which purports to show that Japan's best (Toyota Takaoka) performs a series of standard operations in half the time of America's worst (GM Framingham) So at this point we will consider Michael Cusumano's comparisons of Toyota against the rest.

Cusumano offers two exhibits in support of the proposition that the Japanese in general and Toyota in particular have an advantage. The industry comparison is relevant because Toyota accounts for 35–40 percent of the output of the Japanese industry and, according to Cusumano, the Japanese auto industry produced 8.7 vehicles per worker in 1983 against 5.9 in America in 1981 (Cusumano, 1985, p.193). At a company level Toyota has an overwhelming superiority; 'at a company level as early as 1965, even adjusting for differences in vertical integration, each Toyota worker was producing 70 percent more vehicles per year than employees at GM, Ford, Chrysler or Nissan, where each worker made the equivalent of between 4 and 5 complete vehicles' (Ibid, p.196). In our view, Cusumano's measures overstate the gap because the sectoral comparison does not make adequate allowance for differences in hours worked and the company comparison does not make adequate allowance for differences in vertical disintegration. On hours, Cusumano assumes that the Americans worked 87–94 percent of Japanese hours (Ibid, p.398) which we do not accept because, for much of the 1980s, Toyota workers worked six days of ten hours each week (Williams et al., 1991). As for the company comparison, Cusumano uses the ratio of internal operating costs to total costs as the adjuster for differences in amount of work carried out internally where we would use value-added to sales. Cusumano's adjuster is misleading because it includes payments to subcontractors in the numerator; this is an important consideration when Toyota subcontracts the assembly of a substantial part of its output. It is also misleading because all conversion work which is undertaken and realized as cash or profit vanishes from the calculation; again this is an important consideration in a profitable company like Toyota where the missing conversion work may account for 15 percent of output. The arithmetical effect of Cusumano's procedure is to exaggerate Toyota's apparent productivity because profit accounts for a much larger share of the value-added numerator than of the sales denominator; our value-added/sales adjuster which excludes payments to subcontractors and includes profit gives a span corrected vehicles per employee figure which is around half that of Cusumano.

Our own comparisons are presented in the final chapter of this book which considers the relative position of the American and Japanese industries and of Toyota against other companies, Japanese and American. On the respective car industries, after making realistic allowance for differences in hours worked, our conclusion is that the Japanese and American industries are not that far apart because in recent years there have been around 130 motor-sector hours in a Japanese vehicle against 150 or so in an American vehicle when their more cyclical market is relatively brisk. On the relative performance of the companies, Toyota does add more value per worker, most recently around 100,000 $US per worker against 70-80,000 for Nissan or the American Big Three and that is a fair index of physical difference given the similarity of wage levels since the mid-1980s. But this differential is considerably less than 2 to 1 and it is comparatively recent in origin because it coincides with the Japanese domestic market boom of the late 1980s which provided a major boost to Toyota's performance. The conclusion must be that reports of Toyota's productive superiority have been greatly exaggerated.

The Illusion of Diffusion

In myth and romance, Ford and Toyota are system prototypes whose productive innovations are adopted by national and international imitators who realize the benefits of their systems. This schema about the diffusion of imaginary 'systems' misunderstands the content of history which it represents as a series of binary choices which open the possibility of enhanced performance through adoption of the appropriate new system. We will begin this section by challenging these assumptions.

The idea of binary choice between mutually-exclusive systems is central to most systems thinking; it is, for example, elaborated through the concepts of divides and branching paths in Piore and Sabel's book, *The Second Industrial Divide* (1984) which we have criticized elsewhere (Williams et al., 1987b). This conceptualization offers the semblance of choice so that it is possible to have stages theory without the embarrassment of historical determinism and inevitable succession.

But the schema of choice misrepresents the history of the cars business which displays altogether more complex patterns which include the recombination of productive elements as well as varying mixes of the productive in relation to market and financial variables.

The diffusion of productive techniques, for example, involves loss as well as gain because of the uncertain balance of mechanical imitation and forgetting against understanding and memory. Mechanical imitation at the level of the firm is best illustrated by Lingorno, the Turin factory which Fiat built in imitation of Highland Park without realizing that the multi-story form was one of Ford's unsolved problems. A sectoral process of memory and forgetting is at work in the diffusion and loss of Ford's practice on layout and machine use; the Anglo-American Council on productivity (AACP) reports of the 1940s document the widespread use of Ford-style techniques which were then lost and rediscovered as Japanese novelties by American engineers like Schonberger (1982) in the 1980s. The process of productive forgetting and rediscovery is driven partly by the way in which unsuccessful firms and sectors are forced to compete in new ways. Thus, for better or worse, GM in the 1920s responded to Ford's productive innovations by organizational innovation; Ford's organization was flat, task centered and ran on simple physical measures, whereas GM created a corporate hierarchy which allowed financial and strategic control. Sectorally, the same dialectic of thesis and antithesis is at work in the European industry. As our chapter on that industry will show, the Germans successfully occupied the upper end of the EC market which allowed them to recover their high costs; the French were forced in the 1980s to adopt the option of productive cost reduction. Only exceptionally can a successful firm or sector block all of the options for its competitors.

If the dynamics of the historical process are complex, the end result is something different from step-like increments in performance arising from the adoption of each new system. The idea of performance steps is central to the Womack, Roos and Jones book on the cars business which we have criticized elsewhere. Again, we would argue that this position has an internal logic for those who purvey system fixes; in the case of Womack, Jones and Roos the schema of steps justifies the universalist prescription that all firms should adopt lean production which is simply 'a better way of making things'. As we have seen, Ford's application of repetitive manufacture principles to car manufacture did generate a huge jump in productivity and reduction in cost. Long-run comparisons of Ford against Toyota are difficult, but in the paragraphs below we present comparisons of cars per employee, materials flow and wages and conditions. All of these suggest that Toyota in the 1980s represents no advance on Henry Ford in his heyday.

In the interests of fair comparison, we compare Toyota Motor Company against Ford (Highland Park) and exclude Toyota Motor Sales employees whose equivalents in Ford would often have been employed in Ford's independent-dealer network. The results of this comparison are summarized in Table 7.9 which presents the crude vehicles per employee result for both companies and calculates corrected productivity for Toyota which are comparable to Ford's crude figures because they apply the value-added/sales ratio as a deflator to correct for Toyota's much shorter process span.

Table 7.9: Ford (Highland Park) and Toyota, Vehicles per Employee.

	Toyota crude vehicles per employee	Toyota span adjusted vehicles per employee		Ford crude vehicles per employee
1984	44.2	17.0	1909	8.4
1985	45.9	17.7	1910	7.5
1986	44.3	17.0	1911	13.5
1987	43.2	16.6	1912	12.0
1988	46.1	17.7	1913	13.9
1989	44.8	17.2	1914	19.4
1990	45.7	17.6	1915	19.5
1991	44.3	17.0	1916	17.9

Notes: Col.2 is calculated from Col.1 divided by 2.6, which is the average differential between the value-added to sales ratio of Toyota (1984 to 1991) and Ford (1909 to 1916).

Source: Toyota output and employment data from the consolidated Annual Report and Accounts; Ford Motor Company *Report and Accounts*, various years; Col.2, A.Nevins (1954) Ford: *The Times, the Man, the Company*, p.648.

Toyota has a large apparent advantage in vehicles-per-employee; from 1984-91 Toyota achieves forty-four to forty-six cars per employee against Ford's best of eighteen to twenty in 1914-16. But, after correcting for Toyota's much shorter process span, Toyota's margin of superiority vanishes because Toyota's corrected vehicles per employee ranges from seventeen to eighteen, almost exactly the same as Ford's. It would be unwise to see this as anything more than an interesting coincidence when car type and specification are so different in 1914 and 1984; Toyota undoubtedly produces a more complex, closed car than the open Model T. But, the vehicles per employee comparison does provide a first indication that Toyota may not have overwhelming superiority.

Table 7.10a: Ford 1909–16, Stocks, Value-added and Stocks to Value-added Ratio.

	Value Added $ m.	Average stocks $ m.	Stocks/VA ratio
1909	4.2	2.2	1.91
1910	6.4	3.0	2.13
1911	10.9	4.2	2.60
1912	18.7	7.3	2.56
1913	38.2	12.6	3.03
1914	39.2	12.3	3.19
1915	52.0	15.3	3.40
1916	91.0	24.3	3.74

Source: Payroll, depreciation and profit per car from Ford Archive, Accession 843; Col.2, from Ford Archive, Accession 96, Box 10.

Table 7.10b: Toyota 1984-91, Stocks, Value-added and stocks to Value-added Ratio.

	Value Added Yen m.	Average stocks Yen m.	Stocks/VA ratio
1984	814,521	249,241	3.27
1985	955,007	286,129	3.34
1986	938,141	287,614	3.26
1987	890,972	263,596	3.38
1988	982,524	260,383	3.77
1989	1,104,844	297,973	3.71
1990	1,351,155	336,106	4.02
1991	1,446,735	371,324	3.90

Source: Consolidated Annual Report and Accounts, various years.

Materials-flow measures are altogether more telling because the Ford and Toyota products do represent roughly comparable multi-process fabrication problems; Toyota has not succeeded in producing a car with half the parts or weight of the model T and, if Henry were to tour Toyota factories, he would immediately recognize many of the processes. In the absence of a WIP figure for both firms, we cannot calculate WIP to VA ratios and Tables 7.10 a and b present what we can do which is calculate a stocks to VA ratio.

As we have already emphasized, Ford managed continuous improvement in flow with the stocks to value-added ratio rising from 2.13 in 1910 to 3.74 in 1916; Table 7.10b sets this in comparative perspective because Toyota after 1984 turns in a ratio which fluctuates around 3.75 with no sustained upward trend. If we take the VA to sales ratio as a proxy for physical-process span, Ford's process span was three-times longer than Toyota's span and, other things being equal, it is always more difficult to sustain the same flow over a longer span which involves more process stations. Thus, a comparable ratio of around 3.75 at Ford indicates markedly superior performance.

The impression of Ford's superiority is confirmed if we broaden the performance measures to consider the social dimension of producer welfare. The question of which company offered more fulfilling work can only be answered by arrogant humanists, (Womack et al., p.54, 80, 99) who are prepared to make large assumptions about the essence of homo faber. The evidence, which the MIT book ignores, suggests that both companies were nasty to work for; both Ford and Toyota eschewed formal Taylorism and instead applied intense, informal pressure on the workforce to meet and raise output norms. Oral reminiscences in the Ford archive describe the use of working foremen and pace setters to drive an immigrant workforce; just as Kamata's (1983) memoir of seasonal work at Toyota in the early 1970s gives a first-hand account of the 'work to finish' system which Toyota then operated. If, however, we turn to look at the reward side of the effort bargain, then Ford appears to be the more responsible employer. Ford workers were rewarded with rapidly-increasing real wages; average money wages increased from 22 to 53 cents per hour between 1909 and 1916. When in 1914 Ford offered his line workers $5 for an eight-hour day it was thus dramatically re-emphasized that he offered higher wages and shorter hours than in any other manufacturing firm: by our calculations Ford's wages were 62 percent higher than those paid to all Michigan manufacturing employees in 1909 (Lee, 1957) and this differential was broadly maintained in 1914 and 1919. Ford's strategy of vertical integration was such that his company aspired to become coincident with the sector and these top-dollar wages were paid to an increasing proportion of those employed in the Model T production chain. Toyota's workers have enjoyed rapidly-rising real wages but in all other respects the social reward for effort is inferior. Until the downturn of the early 1990s, Toyota workers routinely worked very long hours and put in a sixty hour week over six days (Williams et al., 1991) which was longer than in any other advanced country. Furthermore, Toyota's strategy of vertical disintegration confines the benefits of high wages to those directly employed by Toyota and Toyota exploits the steep wage gradient into supplier firms. Those who ignorantly disparage 'Fordism' as an industrial system seldom bother to consider these facts about its supposedly superior successor.

Where others see imaginary systems, we see trajectories. A trajectory is defined by the intersection of two sets of conditions; a first set of internal technical and social capabilities establishes the possibility of cost reduction and a second set of external environmental conditions, especially market space, establishes the possibility of cost recovery. The over-used concept of strategy is a tendentious and inadequate way of representing internal conditions which are often embedded and semi-institutionalized or active at the operational level. A trajectory is different from a system or strategy because it entails the idea of an arc of performance. Initially, there is the possibility of higher performance by deploying internal capabilities or exploiting an external environment. But, there are internal limits to the application of productive, market or financial techniques and also the certainty that in the long run the external environment will change. Internal limits and external changes together cause a falling away so that the latter part of any trajectory is a descent into ordinariness. From this point of view, Ford and Toyota are both exceptional companies which got onto high performance trajectories of output growth and cost reduction. And they did so in part because both companies operated in similarly favorable internal and external conditions.

In both cases, the internal condition was an unusual degree of complete control over the labor force. This facilitated forms of productive intervention which relied (differently) on layout change and task recomposition. Ford operated in the open-shop capital of America; the company was non-union and the management prerogative over labor was absolute in a factory where any worker who refused instructions was sacked on the spot. As Arnold and Faurote (1915, p.328) observed, 'workmen are studied individually and changed from place to place with no cause assigned, as the bosses see fit, and not one word of protest is ever spoken'. The only form of resistance was walking off the job into Detroit's external labor market. Toyota created a similarly absolutist regime after the end of the 1950 labor dispute. The possibility of internal resistance is undermined by a system of individualized pay according to the foreman's merit rating and a complicated system of group bonuses which set workers against individuals or groups which fail to deliver; the company union gives little trouble because there is no secret ballot for elected representatives and officers (see, Williams et al., 1991). When, in 1988, we asked a Toyota manager what he would do if he wanted a worker to speed up he said 'tap him on the shoulder and tell him to speed up'. The external labor market is not much of an alternative for this worker because it offers much lower wages and less security.

In terms of external conditions, both Ford and Toyota benefited from rapidly expanding home-market demand in the early stages of motorization. Table 7.11 summarizes the available data which covers both US car production after 1909 which was almost entirely for the home market, and also Japanese home-market registrations and car exports after 1960.

Table 7.11: US and Japanese Passenger Car Output 1909-91.

	United States production		Japan home market registrations	Japanese passenger car exports
1909	128,000	1960	145,227	7,013
1910	181,000	1961	229,057	11,531
1911	199,000	1962	259,269	16,011
1912	356,000	1963	371,076	31,445
1913	462,000	1964	493,536	66,965
1914	544,000	1965	586,287	100,703
1915	896,000	1966	740,259	153,090
1916	1,526,000	1967	1,131,337	223,491
1917	1,746,000	1968	1,569,404	406,250
1918	943,000	1969	2,036,662	560,431
1919	1,658,000	1970	2,379,128	725,586
1920	1,906,000	1971	2,402,757	1,299,351
1921	1,518,000	1972	2,627,087	1,407,340
1922	2,369,000	1973	2,933,590	1,450,884
1923	3,754,000	1974	2,286,795	1,727,396
1924	3,304,000	1975	2,737,595	1,827,286
1925	3,871,000	1976	2,449,429	2,538,919
1926	3,949,000	1977	2,500,095	2,958,879
1927	3,083,000	1978	2,856,710	3,042,237
1928	4,012,000	1979	3,036,873	3,101,990
1929	4,795,000	1980	2,854,176	3,947,160
1930	2,787,400	1981	2,866,695	3,946,542
1931	1,948,100	1982	3,038,272	3,770,036
1932	1,103,500	1983	3,135,610	3,806,396
1933	1,560,500	1984	3,095,554	3,980,619
1934	2,160,800	1985	3,104,074	4,426,762
1935	3,273,800	1986	3,146,023	4,572,791
1936	3,679,200	1987	3,274,800	4,507,530
1937	3,929,200	1988	3,717,359	4,431,887
1938	2,019,500	1989	4,403,745	4,403,060
1939	2,888,500	1990	5,102,660	4,482,130
1940	3,717,300	1991	4,801,000	4,452,233

Sources: US production data: *Statistical Abstract of the US*, US Department of Commerce; Japan: *Motor Vehicle Statistics of Japan*, JAMA, various years.

If we take US output as a proxy for market demand, the table indicates that the American market grew from virtually nothing to nearly 4.5 million in twenty years and increased ten fold to 1.5 million between 1909 and 1916. The Japanese home market grew from insignificance in 1960 to 5 million in 1990 with a twenty fold increase to 2.9 million between 1960 and 1973; if the initial growth rate of the Japanese market was slower that was compensated by export sales which reached 1.5 million in 1973 and 4.5 million in 1990. Ford and Toyota claimed the lion's share of the market increase as they were the established market leaders throughout the two decades of headlong motorization in their home markets. Ford's performance is phenomenal with the firm accounting for 35 percent plus of US production in most years after 1913; between 1921 and 1924 Ford sold more than 50 percent of the market and recovered to 38 percent in 1929 after the debacle over replacement of the T. Table 7.12 shows that Toyota consistently claimed 30–40 percent of its home market. In both companies high shares of rapidly-growing markets provided incentives for productive intervention which raised throughput and eased the process of stripping labor out because sustained expansion prevented redundancies which would otherwise have been necessary.

Table 7.12: Ford and Toyota Passenger Car Market Share 1909-91.

	Ford production	Ford % share of US production		Toyota registrations	Toyota % market share
1909	10,202	7.8	1970	709,000	29.8
1910	17,771	9.8	1971	786,000	32.7
1911	32,053	16.1	1972	927,000	35.3
1912	69,762	19.6	1973	1,074,000	36.6
1913	170,068	36.8	1974	892,000	39.0
1914	195,954	36.0	1975	1,073,000	39.2
1915	299,797	33.5	1976	899,000	36.7
1916	489,202	32.1	1977	893,000	35.7
1917	718,397	41.1	1978	1,083,000	37.9
1918	645,309	68.4	1979	1,142,000	37.6
1919	479,166	28.9	1980	1,064,000	39.7
1920	867,826	45.5	1981	1,098,000	40.7
1921	928,750	61.2	1982	1,174,000	41.1
1922	1,232,209	52.0	1983	1,248,000	42.5
1923	1,915,485	51.0	1984	1,275,000	43.9
1924	1,869,522	56.6	1985	1,323,000	45.0
1925	1,854,489	47.9	1986	1,383,000	46.0
1926	1,549,740	39.2	1987	1,454,000	46.2
1927	389,240	12.6	1988	1,633,000	45.8

Table 7.12 (*continued*)

	Ford production	Ford % share of US production		Toyota registrations	Toyota % market share
1928	788,321	19.7	1989	1,761,000	43.9
1929	1,797,741	37.5	1990	1,893,000	44.0
1930	2,787,400	45.5	1991	1,728,000	42.9

Sources: Ford production, A.Nevins and Hill (1962), *Decline and Rebirth, 1933–1962*, Appendix I; Toyota registrations, *Motor Vehicle Statistics of Japan*, JAMA, various years.

As both companies moved along trajectories of output growth and cost reduction, they gushed cash. We have already emphasized Toyota's low labor share of value-added and Table 7.13 shows that Ford's share was even lower. From 1909–16, Ford's labor share of value-added ranged between 27 and 32 percent whereas Toyota's, over the period 1980-91, ranged between 38 and 44 percent. As the analysis chapters showed most car companies now run with average labor share of value-added at or above 70 percent.

The cash gushed out because most of what was left over after labor had been paid was available as free cash. Both companies were also financially adept at realizing cash from current operations: at Ford, Couzens sold cars for cash to the dealers before he paid suppliers, and at Toyota Kamiya introduced a system of dealer payment by promissory notes which Toyota could immediately turn into cash. Thus both companies quickly built up cash mountains. By 1914 Ford had $22 million in cash which was a sum equal to nearly half of that year's value-added. The extent of Toyota's cash reserves in 1992 were 1,492,651 million Yen equivalent to the value-added of that year; forty years after it was rescued by the banks, the company is now itself referred to as 'Toyota bank'.

Table 7.13: Ford and Toyota Labor Share of Value-added.

	Ford Labor's share of Value Added (%)		Toyota Labor's share of Value Added (%)
1909	27.7	1984	41.0
1910	32.6	1985	37.5
1911	27.1	1986	39.8
1912	28.9	1987	43.2
1913	31.8	1988	42.1
1914	31.1	1989	42.0

Table 7.13 (*continued*)

	Ford Labor's share of Value Added (%)		Toyota Labor's share of Value Added (%)
1915	30.4	1990	42.2
1916	39.0	1991	43.7

Notes: Ford labor's share of value-added is calculated by subtracting purchases from sales and expressing labor costs as a percent of value added, Toyota: labor's share of value-added is calculated as labor costs as a percentage of value-added (calculated as net income, plus depreciation, plus labor costs).

Sources: Ford: Archive, Accession 463, Box 6, gross output, Ford Archive, Accession 96, Box 8 and 10; Total labor costs, Ford Archive, Accession 843; Toyota: *Annual Report and Accounts*, various years and company communication.

Both companies had the resources for discretionary spending and their huge success no doubt encouraged the usual business illusion about skills which could transform any activity. Both Ford and Toyota repeatedly tried to pull the same trick all over again with other product lines. Ford did develop an adjunct business with the Fordson tractor just as Toyota built a strong position in trucks through its Hino affiliate. But the further Ford and Toyota moved away from road vehicles, the less successful were their attempts at redefining products and processes in ways which established dominant positions. The DC3 Dakota and the supermarket succeeded where Ford failed with his trimotor and his commission shops. And Toyota's failure with the prefabricated Toyohome only established that the motor car (and the cheaper consumer durables) offered a unique one-off opportunity for volume repetitive manufacture. The consumer demand for at least a semblance of individuality can always be overcome if the repetitively manufactured product offers a large enough cost saving; but in housing that is not possible because land accounts for a fixed and significant portion of total price and because those who build one-off homes have access to repetitive-manufacture fixtures and fittings.

Because diversification was always a side show, both companies applied large amounts of cash to auto-industry product and process innovation. Toyota approached this in a way which was orthodox and conservative whereas Ford was the heroic and unsuccessful visionary. By the late 1980s, although Toyota's operating standards were high, most of its productive techniques must have long since reached the limits of their sphere of application; like many ageing conservatives, the company spends time in trying to recreate its earlier conditions of success by, for example, opening a plant on Honshu, the southernmost

Japanese island where green labor is still available. Most of Toyota's money went on product churning which steadily replaced one bland product with another and gradually expanded the product range; with the September 1989 launch of the Lexus LS400, which sold in America on price against BMW and Mercedes, the range was complete. As for broader changes in external circumstances, Toyota was unable to accept them: its journal *The Wheel Extended* promotes techno fixes for the growing contradiction between car use and urban life; while, when the market turned down in 1990, the company's annual report could only recommend employees to redouble their efforts. 'In the early 1980s, pessimistic pundits were telling us that our industry was mature, our markets saturated. But we proved them wrong with exciting new models that captured the public imagination and stimulated unprece- dented growth in demand' (*Toyota Annual Report*, 1990, p.17).

Ford, by way of contrast, lived by heroic product and process inno- vation. With the T, Ford had created the first great 'people's car' and the company's subsequent efforts were directed towards developing a high-performance, luxury car which sold at a popular price. Replacement of the T was delayed while Henry tinkered with an X8 engine and an automatic gearbox. And if the Model A of 1927 was mechanically mundane, the same could not be said of the V8 powered Model B of 1932. In 'high boy' coupe form this car created NASCAR, drag racing and hot rods; its vivid acceleration was equally appreciated by Clyde Barrow who died in a hail of bullets at the wheel of his 85th stolen Ford. More remarkably, within ten years of putting the Model T into production at Highland Park, Ford was building a second great factory on different principles at Rouge; no car company, before or since, has ever attempted to sustain flow across such a large span of processes. Rouge is often loosely described as an integrated car factory which it was; here Ford made everything from steel and glass to leatherette in a factory where coal and iron ore went in at one end and finished cars came out at the other. More accurately it could be described as an interconnected conversion machine because all processes, including steel making were to be undertaken continuously and linked by conveyor belts; the scale of Ford's ambition is astonish- ing because the factory contained twenty-seven miles of conveyor belt and, at its peacetime peak, employed 80,000 (Van Deventer, 1923).

Those, like Diego Rivera, who based his 1932-3 Detroit Industry Frescoes on production of the Model B at Rouge, realized they were in the presence of industrial greatness. In his Marxist way Rivera understood the factory much better than most subsequent academic commentators; on the main (North and South wall) frescoes, all the workers are portrayed in unending movement which is the logic of continuous conversion. But Ford's was a flawed greatness and the factory never operated as Rivera envisaged it. That was because the company was autocratically headed by an old man who was increasingly at odds with his times. Thus, Henry could not comprehend or accommodate the countervailing power of independent unionism in the 1930s. Nor, more fundamentally, could he develop an adequate response to changing market circumstances from the middle 1920s. In his usual visionary way, Henry did recognize the problem because he promoted a series of social experiments to increase prosperity and create new circuits of demand which would unite industrial producers and rural consumers; Henry experimented with decentralization of component production to rural factories and with the processing of soyabeans into industrial raw materials from which he could make steering wheels and car panels. Meanwhile, he neglected marketing in the 1920s and paid the price of market fluctuations in the 1930s.

Just as Toyota's marketing efforts shut the door on Nissan in the 1960s and 1970s, so GM Chevrolet's marketing efforts shut the door on Ford in the 1920s. GM concentrated on breaking the connection between lower prices and increased sales which had been the basis of Ford's pre-and post-war successes; Ford used pricing as a substitute for marketing on the assumption that if the Ford car was cheaper than its competitors (and last year's Ford) then consumers would buy the Ford rather than other offerings in the sub-$1,000 category. But the connection was broken by a variety of developments; the natural effects of rising real incomes and a growing number of new entrants offering more power and comfort were purposefully magnified by GM policies on easy payments and second hands. Easy payment-instalment plans of the kind pioneered by General Motors Acceptance Corporation (GMAC), the finance division of GM, were important because they made windscreen sticker price less important; and selling trade-ins at cost was equally important as a way of encouraging replacement new-car sales and filling the forecourts with second-hand substitutes for a new Ford. Ford persisted with its pricing policy after the Model A was introduced; the four door Model A sedan cost $30 more than its Model T predecessor and $125 below the comparable Chevrolet (Hounshell, 1987, p.457). But by this stage, the pricing policy already looked like Ford undermining his own cost-recovery position because Chevrolet had built a substantial market share and was splitting cheap-car sales with Ford. 'Vun for vun' (one for one) was the slogan of Knudsen, the ex-Ford man who headed Chevrolet in the 1920s; by 1926, before the Model T ran out, Knudsen was already selling one Chevrolet for every two Fords and in most years of the 1930s Chevrolet outsold Ford.

Only sustained growth in the market for cheap cars could have saved Ford in the 1930s from its neglect of marketing in the 1920s. In these circumstances, the company's embarrassment was deepened by the macroeconomic cataclysm of the Great Depression which reduced total US car production from a cyclical peak of 4.5 million in 1929 to just 1.1 million in 1932 with slow and unsteady recovery through the rest of the decade. Although Ford was operating the world's greatest car factory, it could never be a super company in the 1930s because it did not have the volume base to achieve decent rates of utilization in a factory where labor content did vary with throughput and belt speed; Rouge was used for raw-material conversion in the early post-war period and only began to function as an integrated factory, turning out finished cars, at the time of the change over from the Model T to Model A; at this time, the Rouge factory had a planned throughput of 5,000 cars a day or approximately 1.5 million cars per year (Van Deventer, 1923, Vol.LXVI, No.2, p.85) while the Ford company retained component production at Highland Park and branch assembly facilities around the country. The American Ford company's production averaged 764,000 per annum in the 1930s so Rouge's utilization must have been no more than 50 percent and in the two worst recession years of 1932 and 1933 utilization was probably worse than 25 percent.

The story of Rouge shows how the history of car manufacture is the struggle of productive flow against market restriction. For most companies restriction is the everyday condition and for super companies it is the fate that awaits them and limits their upward trajectory. In extreme cases, the result of restriction is market failure and the next chapter considers what up to the early 1990s, at least, has been the largest company failure in the history of the world cars business.

✦ ✦ ✦

8
BMC/BLMC/BL:
Market–Led Failure

———— ❖ ————

This chapter provides an analysis of company failure which is a natural and necessary counterpart to the analysis of Ford and Toyota's success; it analyzes the largest failure in the world cars business up to the 1990s and tells a story of merger and company failure which brought down a national champion and a national industry. The national champion, British Motor Corporation, was created in 1952 by the merger of Austin and Morris, the two independent British-owned volume-cars businesses. Reverse merger created British Leyland Motor Corporation in 1968; by this stage the combine was effectively the British-owned motor sector because BLMC brought together all the British-owned specialist producers like Triumph, Rover and Jaguar as well as Austin and Morris. The loss-making BLMC was nationalized as British Leyland in 1975 and, after a decade of unsuccess in the public sector, the firm was denationalized in 1985 through sale to British Aerospace which was then diversifying out of military and civil aircraft; rather confusingly, Aerospace increasingly marketed the product of the old Austin and Morris factories under the Rover badge. This is a drama with a large and confusing cast of characters whose acronyms and marque names mean little to a non-British audience or indeed to younger British readers; it is therefore important to emphasize that this is a tragedy in two acts which will be considered separately in this chapter.

Act one is the BMC period from 1952–68. This was a period of rapid expansion in output which rose from less than 300,000 vehicles in 1951–2 to nearly 900,000 vehicles in 1964–5. In the early 1960s, the company claimed to be the world's fourth largest car company (*BMC World*, November 1961); the company was certainly a major European manufacturer which was fully the equal of VW, Renault and Fiat. When BLMC was formed in 1968, Austin Morris and the specialists together made over one-million vehicles and the merging firms together employed 175,000 employees. Act two covers the BLMC and BL period from 1968 to the present. For much of this period, the media headlines were about the unsolved problems of profitability and cash flow which led to BLMC's collapse and endless crisis at BL. In the latter 1970s, the company entered a period of output decline which more or less halved car output between 1972 and 1979. The launch of new models failed to generate product-led recovery and in the second half of the 1980s car output settled at somewhere around 500,000; in 1992 Rover produced fewer cars than Fiat's Polish assembly plants. Increasingly, the company is not a full manufacturer but a licensed assembler of other companies' designs which are currently supplied by Honda which has a minority stake in Rover. In January 1994, British Aerospace sold its majority shareholding to BMW, without Honda's agreement; Rover factories, except Land Rover, are likely to become branch manufacturing operations.

This failure is not only heroic but also instructive and in this chapter we tell the story and draw three lessons of failure. The first two lessons reinforce and qualify themes about production systems and market shares which have already emerged in the argument so far and the third introduces a new theme about the limits of management. The first lesson of failure is that it reinforces our skepticism about the explanation of success and failure in terms of good and bad production systems; in the case of the British-owned car firms, this argument has been developed by Lewchuk (1987) who attributes the failure of British-owned car firms to their incomplete adoption of the (American) system of mass production and specifically to their persistence with craft-style indirect labor control under group piece-rate systems. Against this, we will present a multi-dimensional explanation of failure which gives proper weight to the external-market variable and thereby underscores the point that firms do not compete on an abstracted terrain of production where victory goes to the firm with the best manufacturing system. As we shall see, under their production guru Woollard, BMC creatively adapted American techniques and pursued an ideal of flow manufacture which could not be realized because of increasing market difficulties.

The second lesson takes the form of a caution or health warning about the role of the market. BMC was a market-leading firm which held nearly 40 percent of the British market; the lesson of its failure is that car firms with large market shares do not have any invariant or general advantage over firms with small market shares. This qualification is necessary because our argument about Ford and Toyota in the previous chapter may appear to endorse the conventional wisdom of the strategy texts about the advantages of large market share. On this point our argument is not in opposition but simply more discriminating. Ford and Toyota show that large shares of growing markets are positive conditions for firms operating along trajectories of expansion. But large shares of mature markets are an embarrassment for firms which must try and defend them; BMC/BL (like GM in our own time) could only defend its share by incurring extra expense on proliferating and replacing a broad range of models which were sold in variant forms through parallel distribution networks. For American and European firms, market spread and decent volume on a limited range of models are important conditions of survival. A minimum model volume is essential because the next generation of product is always developed with cash generated from sales of the existing model; when its new models failed to sell in high volume BL was effectively forced out of the business of developing and manufacturing its own product.

Lesson three concerns the limits of management thought and action: it can plausibly be argued that management was not the saviour but the destroyer of the company in the second act of the tragedy after 1968. The old BMC had been run by car makers who had many achievements in product and process design; if they expanded the company without solving its problems that was probably the best that could be done under the circumstances. BLMC was run down by managers whose actions made things worse because they reflected too little understanding of the realities of the cars business and too much exposure to corporate practice and management theory. In the BLMC era, the company was disastrously remade in the image of Ford UK; newly-installed managers made the classic mistake of mechanically imitating the winning formula regardless of the difference in circumstance. Recipe thinking was replaced by macho action in the BL period when the next management team failed to execute the difficult manoeuvre of downsizing to create a smaller yet viable firm. The priorities and decisions of the Edwardes era showed that, when incrementalism and routine were not enough, managers from outside the business were ineffectual actors because they lacked the necessary understanding of the complex relations between market, financial and productive variables. Von Moltke defined strategy as 'the art of action under pressure of most difficult circumstances'; the failure of BLMC and BL shows that (British) managers had less mastery of this art than their more modest car-making predecessors.

BMC: A Policy of Expansion

In 1952 the newly created BMC was headed by Len Lord who had previously described Austin and Morris as two 'second division teams'. Throughout the 1950s Lord's policy was to get into the first division by going for output growth mainly by defending the company's near 40 percent share of the rapidly-expanding home market. The policy was based on intuition and experience rather than any formal market analysis or forecasting techniques. Thus, in 1956 when the company was temporarily embarrassed by a cyclical downturn, the Annual Report argued simply that 'never in the past, viewed over a reasonable period, has our industry in general, or have we in particular, been wrong in pursuing a policy of expansion' (BMC Report, 1956, p.13). The same kind of intuition was applied to all the company's other problems: in effect the company was run by car makers who knew nothing about the new discourses of management and indeed preferred not to recruit graduate trainees. As car makers, Lord and his team realized that increased output would only generate profit and cash if they revamped product and process and this was the first priority in the 1950s.

There was nothing second rate about BMC's product-design and process-engineering talents. Its design star was Alec Issigonis whose cars included the Minor of 1947 and then the Mini, 1100 and 1800 of 1959–65. Only Dante Giacosa, who designed the Topolino, 500 and 600 for Fiat, had anything like the same flair for packaging small cars. Giacosa was creative but never invented a configuration which everybody else subsequently imitated as Issigonis did with the front wheel drive, transverse engine over gearbox, cars. In process engineering, the company's unsung hero was Frank Woollard whose late career achievements were the construction of a model car-assembly hall (Longbridge CAB1) which opened in 1951 and the design of automatic-transfer lines which were producing a rationalized range of (A and B series) engines and gearboxes by 1954. BMC was, with Renault, one of the two pioneering adapters of American transfer techniques to the lower-volume requirements of European manufacturers. When Nissan in December 1952 signed a license deal to produce the A50 Cambridge in Japan, it obtained a stolid, worthy product design and what would now be called 'world class' production engineering.

If the company's product and process design was excellent, the company's unsuccess is hard to comprehend within the framework of business school and consulting orthodoxies that emphasize the benefits of productive excellence which apparently always solves problems and saves struggling firms. Perhaps, the anomaly of BMC failure is easier to understand if we change Lord's sporting metaphor and invoke a game of chance not skill. Success eluded BMC because the company was 'one lemon short of the jackpot'; specifically, BMC could not line up the market in a way which would allow it to realize the full benefits of product and process innovation. This point can be demonstrated by analyzing Woollard's considerable engineering achievements and their limited benefits.

Like Ohno, Woollard wrote a book when he retired and this unjustly neglected text, *Principles of Mass and Flow Production* (1954), decisively refutes the idea that the space between Henry Ford and the Japanese is occupied with dull, mechanical diffusion and imitation. Woollard's insight into repetitive manufacturing is at least as sharp and distinctive as Ohno's and is considerably more acute than most current Production and Operations Management textbooks. Woollard realized that the key objective was manpower reduction because 'the cost of manpower [is] usually considerably greater than that of machines' (Ibid, 1954, p.104). Improved flow was the means which could take labor hours and cost out of the product so the ideal was flow production with 'the passage of the part from operation to operation in a direct and uninterrupted sequence' (Ibid, p.48). Woollard shared an understanding about instruments with Ford and the Japanese because he realized that changes in materials transfer and process layout were the prerequisite for flow improvement and cost reduction; 'freedom to change the layout of both machine and assembly lines to suit the changing character of, and the modified demands for, the product must be retained' (Ibid, p.83). Like Henry Ford who came before and the Japanese who came after, Woollard believed in continuous layout change as the secret of improvement; like all the past masters he believed that 'machines should not be bolted to the floor' (Ibid, p.82).

Woollard is in many ways an interesting hybrid figure who combines the traditionally American approach with anticipations of the distinctively Japanese. Woollard operated easily and unconsciously in an American-line problematic where the (pre-cellular) task was to take work past the stationary worker. Woollard's concept of flow elides shorter distances and straight-line movements; 'naturally, distances travelled will be as short as possible and all moves will be in straight lines' (Ibid, 1954, p.104). He also shared the characteristic pre-occupation of the time with mechanized materials handling; 'wherever possible the movement of materials should be mechanized and, where circumstances permit, materials should be handled automatically' (Ibid, 1954, p.104). At the same time, he looked to the future with his con-cept of a pull-through factory where the final-assembly line determined the feed rate from earlier machining and subassembly processes; 'the final assembly line can be regarded as a factory metronome beating out the time and marking the pace for all the tributary lines' (Ibid, 1954, p.112). As Woollard grasped, the problem was that flow was imperfectly realized through principles like machines in order of use, in the earlier stages of production; 'even in the most highly integrated factory, there is still a percentage, sometimes a fairly large percentage of work that is not handled on flow production lines' (Ibid, 1954, p.104).

Woollard's mission was to extend the area of flow and he was bril-liantly successful in realizing this objective at single process level through the introduction of automatic-transfer machines (ATM) for cutting metal components used in engines and gearboxes. By 1954, BMC had installed all new ATMs to produce 400,000 engines a year on lines which deployed various kinds of cutting heads in sequence as the workpiece tracked down a linear bed; the machine clamped, cut, released and then moved the workpiece automatically to the next sta-tion. The ATM realized a perfect single unit flow within the bed because there was no stock between the process stages. It also broke the bottleneck of manual loading and unloading at the same time as it dealt with the linear constraint of one worker per station by eliminat-ing direct workers. Woollard laid out cheap modular ATMs which used simple standard machine heads and transfer devices so that they were cheaper than the old manual lines; as Griffith observed 'not only does the new equipment reduce cost per unit greatly, it is also cheaper to buy and operate than the machinery it replaces' (*Machinist*, 21 January 1955). The one transfer machine replacing thirteen single-purpose machines used in finishing A40 cylinder blocks 'saved 26 per-cent in floor space, 30 percent in machine costs per unit of output and 85 percent in direct labor' (*Machinist*, 21 January 1955). The innova-tion was so successful that it was rapidly adopted by all the other European volume manufacturers so that Maxcy and Silbertson (1959, p.56) identified the ATM as 'the principal form which automation takes in the motor industry'.

Woollard also had considerable success in improving flow at factory level. Longbridge CAB1 opened in 1951 was a high-flow, low-stocks line factory. A central marshalling area held two-days stock of small parts which were sent as kits on belt conveyors to sub-assembly work stations so that workers never had to move from their fixed positions. American-style handling systems were used to deliver engines, gearboxes, axles and bodies to the mixed-model final-assembly lines with production sequencing controlled by punch cards. The result was a factory whose productivity was as good or better than that of any mixed-model factory outside the United States. At the cyclical peak in 1960 (before CAB2 opened) Longbridge employed 23,000 (*BMC World*, September 1960) and made nearly 300,000 complete cars and a similar number of engines and gearboxes for use in other BMC factories; thus factory productivity was around 12.5 finished cars plus 12.5 engines and gearboxes per employee.

But the company was not transformed because BMC never realized companywide flow; this is the central point which commentators on Woollard fail to confront. A high-flow company on a trajectory of expansion should have low stocks and rising cars per employee; as was emphasized in the analysis chapters, stocks are a basic indicator of materials flow which is only desirable because it takes labor out. Table 8.1 summarizes the basic evidence on stock levels by providing data on the stock levels which are expressed as an orthodox stock/turnover ratio and then as number of weeks sales cover; in the absence of a WIP figure we have calculated a stock/value-added ratio which corrects for differences in vertical integration. These corrections are important if we want to make a comparison with recent performance by Rover which is less vertically integrated because it partly assembles Honda parts.

Table 8.1: BMC/BLMC/BL/Rover Stock Cover, 1955–91.

	Stock/turnover ratio	Stock cover (weeks)	Value added/ stock ratio
1955	5.01	10.4	1.39
1960	6.30	8.3	1.58
1965	4.87	10.7	1.71
1970	3.17	16.4	2.50
1975	3.23	16.1	3.08
1980	3.04	17.1	3.24
1985	4.33	12.0	1.69
1990	6.00	8.7	1.01
1991	8.63	6.0	0.98

Source: Annual Report and Accounts, various years.

As Table 8.1 shows, BMC's stock levels in the 1950s were reasonably, but not outstandingly, low; the best-ever performance was 8.25 weeks of stock in 1959–60. This slightly disappointing performance undoubtedly reflects the drag of Cowley; BMC modernized Longbridge as a show-piece but never reequipped Cowley to the same standard. Those who savor historical ironies will appreciate the point that BMC's best is better than anything Rover has achieved in recent years after its much vaunted Japanization; in 1990 Rover had 8.67 weeks of stock and in 1991 6.03 weeks of stock which is arithmetically better but materially worse when we remember that the current company is a smaller, less vertically inte-grated firm with substantially simpler material flows. But, more to the point, BMC never shows any sign of steadily improving flow and dimin-ishing stock cover; stock levels are on a plateau around 8-9 weeks between 1956–7 and 1964–5 and then drift upwards to a much less cred-itable 13 weeks plus in the last two years of the company after BMC's takeover of the Pressed Steel bodies business and Jaguar Cars.

Much the same picture emerges from any consideration of vehicles per employee. The relevant evidence is summarized in Table 8.2 which presents the results of a crude calculation of vehicles per employee which is also expressed as man months per vehicle; as a cross check and aid to long-run comparisons, Table 8.2 also presents a span-corrected calculation of vehicles per employee which applies the value-added to sales ratio as a correction factor.

Table 8.2: BMC/BLMC/BL/Rover Vehicles per Employee, 1955–90.

	Vehicles produced 000 units	Number of employees	Crude vehicles per employee	Span corrected vehicles per employee	Man months per vehicle
1955	439.6	60,000	7.3	2.0	1.64
1960	601.4	79,000	7.6	2.1	1.58
1965	845.6	120,000	7.0	2.4	1.71
1970	961.7	199,524	4.8	1.4	2.50
1975	738.2	191,467	3.9	1.2	3.08
1980	585.0	157,000	3.7	1.2	3.24
1985	555.5	78,000	7.1	2.0	1.69
1990	500.5	41,900	11.9	2.7	1.01

Source: Annual Report and Accounts, various years.

Here again the pattern is that there is no sustained improvement; vehicles per employee fluctuates between a high of 9.2 in 1963–4 and a low of 5.9 in 1956–7. An examination of the vehicles-produced totals in Table 8.2 suggests that the variation in vehicles per employee is driven by cyclical fluctuations in demand; when output falls as it did between 1955 and 1957 or between 1959 and 1962 then vehicles per employee also falls. Again BMC's best level of performance is quite respectable and beats anything which Rover has more recently achieved; in 1990 and 1991 Rover achieved a crude best ever of 11.9 and 12.2 vehicles per employee but when span correction is applied the result is 2.68 and 2.72 vehicles per employee which is not much better than BMC achieved in any year from 1955 to 1963. Nevertheless the basic point remains that BMC was not taking labor content out but enduring a market-driven variation in labor content; this emerges most clearly from the calculation of man months per car which ranges in the short run from 2.03 man months in the trough of 1956–7 to 1.36 man months at the peak of 1959–60. Put another way, the point is that 30 percent of the labor content comes out on the upswing as the market exerts a pull-through vacuum effect and 50 percent of labor content goes in on the downswing when flow cannot be sustained against the market. BMC and Longbridge teach the same lesson as Ford and Rouge: a high-flow, low-labor content factory is useless if the firm cannot sell enough output to load the factory.

If we ask why BMC could not load its factories, the answer is that the firm could not develop a model range which surmounted market limitations. This problem is complex because it has a financial as well as a physical aspect. BMC's problem was not simply a problem about sales volume, it was also a problem about cost recovery. As Anders Clausager, the archivist at BL Heritage argues, the company could have solved its problems if it had been able to charge higher prices for its product; on too many high-volume models, the market price was too low in relation to conversion cost and on the low-volume models, the market price was too low in relation to development and tooling costs. The market was a double constraint because it impeded cost reduction in the factory and cost recovery in the market place. BMC's car makers made two serious attempts to solve this problem by introducing new models and maneuvering within and between different national markets: the new models of 1952–4 represented the first 'Olde English' phase and the new models of 1959–65 represented the second 'space efficiency' phase.

Between 1952 and 1954 BMC introduced a spate of new models which had been planned by Austin and Morris before the merger.

These Olde English models were designed for an English bourgeoisie which appreciated a class semiotics of carpet, leather and wooden dashboards. The company aimed to occupy the aspirational space in four-cylinder cars between cheap Fords and up market Rovers and Jaguars. To do this it fielded no less than three completely different 1500cc unitary body shells for Austin, Morris and MG/Wolseley; while the A30/35 added a second small body shell to the existing Minor line. Cost reduction was addressed by rationalizing engine and gearbox production for all these cars around the newly designed A and B types of overhead-valve engines and four-speed gearboxes which were produced cheaply on Woollard's ATMs. While body shells proliferated, engine and gearbox types were rationalized; the company, which produced no less than eleven engine types in 1952, produced just four car engines by the end of 1956 and all its volume was in the A and B types.

The company had done enough to win volume increases but it encountered problems about cost recovery and market space. The price premium charged for low volume variants like the MG Magnette/Wolseley 4/44 was almost certainly insufficient to justify the expense of separate shells; according to Autocar price lists, the company obtained only a small premium over the volume Morris Oxford. The company admitted as much in 1959 when all these models were replaced by the Farina A55 and the other marque variants survived as 'badge engineered' models, distinguished only by grille, wing and trim differences. As for the Olde English volume sellers by Austin and Morris, they encountered difficulties in export markets which, as Table 8.3 shows, were taking no less than two-thirds of output in 1951–2 because the post-war Labor government had effectively diverted car production into export markets. Commonwealth export markets were spoilt by content regulations which required local manufacture and the company responded by developing the American market which was then the only large car market that was open to imports; between 1954–5 and 1959–60, exports to Canada and the USA increased from 19,000 to 110,000 (Williams et al., 1983, pp.236–7). But in 1960 the American manufacturers introduced their compact cars and spoilt the market for BMC and other European importers because the Americans, as low-cost producers, were able to offer more car for less money.

Table 8.3: BMC/BLMC/BL/Rover Production, Home and
Export Sales, 1955–90.

	Total production 000 units	UK sales 000 units	Export sales 000 units	Exports as percent of production
1955	439.6	252.0	187.1	42.6
1960	601.4	402.0	179.0	29.8
1965	845.6	531.4	314.2	37.2
1970	961.7	521.1	440.6	45.8
1975	738.2	422.1	316.1	42.8
1980	585.0	309.7	215.8	36.9
1985	555.5	415.6	139.9	25.2
1990	500.5	317.9	182.6	36.5
1991	419.7	220.4	199.6	47.6

Source: SMMT, various years.

In most years of the 1950s the company struggled to raise export volumes much above the 180,000 level of 1951–2 (Table 8.3). Effectively, the company expanded by diverting a growing proportion of output onto the home market which was expanding rapidly as motorization resumed after a decade's interruption caused by the Second World War and post-war austerity: home sales accounted for 97,000 vehicles in 1951–2 and 402,000 in 1960–1. The problem was that the home market was always cyclical and the company disposed of its output increase on the upswing when there were remarkable surges in demand which more or less doubled new-car registrations from 1951–5 and 1957–62 (Williams et al., 1983, p. 275). The company was vulnerable because as the market matured, demand surges would inevitably fail; indeed after a weaker surge between 1962–4, the home market was steady around 1.1 million new cars through the rest of the 1960s.

A second phase was inaugurated by the spate of new models launched between 1959 and 1965 with 'the advent of designs specifically BMC' (BMC, *Annual Report*, 1959, p.14). The Issigonis Mini, 1100 and 1800 were design breakthroughs in space efficiency. The transverse-engine, front-wheel drive layout allowed the smallest cabins in class and the 'wheel at each corner' package opened up a new classless semiotics of functionality. Cost reduction was addressed by carrying over the old A and B powertrains and going for volume. From the Mini onwards, the company began to plan model production in modules of 200,000 per annum. In 1959 no British car had been produced in volumes of much more than 100,000 per annum and BMC's long standing best seller, the Morris Minor, had been produced at a rate of 70,000 per annum in its first fifteen years. The Longbridge factory was extended to meet the new requirement for volume; a second assembly hall (CAB2) was ready by late 1961 (*BMC World*, October 1960) and the A series lines were re-equipped to build 12,000 engines and gearboxes a week (BMC, *Annual Report*, 1962).

If the company was going for volume, problems about cost recovery and market space were still not solved. By 1965, the new front-wheel-drive models accounted for 73 percent of BMC's car output (BMC, *Annual Report*, 1965, p.10). But, of the three new models, only the 1100/1300 offered both adequate cost recovery and high volume. The Mini was proof of the 'small-car, small-profit' proposition; when it was introduced in 1959 it was priced at £496, a full £100 below conventional small cars like the Ford Anglia and Triumph Herald. With this kind of pricing, it was impossible to make money on the Mini except in boom years of high demand and this was a serious problem because the Mini accounted for half of Longbridge's output and a quarter of Cowley's for much of the 1960s. BMC's other problem was the 1800 which, like the later Maxi, did not sell in volume; BMC planned to make 200,000 1800s per annum but production only topped 50,000 for two years (Williams et al., 1983, p.271). The 1800 failed in the market because, as the car grew larger, the advantage of space efficiency diminished and the power of snobbery increased. Thus, the pursuit of space efficiency turned into a move down market into small, cheap cars.

As home-market growth slowed in the 1960s, the company tried to find export volume. The United States was irrelevant because the space-efficient configuration of the new models was unsaleable in America which required low volume sports cars like the MGB of 1962. BMC's 1960 *Annual Report* (p.16) concluded that 'we must look to a wider variety of markets including, if Common Market/European Free Trade Association developments permit, those nearer home in Europe'. At this point General de Gaulle intervened decisively by vetoing the 1963 British application for membership of the EC. French opposition to British membership did not reflect economic fears about the consequences of free trade; the French had already accepted free trade with West Germany for the good of Europe and the benefit of French farmers. De Gaulle's veto was a political response to the viscerally pro-American (and anti-European) foreign policy of the British political classes whose public school and Oxbridge backgrounds were of course very different from those of the hard-nosed provincial car makers at Longbridge. But this political action at a distance now determined the future of the company and undermined the best efforts of the car makers.

Access to the European market was crucial for a company that was pursuing volume and trying to load its factories. The West European markets together were much larger than the British market and offered a partial offset to domestic cylicality; four to five million cars a year were sold in the EC markets in the early 1960s. But BMC now found itself in a paradoxical position; after single-handedly (re)inventing the European small car, BMC had the product, but volume exports of that product to the major West European markets were blocked by EC tariffs. As always, BMC's car makers responded by making the best of a bad job and rapidly developed EC assembly of British-sourced kits in Belgium, Spain and Italy as a substitute for direct export; by 1966, 40 percent of exports were in 'KD'(knocked down) kit form and the European plants assembled nearly 100,000 cars per annum (BMC, *Annual Report*, 1960, p. 19). As Table 8.4 shows, in the years after 1963, export markets took more than 300,000 cars which was very useful but not enough to save the company.

BMC's problems about cost recovery and market space knocked through into increasingly-dismal financial results. The visible problem was that the results of expansion, in terms of profitability, were very disappointing. The car makers had more than doubled the size of the company and halved the profit per unit; from 1953–4 to 1959–60 real profit per unit averaged £34.1 while from 1960–1 to 1966–7 real-profit per unit averaged £16.3 (Table 8.4). Even more worrying was the increasing volatility of this meagre profits stream through the 1960s; when the home market turned down in 1966–7, the company moved into loss.

Table 8.4: BMC/BLMC Profit, 1955–68.

	Net pre-tax profit £000s	Pre-Tax profit per vehicle £	Real pre-tax profit per vehicle 1955 = base	Distributed profit £000s	Distributed profit as percent of net profit
1956	18,571	42.7	40.7	2,554	13.8
1957	8,269	23.4	21.5	2,554	30.9
1958	20,991	41.6	37.1	2,554	12.2
1959	16,304	33.6	29.8	5,813	35.7
1960	26,933	40.3	35.4	5,354	19.9
1961	10,154	16.9	14.3	5,354	52.7

Table 8.4 (*continued*)

	Net pre-tax profit £000s	Pre-Tax profit per vehicle £	Real pre-tax profit per vehicle 1955 = base	Distributed profit £000s	Distributed profit as percent of net profit
1962	4,060	6.8	5.5	5,354	131.9
1963	15,054	20.1	16.1	5,376	35.7
1964	21,172	24.7	19.1	6,010	28.4
1965	22,780	25.7	19.0	6,740	29.6
1966	20,471	24.2	17.2	10,382	50.7
1967	3,227	4.7	3.2	6,941	215.1
1968	37,946	36.1	23.9	15,484	40.8

Source: Annual Report and Accounts, various years.

Profit is of course a relatively small and ambiguous residual but a more forensic approach to the accounts confirms the existence of grave problems. As Table 8.5 shows, the underlying problem was a high and rising labor share of value-added: in the 1950s, this ranged from a very acceptable 59 percent to an embarrassing 78 percent in 1956–7; the range of variation in the 1960s starts at a lower limit of 78 percent and ranges upwards to a disastrous 90 percent in 1966–7. If we remember that depreciation took an average 7 percent extra on top of labor's share, the fact is that in the 1960s the company failed to generate the free cash necessary for model renewal and factory re-equipment. By the mid-1960s BMC could carry on doing that which it was already doing but had no long-term future; the car makers had reached the end of their road.

Table 8.5: BMC/BLMC Value-added, Labor Costs and Cash Flow, 1952–68.

	Value added £000s	Labor costs £000s	Labor share value added %	Cash flow £000s	Cash flow per vehicle £	Real cash flow per vehicle 1955 = base £
1955	57,000	33,636	59.0	23,364	53.2	53.2
1956	61,396	39,720	64.7	21,676	61.4	58.6
1957	53,686	41,860	78.0	11,826	23.4	21.5
1958	69,369	44,525	64.2	24,844	51.1	45.6
1959	71,131	50,163	70.5	20,968	31.3	27.8
1960	93,892	61,712	65.7	32,180	53.5	47.0
1961	86,468	70,863	82.0	15,605	26.0	22.1
1962	88,752	78,560	88.5	10,192	13.6	11.1
1963	113,118	92,829	82.1	20,289	23.6	18.9
1964	137,202	107,136	78.1	30,066	33.9	26.2
1965	150,451	118,700	78.9	31,751	37.6	27.7
1966	178,795	146,640	82.0	32,155	46.3	32.9

Table 8.5 (*continued*)

	Value added £000s	Labor costs £000s	Labor share value added %	Cash flow £000s	Cash flow per vehicle £	Real cash flow per vehicle 1955 = base £
1967	159,601	143,298	89.8	16,303	15.5	10.8
1968	314,103	249,615	79.5	64,488	59.6	39.4

Notes: Value-added is net profit pre-tax plus depreciation and labor costs. Pre 1968 labor cost per employee derived from PA1002, The Census of Production, Class 35 (Motor Vehicles) and multiplied by employees in each year. Cash flow equals depreciation plus profits pre-tax.

Source: *Annual Report and Accounts*, various years and *Census of production*, various years.

If market limitations on volume and cost recovery are a necessary and sufficient cause of BMC's failure, by implication labor control and work practices must have played a limited role in the company's downfall. Lewchuk's (1987) influential work presents a very different interpretation where labor control figures as the major cause of the failure of the British-owned car industry. According to Lewchuk, the British failed because they did not adopt the complete Ford system of mass production. Instead, the British allegedly created 'the British system of mass production' which combined the assembly-line system of production with indirect systems of labor control, relying on group or gang systems of payment by results which were a relic of earlier 'craft technology' (Lewchuk, 1987, p.110). These British payment and control systems were inherently inferior to Ford's day work as a way of converting labor time into effort and the result was 'disaster from the employer's point of view' after the Second World War when British employers lost control of effort levels (Lewchuk, 1984, p.222).

Like most other 'production system' arguments, Lewchuk's thesis rests on historical misunderstanding; the gang system was not peculiarly British because it was widely used in pre-war America and post-war Europe, including VW Wolfsburg (Melman, 1956). Contemporaries were generally positive about the control and cost advantages of these systems. Thus Woollard, who had a shrewd understanding of cost composition and variation, recommended the use of 'group bonus' under which a gang of workers was collectively incentivised to get metal out of the door: 'flow production is admirably suited for group bonus whereby the gang is paid for the net number of parts passed correct by the inspector' (Woollard, 1954, p. 133). Melman's academic study of the gang system at Standard Triumph observed that the Coventry system used manual labor to co-ordinate many activities on the shop floor so that Standard

Triumph was able to operate with fewer supervisors and managers, thereby reducing overhead expense (Melman, 1956). We do not wish to side with Woollard and Melman against Lewchuk; in our view both sides of this debate are mistaken because they credit labor-process control with inherently vicious or virtuous effects. This is just another instance of the one dimensional thinking which we have criticized throughout this book. Against this we would argue that the results of most forms of labor control depends on market demand whilst the effects must be also analyzed in the context of an understanding of the mechanics and financial dynamics of car production.

Car firms which operate in cyclical markets capture the benefits of upswing into brisk demand by increasing production of recently-introduced volume models which the market wants to buy. BMC managed to do this easily; in the first three post-war upswings it increased the output of the Longbridge volume lines by 100-200 percent within two to three years (Table 8.6).

Table 8.6: Austin, Morris and BMC Output Surges, 1947–64.

Trough to peak	Longbridge volume line output	Longbridge and Cowley output	BMC combine employment	BMC percent above break-even point
1947–8	33,000	121,000		
1949–50	102,000	231,000		
	+ 209%	+ 91%		
1952–3	114,000	220,000		
1955–6	242,000	366,000	60,000	30.3%
	+ 112%	+ 66%		
1956–7	111,000	281,000	60,000	15.4%
1959–60	243,000	530,000	76,000	29.7%
	+ 118%	+ 89%	+ 27%	
1961–2	259,000	243,000	80,000	4.6%
1964–5	353,000	680,000	93,000	15.4%
	+ 36%	+ 179%	+ 16%	

Notes: Longbridge volume lines are those producing recently introduced volume cars which were important in product-planning terms and whose best annual sales exceed 70,000 units. The models are: A40 Devon/Somerset 1947–50; A40, A30 and A50 1952–6; A55, A35, A40 Farina and Mini 1956–60; Mini, 1100 and 1800 1961–5. All listed models meet the criteria except for (i) the carry over A40 of the early 1950s which remained fresh because it was a post-war design in a world of car shortage and (ii) the 1800 which never sold much over 50,000. Percent above breakeven indicates the margin by which sales revenue (or physical units produced) exceeds labor and depreciation costs incurred within the firm.

Source: Austin Rover Group, Historical Production Figures, 1983; BMC Report and Accounts, various years.

Expanded output was partly achieved by laying out extra lines but much of it must have been achieved by speed up on existing lines; Table 8.6 shows that, during the output surges, employment for the whole combine increased much less than output at Longbridge and Cowley, the two volume factories. The workforce had to be bribed to produce the output but the net benefits to the company were considerable because the company was above breakeven at the beginning of the output surges (Table 8.6); in this case, as output increases, extra units are mainly free cash and any car firm can afford to offer generous pay incentives to the workforce. The implication is that the gang system worked for BMC in the 1950s and early 1960s when the company was trying to meet demand and generate cash by getting more best sellers through the factory. We cannot answer the counterfactual about whether some alternative payment system would have worked better in the demand surges of the 1950s; the point we have made is that the gang system worked well enough.

As demand weakened after the mid-1960s, when the company no longer required output increases on the volume lines, the gang system provided no incentives to increase output and this was hardly a problem for a company where effective pay incentives would only have generated unsaleable output. With or without payment by results incentives, most payment systems work badly when demand and output sags, and the worse the market failure, the more irrelevant the payment system becomes. This last point is proved by the fact that the introduction of measured day work in BLMC between 1971 and 1974 had no discernible effect on performance in terms of cars per man; by this stage the whisky of the wage-payment system was entirely drowned in the water of market failure. If the BLMC managers who introduced measured day work had unreasonable expectations of large benefits, that was partly because through the 1950s and 1960s Ford UK used measured day work and Ford performed better than BMC. But, as we will now argue, higher performance came easily at Ford because this company was not on BMC's market-leading mission impossible.

Whereas BMC struggled to get into the first division of the cars business, Ford UK was happy to stay at the top of the second division. While BMC defended its near 40 percent share of the home market, Ford was content with 25 percent. Ford was able to defend its smaller share with just three body shells; whereas, when the specialists joined Austin and Morris to form BLMC, the combine reputedly made nineteen different body shells. If Ford started with a huge in-built advantage, this was reinforced by intelligent product development and targeting of market sectors. Ford's breakthrough product was the Cortina 1 of 1962, a light-weight car which could be made and sold more cheaply than the old-style 1500cc British family cars like the A55. As home-market growth slowed in the late 1960s, Ford was able to pitch two of its new style products (Escort 1 and Cortina 2) into the company car sector which was then rapidly increasing in importance. Ford's financial results were erratic because the company was not immune to cyclical fluctuation. But Ford always made money in the good years and held its market share in the bad years while its senior managers waited for the market leader to go out of business.

BLMC/BL: Under New Management

When BLMC was formed by merger in 1975 a 'statement of manage-ment principles' was laid down by Leyland management as a condition of the merger; the statement prescribed divisionalization with strategy and financial control centralized at corporate headquarters and Austin Morris as the largest of seven divisions. Leyland did not have the man-agement team to run an operation of this size and it responded by recruiting ex-Ford executives such as John Barber who was the dom-inant figure at corporate headquarters. The Austin Morris division was headed by an ex-Triumph executive but all the other key functional positions were occupied by ex-Ford men such as David Andrews and Filmer Paradise as finance and sales directors. Some of the Ford men left quickly but they were replaced by other 'Ford graduates'; Michael Edwardes' two lieutenants in the 1977–82 period were David Andrews and Ray Horrocks who had joined from Ford in 1972. Barber had been finance director of Ford but none of the recruits had high-level product planning or production experience in Ford.

Most of the recruits were not car makers but general managers whose careers had included a spell at Ford. Barber, for example, had been a Principal at the Ministry of Supply before joining Ford which he left to become finance director at the AEI electrical conglomerate. Ray Horrocks had worked for Marks and Spencer and Littlewoods in retailing before joining Ford. The importance of general management was reinforced when nationalized BL was created in 1975 because the initial strategy was set in a plan authored by Don Ryder whose expe-rience was of periodicals and paper at International Publishing Corporation and Reed International. Between 1977 and 1982, strategic direction was provided by a new chairman, Michael Edwardes, who had risen meteorically in the Chloride batteries company. Edwardes was succeeded by Graham Day whose previous employers included Canadian Pacific and British Shipbuilders. In effect, the British entrusted the future of their largest employer and exporter to general managers who in most other countries would have been perceived to lack the necessary expertise to run a giant car firm.

The productive and financial results achieved 'under new management' were much worse than those achieved by the old-style car makers before 1968. The increasingly dire results were driven by the management's failure to maintain, leave alone increase, output as the car makers had done in the BMC era. Table 8.7 presents the results for the combine as a whole which made specialist cars and trucks as well as Austin Morris cars. Output held up for a few years on the upswing of the early 1970s which allowed the company to maintain sales. But the company then lost output in eight of the nine years after 1972 so that its output levels were more or less halved. Home sales fell by this amount from 614,000 in 1973 to 310,000 in 1980; export sales held up reasonably well up to 1978 when 304,000 vehicles were exported but then collapsed to 99,000 in 1980. The results of market failure were initially disastrous because, as Table 8.7 shows, up to 1979 although output had (permanently) fallen away the workforce had not; wholesale sacking (and some divestment) then reduced employment from 177,000 in 1979 to 78,000 in 1985. The output fall was such that even sacking on this scale did not restore vehicles per employee to the level achieved by BMC in its best years.

Table 8.7: BLMC/BL Output and Employment 1968–85.

	Output units 000s	Home sales units 000s	UK car market share %	Export sales units 000s	Employment 000s	Vehicles per employee	Span corrected vehicles per employee
1968	1050.0		41		188.3	5.6	1.96
1969	1083.0	· 483.6	41	483.6	196.4	5.5	1.78
1970	961.7	521.1	38	440.6	199.5	4.8	1.48
1971	1061.0	602.3	41	301.7	193.7	5.5	1.44
1972	1056.3	657.8	35	398.5	190.8	5.5	1.78
1973	1012.5	614.2	31	398.3	204.2	5.0	1.41
1974	863.2	491.3	32	371.8	207.8	4.2	1.41
1975	738.2	422.1	30	316.1	191.5	3.9	1.10
1976	808.1	425.4	27	382.7	183.0	4.4	1.36
1977	771.4	423.2	25	348.2	195.0	4.0	1.15

Table 8.7 (continued)

	Output units 000s	Home sales units 000s	UK car market share %	Export sales units 000s	Employment 000s	Vehicles per employee	Span corrected vehicles per employee
1978	743.1	439.1	23	304.0	192.0	3.9	1.08
1979	628.5	375.8	20	252.6	177.0	3.6	1.04
1980	585.0	309.7	18	215.8	157.0	3.7	1.17
1981	517.9	316.7	19	180.1	126.0	4.1	1.27
1982	491.5	313.6	18	158.4	108.0	4.6	1.42
1983	545.4	408.9	19	122.7	103.0	5.3	1.58
1984	470.5	356.6	18	99.3	96.0	4.9	1.39
1985	555.5	415.6	18	139.9	78.0	7.1	2.04

Note: Span-corrected vehicles per employee is calculated by deflating crude productivity by the value-added to sales ratio for each year. This calculation allows comparisons of productivity to be made when the degree of vertical integration of the company is changing.

Sources: Annual Report and Accounts, various years and SMMT, various years.

Precise long-run comparisons are impossible because the composition of combine output (volume cars/specialist cars/trucks) changes over time according to market success and corporate reorganization. It is therefore useful to isolate the performance of the volume-cars business which metamorphosed from the Austin Morris division of BLMC into the Rover division of British Aerospace.

Table 8.8: Austin Morris/Rover Output and Employment, 1969–91.

	Production units 000s	Employees 000s	Vehicles per employee
1969	634	81	7.8
1970	588	88	6.7
1971	666	81	8.2
1972	698	80	8.7
1973	673	85	7.9
1974	561	81	6.9
1975	450	81	5.6
1976	n/a	n/a	n/a
1977	n/a	n/a	n/a
1978	466	86	5.4
1979	348	81	4.3
1980	315	55	5.7
1981	348	55	6.3
1982	370	55	6.7
1983	433	55	7.9
1984	404	48	8.4
1985	467	46	10.2

Table 8.8 (*continued*)

	Production units 000s	Employees 000s	Vehicles per employee
1986	420	38	11.1
1987	471	35	13.5
1988	n/a	n/a	n/a
1989	n/a	n/a	n/a
1990	501	42	11.9

Source: Annual Report and Accounts, various years.

Table 8.8 presents a picture of divisional output and employment loss which is broadly similar to that for the combine as a whole. As in the combine as a whole, volume-car output is halved between 1973 and 1980 when it bottoms at 315,000. Again there is a lagged employment adjustment with employment nearly halved to 55,000 between 1979 and 1983. The continuation of the story up to 1991 shows that in this case lost output and employment was never found again. Even at the cyclical peak in the late 1980s, output was below 500,000. In a year like this, the slimmed-down volume-cars business can reach vehicles per employee figures which look good; in 1990 the crude productivity was 12 vehicles per employee year. As we have already observed, all of this improvement reflects increasing vertical disintegration and the fact that, as an assembler of Hondas, the company is now making less of each car.

All the strategy plans after 1968 promised to restore profitability but none of them delivered on this promise. As Table 8.9 shows, the cyclical profits crises in successive downturns grew worse, not better, despite the application of increasingly creative accounting principles (e.g. Williams et al., 1983, pp. 246–50; 1986, pp. 118–24): BLMC recorded a loss of £76 million or £103 per vehicle in the trough year of 1975; while BL lost £388 million or £662 per vehicle in 1980. Not much changed in the following years, in the trough of the next downturn the Rover division lost £279 million or £600 per vehicle in 1991. While the loss of 1975 could be represented as the last and the worst in a series of cyclical 'blips', since 1979 good news has been hard to find in any year; the volume-cars business made pre-tax losses in eleven of the thirteen years after 1979 and the pre-tax losses per vehicle sold averaged £290.

As Table 8.9 shows the underlying problem is that labor's share of value-added goes well over 100 percent in each downturn (Table 8.9); in 1980 labor's share of value-added in the BL combine peaked at an all-time high of 158 percent and there was still no sign that this problem had been resolved when labor's share of value-added reached 151 percent in the Rover division of Aerospace in 1991. This pattern is outside the usual experience of private-sector firms because it implies the firm is not only making losses at the end of each year, it is also cash negative each week because it has to borrow to pay the wages bill. Thus BLMC and BL kept going by borrowing money initially from the banks and then, after nationalization, from the state. BLMC sank under the weight of short-term borrowings which had reached £248 million by 1975 and these debts rose again to £296 million in 1980 in the middle of the next downturn. The corporate logos changed over the years but the company's colour was always red.

Table 8.9: BLMC/BL Profit/Loss and Cash Flow, 1968–85.

	Labor share of value added %	Break-even 100 = BEP	Cashflow £000s	Cashflow per unit £	Profit/ loss £000s	Profit/ loss per unit £
1968	79.5	125.8	64.5	59.6	37.9	36.1
1969	82.8	120.8	53.9	56.0	40.4	37.3
1970	93.7	106.7	19.2	18.1	3.9	4.1
1971	80.2	124.7	79.3	75.1	32.4	30.5
1972	82.7	120.9	74.4	73.5	31.9	30.2
1973	82.2	121.7	95.3	110.4	51.3	50.7
1974	91.7	109.1	44.0	59.6	2.3	2.7
1975	n/a	n/a	n/a	n/a	-76.1	-103.9
1976	87.3	114.6	113.8	147.6	70.5	87.2
1977	94.0	106.4	44.7	60.1	3.1	4.0
1978	92.0	108.7	68.5	109.0	15.3	20.6
1979	106.3	94.1	-47.3	-80.9	-112.2	-178.5
1980	158.8	63.0	-306.8	-592.4	-387.5	-662.4
1981	138.0	72.5	-199.0	-405.0	-332.9	-642.8
1982	110.3	90.7	-74.9	-137.3	-222.7	-453.1
1983	77.4	129.2	245.0	520.7	67.1	123.0
1984	91.7	109.1	73.9	133.0	-73.3	-155.8
1985	94.9	105.4	44.2	93.5	-110.3	-198.6

Source: Annual Report and Accounts, various years.

BLMC/BL was different from BMC because BLMC/BL's productive and financial results were much worse and because the relation between those results and the actions of those inside the firm was different in the two cases. As we have seen the car makers of BMC could with some justice plead 'diminished responsibility'; they had consistently made the best of a bad job and inventively expanded the company up to and beyond the point when General de Gaulle said no.

Against this the Ford executives and general managers are clearly guilty of 'manslaughter'; they did not intend mass sacking and all the rest of it but their actions caused or seriously aggravated the outcome. In the rest of this chapter, we will demonstrate this point by critically considering in turn the two main attempts to save the volume-cars business: from 1968–75 the BLMC managers pursued a policy of Fordization through imitating Ford UK's previously winning formula; from 1979–82 BL under Michael Edwardes pursued doxic/common-sense priorities through macho action which was seldom off the front pages. An adverse verdict on the two groups of managers is not (and should not be taken to be) a general judgement on 'management' whatever that may be. We would however argue that the new BLMC/BL managers understandably lacked the car makers primary knowledge of productive, market and financial interrelations; we can also show that they gained little from the secondary discourses of management whose established representatives at MIT sanctioned and encouraged the final mistake of creating a company that was too small to be viable. Recipe thinking, doxa and macho action all vainly attempted to cover up the basic fact that the emperor of management had no clothes.

John Barber's claim that 'it's more important to understand the business than the techniques of finance' (*Management Today*, October 1969, p.69) could serve as an ironic epitaph on the BLMC era. His team of managers did not struggle to understand the cars business but mechanically imitated Ford UK's winning formula: Ford cost-engineering techniques were to be applied to develop a high-style, cheap to manufacture, Cortina-type motor car which would attack Ford's market for company cars; the dealer network would be pruned to create a Ford-style distribution system where fewer dealers sold more cars; and the factories were to be reformed by the introduction of measured day work which was Ford's payment principle. The working assumption was that the formula which had worked for Ford against BMC would now work for BLMC against Ford. But this policy entirely neglected the situational factors which would ensure that imitation was bound to fail; in most businesses the unsuccessful cannot solve their problems by imitating the successful because their requirements and resources are different as long as the successful occupy the market space which generates the cash. The failure of Fordization at BLMC is a cautionary tale which emphasizes this message and should have been carefully considered by all those who have blithely recommend Japanization as a panacea.

BLMC's first priority was the Marina which was launched in 1971 as a rear-wheel-drive three-box motor car designed to attack Ford in the company-car market. The Marina represented the managers' discretionary choice of an objective that was nearly impossible. The previous concentration on front-wheel-drive models had left the company without the product building blocks for a Ford-beating rear-drive car of 1500/1600cc; the result was a high-style body which covered geriatric mechanicals including a front suspension taken from the Minor. Furthermore any consideration of market space and composition of demand would have shown that the volume prospects were discouraging. BMC had done well in the 1100/1300cc market partly because this market segment accounted for around one-third of British sales between 1968 and 1978 and was therefore large enough to support several best sellers in the late 1960s when the Austin/Morris 1100/1300, Ford Escort and Vauxhall Viva had all sold well. But the 1500/1600cc segment accounted for under 20 percent of British sales in the same period (Williams et al., 1983, p.278); as a result, there was only room for one best selling car in that class and Ford already occupied that position with the Cortina which was an excellent product supported by strong distribution and service.

Predictably, the Marina failed in the market place. The newly launched car had two good years when it sold 100,000 and pushed towards 7 percent of the British market and then its sales fell back towards 80,000 or worse (Ibid, p.241). High-style cars which go off quickly are a form of competition which cash-rich companies can afford but for their poor relations like BLMC unstyled long-life cars (like the old BMC product) are a much more sensible choice. After making the wrong choice at the beginning of the 1970s, the managers at BLMC could do little for the rest of the decade except watch the Ford Cortina and Escort effortlessly take number one and two positions in the British sales charts; by 1979 the Cortina outsold the Marina by 3:1. BLMC and BL never made much of an impression on the company-car market; the Montego of 1984 failed to increase the company's share of the company-car market like the Marina of ten years previously (Williams et al., 1987a, p.74). What the Marina did do was kill off the ageing Austin/Morris 1100/1300 whose sales fell by one third after the Marina was introduced; the company was surviving precariously as its traditional private customers transferred their loyalty from one generation of its product to another.

The company's next product launch, the Allegro of 1973, aggravated the problem because the number of these traditional customers was rapidly dwindling. The Allegro was a rebody of the old 1100/1300 which showed only that the Fordists did not understand small functional front-wheel-drive motor cars; they included a bizarre squared off 'quartic' steering wheel and omitted the hatchback which importers included in competing offerings like the Renault 5, Fiat 127, Nissan Cherry and VW Golf, all of which sold mainly or entirely in hatchback form. Imported cars were rapidly increasing from 10 percent of the market in 1969 to 56 percent in 1979; tied imports by Ford and Vauxhall accounted for a substantial part of this increase, but identifiably foreign built and foreign badged cars accounted for around one-third of the market by the end of the decade as they did in most other West European countries. And import penetration was concentrated in the private-customer market where BMC had traditionally taken its sales; by 1974, the new-car market divided roughly 50/50 between company and private purchases and 45 percent of private customers bought imports (Williams et al., 1983, p.234). The Allegro was a powerful inducement to go buy an import and its market performance was disastrous. At its peak, it sold 55–65,000 units or less than 5 percent of the market from 1974–9; by way of contrast, the old 1100/1300 had been the company's best-selling car of the 1960s and sold 150,000 or nearly 15 percent of the market after it was launched (Ibid, p.241).

The preoccupation with beating Ford UK led BLMC to concentrate almost entirely on the domestic market; the managers of BLMC were very much less global and international in their thinking than the old car makers of BMC. The 1100 of 1962 was explicitly launched by BMC as 'a world car' (*Autocar*, 1100 launch issue, 1962) and the claim was to some extent justified subsequently by manufacture or assembly in the UK, Belgium, Spain, Italy and Australia as well as export to many other markets. The Marina of 1971 might well have been launched as 'the unexportable motor car'; between 1975 and 1977, 57 percent of Mini production and 49 percent of Allegro production was exported compared with just 21 percent of Marina output. The paradox was that, after Britain's entry to the EC in 1973, BLMC had the market access but increasingly lacked products that the mainland European consumer wanted to buy, except for the evergreen Mini which it had inherited from BMC. BLMC planned to overhaul European distribution by buying out its independently-owned importers and did take full ownership of AUTHI which was assembling its product in Spain (BLMC *Annual Report*, 1973); but these plans were overtaken by BLMC's financial crisis in 1975 during which loss making AUTHI was closed and nothing was done to save the company's Italian assembler, Innocenti, which went into liquidation. The general impression is reinforced by the results of a short, unsuccessful attempt to sell an Austin-badged Marina in America; stale, unsold cars were reimported and sold off cheaply to the workforce which had built them.

The managers of BLMC were effectively making their company more national when every other major European car company was becoming more international. Their Fordization was *passé* because it imitated Ford UK in the period before 1968; in the BLMC period, Ford of Europe was being created so that by the mid-1970s Ford had an integrated pan-European network of factories with flows of components and finished product criss-crossing national boundaries. If that model was irrelevant, BLMC failed to construct the kind of Euro-company that the indigenous majors like VW, Renault and Fiat were creating in the 1970s. These companies planned to hold 25 percent of their domestic markets and take 3–5 percent shares of other major European markets; thus they would build volume sales of their 1980s best-selling models by selling 200,000 plus units each year at home and then taking 20,000–80,000 sales in each of the major European markets (Williams et al., 1987a, p.68). In the first stage of this development in the mid-1970s sales to adjacent West European countries were crucial; in 1975, two-thirds of West European car exports and four-fifths of French and Italian exports went to neighboring West European countries (Williams et al., 1983, p.237). The managers of BLMC failed to appreciate that their national car company, like all the rest, could only be saved by going Euro-regional for the 1980s.

Thus BLMC managers put the company in the least desirable position for any late-twentieth-century major car company; it was pinned down on a domestic market where import competition was eroding its volume base and unable to find compensating volume by expanding export sales across a broad spread of foreign markets. This 'wasting major' syndrome, which once afflicted BLMC and BL, in the late 1980s came to afflict GM which could not export from its American factories without spoiling the factory loading of its independent European operations. BLMC's problems went critical when the Marina and Allegro failed in the domestic market place; in its first five years the Marina sold at half the planned rate of 300,000 and the Allegro at half the planned rate of 200,000 (Ibid, p.242). By this stage the company had developed and tooled up for two saloons (Marina and Allegro) which together achieved the volume of their one predecessor (1100/1300). Both cars had been cost engineered to some effect; the Allegro, for example, eschewed the front and rear subframes of the 1100/1300. But any benefits from cost engineering were cancelled when the substantial burden of development and tooling costs was spread over low model volumes; development charges of up to £50 per unit killed all the profit (Ibid, 1983, p.243). The shortfall in Marina and Allegro sales created additional problems because it left the company with excess capacity of around 350,000 units in most years; after the 1972–3 boom collapsed, both Longbridge and Cowley never ran at much more than two-thirds of capacity which was well below breakeven (Ibid, p.245).

In 1975, loss-making BLMC was nationalized as BL. Under the Ryder Plan the incumbent management were then offered state funding to do that which they had been unable to do from BLMC's own resources; some £2,000 million was to be spent over eight years on replenishing working capital, re-equipping factories and developing new models. The Ryder plan never made any sense because it ignored output loss and dire financial results: Ryder assumed that the company, which was losing volume, could sell nearly one million cars by the mid-1980s; and, equally optimistically, assumed that public funding could be matched pound for pound from BL profits. Michael Edwardes, who became chairman in 1987, introduced his 'recovery plan' in 1989 when it became clear that Ryder's assumptions were unrealistic. The Edwardes plan essentially added two elements of new realism. Firstly, Edwardes recognized that Ryder's volume targets would never be achieved and planned a downsized company which would make 750,000 vehicles per year, an output which was not much more than half the nominal 1.2 million capacity of BL (Williams et al., 1987a, p.4). Secondly, Edwardes planned 'to regain control of the company' (Edwardes, 1983, p.181) by confronting the workforce and reforming work practices so that the company could gain the full benefit of the investment in new equipment and new models.

As a general manager who was new to the cars business, when Edwardes formulated strategy he did little more than the Vichy chief of police in Casablanca when he gave the order to 'round up the usual suspects'. In the media stereotype of the mid-1970s the declining

British car industry and failing BLMC were powerfully associated with a supposedly work shy and strike happy labor force; in 1975 *The Times* carried 523 items about the British car industry and three-quarters of those items were about labor disputes (Williams et al., 1983, p.251). The labor problem was given a veneer of academic respectability by the Central policy Review Staff (CPRS) report of 1975 which used (misleading) process comparisons to identify bad work practices as the cause of low productivity (Nichols, 1985). Second rate product was again a highly visible problem when the future of the company was increasingly being discussed and decided by individuals who generally preferred not to buy and run a BL product. Factory re-equipment was a more quasi-academic priority that Edwardes carried over from Ryder and the 1975 Commons Expenditure Committee Report which had emphasized the age and inferiority of the capital stock in a firm that, on a fixed assets per employee basis, trailed behind every other European manufacturer.

BL under Edwardes took purposive action to solve all these perceived problems. In October 1979 a workforce vote in favor of the recovery plan provided a basis for mass sackings which began symbolically with the union convenor who had refused to recant his public opposition to the plan. All the peripheral plants (Speke, Canley, Solihull and Seneffe) were closed so that production could be concentrated at Longbridge and Cowley which were re-equipped at a cost of at least £500 million (Williams et al., 1987a, p.21). The right to manage was reclaimed when management unilaterally imposed new work practices in April 1980. Three new front-wheel-drive models (Metro, Maestro and Montego) were launched between 1980 and 1984 and all of them were honest designs and credible class contenders of a kind which the company had not managed since the 1100 nearly twenty years previously. There was a huge disproportion between all this frenetic activity and results achieved because, as we have already seen, success was elusive. The return to profit, which the recovery plan had envisaged in 1982 and 1983 was permanently postponed. The company aimed for 'product-led recovery' and volume-car output of 750,000 but missed that target and never got much above 500,000 because home sales were disappointing and export sales never recovered fully from the collapse which took them below 100,000 in 1980. Partly for this reason, labor productivity after reform of work practices in re-equipped factories was no better than BMC had achieved twenty years previously.

Edwardes' failure shows that doxa is seldom a good guide to business policy because it does not adequately specify individual problems or tightly define the relation between interrelated problems. The Edwardes plan was only credible in a naive productionist framework where if (downsized) factories were re-equipped, work practices were reformed and decent product was introduced, then the product would sell itself and the profit would come through. This reassuring syllogism did not address the productive and financial issues of downsizing and, specifically, failed to confront the issue of what was the minimum size of firm and length of model run necessary to achieve adequate cost reduction and recovery. Nor did it address the relation between these internal factory variables and external market opportunities and constraints; the benefits of re-equipment and workplace reform will only come through if management has an overall strategy which is sensible in relation to the market outside the firm. Essentially, the Edwardes plan had misjudged the significance of what was within management control inside the factory and underestimated the importance of what was outside management control in the market place.

The first issue is whether a downsized volume-car producer with sales of 750,000 units per annum was viable. According to the first MIT International Automobile Programme (Altshuler et al., 1984) the answer was yes, because recent changes in production technology, particularly the advent of flexible robotized body lines, had fundamentally changed the economics of the business; 'a producer with modest volume in several individual [product] lines can [now] offer these at a competitive cost' (Ibid, p.182). The relevance of this argument to BL was always unclear because one of the firm's major blunders was the installation of a dedicated Metro body line at Longbridge which left it with unusable excess capacity of 200,000 vehicles (Williams et al., 1987a, pp.60–62). In any case, as we argued at the time, MIT produced no statistical evidence to back its claims about production costs and was guilty of single-process thinking; minimum economic scale might have changed in body building but engines were still being produced on Woollard-style transfer lines which required volume of 300,000 or more for each engine type. (Ibid, pp.50–2). Furthermore, the MIT position ignored the financial issue of cost recovery; as long as tooling and development for each new model cost several hundred million pounds, larger manufacturers with longer model runs would have a substantial advantage when it came to recovering pre-production costs. It was, and is, hard to see how a small-volume manufacturer can compensate for this disadvantage as long as its products sell at average prices and generate no more cash per unit than those of larger manufacturers. In the mid-1980s, small specialist producers, like Jaguar, Saab and Volvo did well because their luxury cars gave them the cushion of large profit margins per unit (Ibid, p.53); but when the dollar exchange rate turned against them, they were all forced to seek the protection of a larger group.

The second issue is why the company missed its output target. And the answer is that the Edwardes plan ignored demand problems and market limitations which prevented the firm reaching its target output level of 750,000 units by capturing 3–5 percent of the European market, as Ryder had planned, and 25 percent of the domestic market, as Edwardes intended. As late as Spring 1982, these objectives were publicly reiterated by the company's sales and marketing director who then claimed 'it has to be on' (Williams et al., 1983, p.70). In fact the company ended up with less than 1 percent of the European market because export sales collapsed in the years when Edwardes was chairman and reached a nadir of 80,000 in 1983 when two of the three new models had been introduced. As for home-market share, that fell below 25 percent when the old low-volume models such as Maxi, Dolomite and Princess were discontinued and 'product-led recovery' never happened. As Table 8.7 shows, the company's home-market share stabilized around 18 percent and then began a slow unsteady downwards drift which left the company in the early 1990s with 12 percent of the market, in third place behind Ford and Vauxhall-GM. The company which planned product-led recovery suffered market led failure.

The export debacle was a self-inflicted wound which resulted from over-emphasis on product and neglect of distribution; in the cars business good product does not sell itself unless it is backed by adequate distribution. This first principle of the business was neglected by Ryder and by Edwardes; BLMC obtained £2,100 million of interest-free state funding and drew private loans of £1,500 million but never budgeted for the expense investment of setting up a European distribution system. Seneffe, the last of BMC's European assembly plants, was closed as part of the Edwardes rationalization but the company failed to create a European dealer network which would have generated demand for the British factory product. In Germany BL had no distribution, even though this was an important market for Renault and Fiat small cars. BL bought out its German importer in 1976 and six years later had 280 German dealers who sold just 6,000 cars. Its German-dealer network existed only on paper and BL admitted as much in 1984 when it signed a bizarre agreement with the Massa hypermarket chain to sell BL cars as 'own brand products' (Williams et al., 1987a, pp.90–1). The company was also unduly influenced by the short-term effect of exchange-rate fluctuations on export margins which have traditionally been slim on intra-European car trade and did not sufficiently consider the implications of export sales for capacity utilization. Exports to Europe collapsed at the beginning of the 1980s because BL was not trying; Edwardes complained in 1981 that export sales were unprofitable because of the high pound and at this stage the company was effectively cutting markets which could have loaded the factories and raised model volume in the long run (Williams et al., 1987a, p.88). The lure of export profits later diverted the company into a forlorn and unsuccessful attempt to reenter the highly-competitive American luxury market with the Rover 800/Sterling.

The neglect of European export markets was culpable because volume sales on the home market were increasingly difficult because of new patterns of market fragmentation. In the mature markets of West Europe and North America maturity is associated with increased volatility of demand and market fragmentation as more manufacturers offer more look-alike models in each market segment. The only way for manufacturers to resist the process of fragmentation is to assist it elsewhere by piling into another national market and taking small shares elsewhere. The Japanese up to the early 1990s have been beneficiaries of this process because their home market was less volatile and their peculiar distribution and low costs have made their market more resistant to imports while they have been active fragmenters first in the United States and now in Europe. BL represented the Japanese turned upside down; it had renounced exports and so could not benefit from mainland European fragmentation and was pinned down in a home market which was fragmenting rapidly with the advent of full-line direct competition.

In the late 1960s BLMC was shielded from direct competition by differences in product configuration; the British customer of the late 1960s had a choice of BLMC front engine/front drive, Ford front engine/rear drive or a variety of imports with variant configurations and even a choice of air-cooled and two-stroke engines. Even in the early 1970s, when BLMC espoused direct competition with Ford through the Marina, its two American-owned competitors did not field small front-drive cars to compete with BLMC offerings and European competitors like Renault and Fiat effectively did not produce large cars. The old era of indirect competition ended when Ford launched the small front-drive Fiesta in 1977 and the new era of full-line direct competition opened in 1983–4 when Vauxhall entered the small-car class with the Nova and BL launched the Montego, its third new model, into the medium class. From that date onwards all three domestic majors had a full line of similarly packaged directly competing models; Metro, Fiesta and Nova fought it out in the small class as Maestro, Escort and Astra did in the light class and Montego, Sierra and Cavalier did in the medium class. The immediate effect of imports from the late 1960s was to reduce the share of the market collectively claimed by the major manufacturers; the share of the market claimed by the top-ten sellers in the UK decreased from 70 percent in 1965 to 49 percent in 1975. But, as long as indirect competition persisted, it was still possible in the 1970s for a class-leading model to take 10 percent of the market as the Cortina did in most years and the Escort did in good years. With direct competition splitting sales in each class, this became simply impossible in the 1980s; thus, in the medium class after the J series Cavalier was launched, the Cavalier and Sierra disputed class leadership without either selling more than 7 percent of the market and the Montego came a distant third with never more than 4 percent. By 1983–4 it was impossible for any one model to claim more than 7 percent of the market and the average model from one of the three domestic majors sold only 5 percent. Thus Edwardes was bound to fail because three-times five equals 15 percent, not the 25 percent which BL needed.

The company which had once fielded too many models to make a profit ended up with too few models to defend its market share and that undermined profit even more fundamentally. And it is appropriate to end the chapter with this point because the whole story of BMC/BLMC/BL is a cautionary tale about the limited benefits of productionism without the market. It reinforces the message that the market in cars has much the same significance as location in property; it is not of course the only thing but it is the first and most basic prerequisite without which nothing else comes right.

❖ ❖ ❖

9
Western Europe:
The Weak Industry and the Irresolute Confederation

———— ❖ ————

Everybody agrees the West European car industry is weak; the question is what this weakness represents and how it will be resolved. The answer to this question depends on the framework within which the industry's problems and opportunities are represented and this chapter works by counterposing two frameworks: negatively, the chapter criticizes the orthodox-economic framework of efficiency which dominates existing discussion and positively, the chapter proposes an alternative political framework of power as a basis for a problem shift.

Since the late 1940s, when comparative input-output ratios were invented and popularized by Rostas and other pioneers of productivity comparisons, the European industry has been represented as an industry whose problem is inefficient and high cost production. This problem definition rests on the repeated observation of a physical-performance deficit in the European relation between labor input and output. From Rostas to the IMVP only the point of reference changes; the comparisons with America in the 1940s like those with Japan in the 1980s both suggest that Europe's best-practice competitors build with half the labor hours. Most recently, the Boston Consulting Group reported on an 'alarming gap' in productivity in the auto-components sector where Japanese productivity is allegedly 2.5 times greater (*Financial Times*, 18 October 1993). Europe's relative inferiority has persisted for more than forty years because the 2 to 1 productivity gap against best practice has not been closed or reduced and that observation suggests that the European industry has (for whatever reason) a limited ability to manage change. Nevertheless, within the efficiency framework, consultants, academics and governments continue to believe that the inefficiency problem can be resolved through a virtuous process of rationalization; under pressure of competitive market forces (and without political direction or regulation), the producing industry can economize on its unnecessary labor input and thereby secure a competitive and viable future. The mechanisms and processes of adjustments are unclear and the calculations are mainly about how much labor must go in order to secure a competitive future; thus Boston concludes that a 40 percent decline in the component industry workforce is 'the absolute minimum for the industry to be viable after 1999'. From this point of view, the promised solution is little more than a restatement of the supposed problem.

Against all this we propose a problem shift which redefines the West European industry's problems in a political framework about power. Our concept of political power is taken from Machiavelli because his analysis of Renaissance Italy provides an exemplary analysis of fragmented power which is divided between many weak internal players and subject to external threat: the concepts of *virtu*, *fortuna* and *occasione* from *The Prince* provide the basis for understanding the dynamics of a weak and divided industry while *The Discourses* provide the theory of European Union (EU) politics in the absence of a unified state. The industry's problem is insecurity which arises from the absence of economic power within the industry and of political power at the regulatory level. The nationally-based assemblers in the fragmented European industry have pursued strategies of cost reduction and cost recovery without finding competitive advantage. They are now unable to recover their costs as they face the productive threat of competition from outside against a background of worsening internal-market problems. At the regulatory level the problem is that the EC cannot become an effective supra-national state and the industry is therefore the victim of negative integration; the assemblers have lost the protection of their national governments without gaining the protection of the EC. In the absence of appropriate political regulation, the resolution of the insecurity problem will take the form of a vicious process of restructuring. The outcome of this process is uncertain but we doubt whether the industry will find a happy ending of competitiveness and viability through restructuring. Instead we expect that, in the absence of regulation, restructuring will be at the expense of the interests of the worker stakeholder when desperate productionists seek advantage through shedding more labor while cynical financial engineers break their obligations to the workforce as they prepare to exit an unprofitable business.

This chapter which develops our alternative Machiavellian view of the European industry is organized in a fairly straightforward way into two sections; the first section articulates a general analysis of the European industry and its problems while the second section uses the attempted Renault-Volvo case to illustrate the process of predatory restructuring.

(1) Cars in the EC: The Weak Industry and the Irresolute Confederation

Where men have but little virtue, fortune makes a great display of its power. (Machiavelli, *The Discourses*)

No country has ever been united or happy unless the whole of it has been under the jurisdiction of one ruler or prince. (Machiavelli, *The Discourses*)

The European industry lacks *virtu* in the Machiavellian sense, that is, it lacks the internal ability to initiate actions which can master or direct events. As Machiavelli predicted, in such cases *fortuna* or external conditions and circumstances become important. If the European industry now faces difficult times, that is because an earlier period of good fortune is over and the weak firms of a fragmented industry must now face internal market difficulties as well as external productive threats.

The industry's absence of virtu is above all the result of its fragmented structure which prevents any firm from acquiring the market and productive power of Henry Ford or Toyota. The European Community (EC) has created a large unified regional market which is capable of absorbing more than 12 million new cars each year; in the past twenty years the EC has accounted for 40–45 percent of all the cars sold in the three major world markets (Europe, North America and Japan). But the supplying industry still looks much the same as it did 30 years ago when individual firms mainly served much smaller national markets in a Europe divided into the equivalent of 'small princely states'. As Table 9.1 shows, there are thirteen distinct marques with market shares of more than 1.5 percent and no fewer than nine independent firms producing their own designs. The largest volume-car assembler is VW whose market share (excluding Audi and Seat) was 15 percent in 1991: all the other volume-car assemblers like Renault, Fiat and Ford (Europe) have market shares of only 10–12 percent. Chapter 6 on trade observed that the American-owned companies (Ford and GM) responded to regional-market opportunity by creating integrated European operations, but the indigenous assemblers remain productively centered in one country and all the assemblers (with the exception of Ford and GM) are heavily dependent on the sales that they achieve in that one national home market. As Table 9.1 shows, all the indigenous assemblers take 45–65 percent of their total EC sales on one national home market and this is as true of BMW and Audi as it is of Renault and Fiat. If we consider Ford and GM as firms which span two national home markets (UK and Germany), then they are no different from any of the rest.

Table 9.1: EC Car Assembler Shares of EC Passenger Car Registrations and Home Market, 1991.

Assembler	EC car sales	EC market share	Home market sales	Home market sales As % of EC total
Alfa Romeo	177,966	1.5%	113,969	64.0%
Audi	335,306	2.8%	203,648	60.7%
BMW	376,951	3.2%	222,559	59.0%
Citroen	573,149	4.8%	239,927	41.9%
Fiat	1,192,560	10.1%	762,036	63.9%
Ford (Europe)	1,431,143	12.1%	731,664	51.1%
GM (Europe)	1,317,971	11.1%	829,367	62.9%
Mercedes	416,400	3.5%	281,549	67.6%
Peugeot	951,381	8.0%	432,778	45.5%
Renault	1,234,582	10.4%	540,479	43.8%
Rover	351,196	3.0%	229,291	65.3%
Seat	277,395	2.3%	90,357	32.6%
VW	1,249,480	10.6%	687,484	55.0%

Note: Home market sales are those achieved in the one national market around the assembler's main factories (e.g., Italy for Fiat, France for Renault etc.). In the case of Ford and GM, UK and German market shares are added together.

Source: SMMT, 1992.

National home markets remained important through the 1970s and 1980s because their different characteristics and requirements provided a basis for the distinctive pattern of product-type specialization in the European industry and that pattern of product specialization in turn conditioned the firm and industry choice between cost-reduction and cost-recovery strategies. The Germans (and to a lesser extent the British and the Swedes) have long had a substantial home market for larger cars above 1600cc whereas the French and Italian markets, like the more recently developed Spanish market, require small cheap cars. Thus the indigenous German firms (VW, Benz and BMW) were able to develop Euro-bourgeois motor cars like the Golf 2, E30 BMW 3 series and W201 Mercedes 190 which were all launched between 1982 and 1984; this kind of compact four-seat product with mainly

1600–2000cc engines dominated the German market and allowed the Germans to win sales in other EC markets at the expense of national specialists like Rover, Peugeot, Citroen, Alfa and Lancia. All the other assemblers responded to German dominance of the middle-class market by maintaining or developing their specialization in volume production of small cheap cars. Partly for this reason the most successful volume products of the French and Italian industries in the 1980s were the Peugeot 205 and the Fiat Uno both of which sold at a rate of 450,000 a year for a decade. The case of Peugeot is particularly interesting because Peugeot had traditionally left small cars to Renault and succeeded as a specialist supplier of stodgy cars like the 404 and 504 to the French middle classes; as Peugeot was being pushed out of this segment by the Germans, the French company found unexpected success with the 205 which was only the second small car which the company had ever made.

German success against the specialists in other European countries reinforced and widened existing differences in product type. The British may have been in the middle but the other national industries were clearly specialized in bottom or upper-market product. Thus, in 1983 and 1989 small cars with engines below 1400cc accounted for the bulk of the output of the French and Italian industries and all the output of the Spanish factories; by way of contrast, by 1989 roughly 40 percent of the output of the German industry was 1500cc and over. The small cars produced outside Germany in the 1980s were also fairly cheap and basic vehicles without extras such as power steering and electric window lifts; Table 9.2 also shows that Italian, French and Spanish value-added per unit was never much more than 55 percent of the value-added per unit realized by the German industry.

Table 9.2: National Differences in Product Type in 1983 and 1989.

1983

	Value added per unit as % of Germany	Car output up to 1500cc (%)	Car output above 1500cc (%)
Germany	100.0	75.9[1]	24.1[2]
Spain	30.1	n/a	n/a
France	53.9	72.8	27.2
Italy	52.9	71.4	28.6
UK	81.5	83.9[3]	16.1[4]

Table 9.2 (*continued*)

1989

	Value added per unit as % of Germany	Car output up to 1500cc (%)	Car output above 1500cc (%)
Germany	100.0	81.2[1]	18.8[2]
Spain	45.1	n/a	n/a
France	54.1	65.2	34.8
Italy	56.1	74.4	25.6
UK	82.6	65.4[3]	34.6[4]

Note: 1. German output up to 2000cc, 2. Above 2000cc. 3. UK output figures up to 1600cc, 4. above 1600cc.

Source: Eurostat, 1984 and 1989, *SMMT,* 1983 and 1989.

These differences in product type conditioned the different choices which various companies and industries made between the two basic options of cost reduction and cost recovery. For the indigenous German firms, volume-selling middle-market product was the crucial means to cost recovery. VW retained volume when it upsized with the Golf 1 and 2 whose standard engine became a 1600cc; BMW found volume when it downsized with the 1602/2002 which begat the 3 series; whilst Mercedes also downsized with the W201/190 which was smaller than its previous taxi-sized main line product, the W123. By the early 1990s in the UK market, the German product range effectively started at around £10,000 for a standard Golf 2 and the marketing men did everything else that was necessary by devising highly-specified versions of the German cars for which the Euro-bourgeois customer willingly paid extra. The symbol of the yuppie 1980s was the Golf GTi and, in the UK, the yuppie customer paid nearly 50 percent more for a mark 2, 16 valve GTi than for a standard 1600 CL. For the Germans cost reduction was not the major consideration because they were able to position their product so as to recover their costs. For the rest of the European industry, there was no alternative to cost reduction because their firms and factories were effectively trapped down-market by increasing German success in the Euro-bourgeois market. Consider, for example, the position of Renault in the UK market; shortly after the introduction of the Clio in 1991, this one small car was accounting for 50 percent of Renault UK's sales and effectively all these sales were being made in the range of £7,000 to £10,000. For non-German firms like Renault which sold cheap and cheerful products, the crucial means to cost reduction was process reorganization which aimed to reduce the number of motor-sector build hours in the factories of the assemblers and their component suppliers. At Renault, Fiat and Peugeot the factories received quite as much attention as was given the product and its marketing in the indigenous German companies.

The productivity of the European car industry as a whole may still lag behind that of Japan (and of America) as the productivity comparisons insist. But the equally important point is that most of the non-German firms and factories did, in the 1980s, reduce hours to build and increase cars per employee in a way which considerably improved their league position relative to the German firms for whom this was not an important objective. This point emerges from Table 9.3 on the growth of vehicles per employee in various national industries since 1981 and Table 9.4 on the trend in motor vehicles per employee in various national industries between 1979 and 1989. The real contrast is between the Germans and all the rest; in the upswing after 1981, the Germans do no better than a 13 percent increase in productivity whereas all the rest, including the British, manage increases in vehicles per employee of 42–52 percent which are three to four times as large (Table 9.4). The observed increase in productivity was achieved in a period of economic upturn and it is fairly certain that some of it will have been lost in the subsequent downturn after 1989.

Table 9.3: Motor Vehicles per Employee in Various National Industries Since 1979.

	France	Germany	Italy	Spain	UK
1979	7.3	5.9	5.5	n/a	3.1
1980	n/a	n/a	n/a	7.4	n/a
1981	6.6	5.4	5.3	6.8	3.3
1982	7.2	5.6	5.5	8.9	3.7
1983	7.6	5.7	6.5	9.2	4.4
1984	7.3	5.5	7.1	9.5	4.0
1985	7.7	5.9	7.5	10.5	4.9
1986	8.7	5.9	9.1	11.5	4.9
1987	9.8	5.9	9.6	12.3	5.5
1988	10.5	5.9	10.4	13.5	6.0
1989	11.4	6.2	10.7	14.3	6.3

Source: Eurostat, various years and SMMT, various years.

Table 9.4: Percentage Increase in Vehicles per Employee in Various National Industries Since 1981.

	France	Germany	Italy	Spain	UK
1982	7.9	4.9	5.0	23.5	10.2
1983	13.1	5.9	19.3	25.8	25.4

Table 9.4 (*continued*)

	France	Germany	Italy	Spain	UK
1984	8.9	1.6	25.4	28.1	18.1
1985	13.5	8.7	29.6	35.4	31.1
1986	23.5	9.5	42.3	40.7	32.7
1987	32.2	8.9	44.9	44.7	40.1
1988	37.1	9.3	49.1	49.7	44.5
1989	41.8	12.8	50.6	52.4	47.0

Source: Eurostat, various years and *SMMT*, various years.

But the increase in non-German productivity is not simply a cyclical phenomenon driven by increases in output with the workforce constant; a comparison between the cyclical peaks of 1979 and 1989 shows, for example, that whilst French vehicle output was 10 percent higher in 1989 but the workforce was actually 30 percent smaller than in 1989 than in 1979. The same was true of the Italian industry. By taking out labor the non-Germans succeeded in transforming their productivity league-table position relative to the Germans. As Table 9.3 shows, in 1979 the non-Germans had no advantage in terms of vehicles per employee although they specialized in simple, small cars which should have required fewer build hours; but by 1989 the Spanish and the French factories were building roughly twice as many (small, cheap) vehicles per employee as their German counterparts. The value-added per employee (VAPE) measure of productivity is even more revealing because it corrects for the differences in product and vertical integration which complicate comparisons of vehicles per employee.

Table 9.5: Value-added per Employee in ECU in Various National Industries.

	Germany	France	Italy	Spain	UK
1983	32,000	23,000	19,336	15,469	20,294
1984	32,457	22,795	23,276	17,377	22,444
1985	35,657	25,392	25,865	19,672	26,391
1986	37,026	30,766	29,729	25,007	26,789
1987	39,060	36,036	33,496	37,059	28,398
1988	39,970	40,608	38,213	42,337	32,185
1989	42,309	42,239	41,023	44,250	35,489

Source: Eurostat, various years.

The Germans started the 1980s with a substantial advantage over all the rest; in 1983, Spanish VAPE was just 48 percent of Germany's and the French was only 72 percent. As Tables 9.5 and 9.6 show, by the end of the 1980s Germany had a VAPE advantage over the UK industry: all the rest had closed the productivity gap.

Table 9.6: Value-added per Employee in the Major EC Car
Producing Countries as a Percentage of Germany.

	Germany	France	Italy	Spain	UK
1983	100.0	71.9	60.4	48.3	63.4
1984	100.0	70.2	71.7	53.5	69.2
1985	100.0	71.2	72.5	55.2	74.0
1986	100.0	83.1	80.3	67.5	72.4
1987	100.0	92.3	85.8	94.9	72.7
1988	100.0	101.6	95.6	105.9	80.5
1989	100.0	99.8	97.0	104.6	83.9

Source: Eurostat, various years.

The 1980s was therefore a decade of effort, action and change in
Europe's car industry as various firms and industries moved purpo-
sively along different trajectories of cost recovery and cost reduction.
The disappointing result was that the financial returns to cost recovery and reduction efforts were equally negligible; some of the
European manufacturers sold more solid motor cars, none of them
had solid financial results. Because profit is a small and ambiguous
residual, Table 9.7 presents the financial results for various national
industries in terms of their labor share of value-added and cash flow
per unit produced; as readers will recall from the earlier analysis chapters, a financially successful firm or industry will have a labor share
which is steadily at or below 70 percent and that will leave most of
the rest of the value-added fund available as cash. The failure of cost
recovery to generate any margin over and above labor costs is most
obvious in the German case where the upturn of the 1980s covered
German financial weakness rather than generated strength; as Table
9.7 shows, the upturn from 1983 to 1989 does no more than stabilize
labor's share of value-added at the unacceptably high level of 77–81
percent. The German industry's cash flow per unit is understandably
never impressive and in relative terms is disastrous by 1989. As Table
9.7 shows, the German industry started the period with a large cashflow per unit advantage over its competitors but by 1989 it was realizing no more cash per unit from selling its large, expensive cars than
the French, Italian and Spanish industries realized from selling small,
cheap cars whose value-added per unit was little more than half the
German product.

Table 9.7: Labor's Share of Value-added and Cash Flow per Unit in Various National Industries.

	Germany		France		Italy		Spain	
	Labor share of value added (%)	Cash flow per unit ECU	Labor share of value added (%)	Cash flow per unit ECU	Labor share of value added (%)	Cash flow per unit ECU	Labor share of value added (%)	Cash flow per unit ECU
1983	76.6	1,313	84.8	458	74.5	756	85.5	244
1984	78.3	1,289	91.4	270	66.6	1,100	83.0	311
1985	74.5	1,547	87.1	429	66.7	1,152	81.1	353
1986	80.6	1,210	84.1	564	77.6	729	78.4	471
1987	77.9	1,463	66.0	1,256	65.3	1,215	48.0	1,567
1988	78.6	1,446	59.9	1,550	63.9	1,332	47.7	1,637
1989	76.9	1,585	60.7	1,461	66.9	1,274	56.6	1,345

Source: Eurostat, various years and SMMT, various years.

As for the other national industries, they show a more normal cyclical pattern with upturn reducing their labor shares of value-added. But this never translates into sustainable financial strength because the French and Italians, like the Spanish and the British, all start from unacceptably high levels of labor share in the 75–85 percent range around 1983. The financial results of cost-reducing efforts to increase vehicles per employee were generally disappointing no doubt because all the non-Germans achieved substantial productivity increases; it was running to stand still. At all events cost reducing firms like Renault and Fiat never achieved the financial strength to ride out the next market downturn.

None of the major national industries or assembler firms had achieved a sustainable competitive advantage through their efforts at cost recovery and cost reduction; at the end of the 1980s, the precarious financial position of most firms and most national industries was much the same as it had been ten or even twenty years previously. The main development of the 1980s was the absolute and relative weakening of the German industry whose indigenous firms were close to financial crisis even as their products dominated the bourgeois market right across Europe in the later 1980s. Fundamentally, the decade had changed nothing because at the end of it the European industry consisted, as it had always done, of weak firms which did not have the financial strength to withstand a market downturn. This continued weakness is publicly indicated and advertised by the failure of most assemblers in the 1970s or 1980s to avoid financial losses whenever their markets turn down; this is an industry where all the firms have high break-even points and mediocre cash flow. Over the past twenty years, the minor assembler BMW is the only one which has recorded a profit every year. In the downturn of the early 1990s every one of the 1990 volume-car assemblers was losing money in 1993 except for Renault which was more or less breaking even. According to its own calculations just before the downturn, VW, the largest-volume car assembler, had a break-even point which was at or just above 100 per-cent (*Financial Times*, 21 June 1993). By the middle of the downturn in 1993 Fiat was restructuring its finances and in effect borrowing money to finance the development of a new generation of models.

Industries with a multiplicity of weak firms are typically unstable and prone to structural change as merger and exit remove the tem-porarily embarrassed. The paradox of European cars over the past twenty years is that this is a weak industry with a very stable structure. General restructuring has been confined to the minor assemblers who in an earlier generation typically produced larger or sporting cars for national customers. The minors like Alfa or Volvo had special prob-lems about cost recovery. All car manufacturers find volume by pro-ducing a range of differently-sized cars which may perhaps include a European-class leading best seller and will certainly include an assort-ment of relatively low-volume range fillers; in the volume end of the business, class-leading cars like the Golf 2 or the Peugeot 205 in the 1980s accounted for no more than 55 percent of the parent-assem-bler's sales. The same '55 percent with one model' rule applies equally to the specialist end of the business; in recent years (1987 to 1991), the BMW 3 series has accounted for no more than 56 percent of BMW's sales and specialist companies like Jaguar and Saab which only field one or two models are seriously handicapped. The problem of the specialists is how to generate the cash for the renewal of a range of models when individual model runs are very short and the cus-tomer is not prepared to pay a substantial premium for exclusiveness; the arithmetic of development-cost recovery simply does not add up for any firm whose best-selling model is sold in quantities of around 150,000 a year or less. As a result in the last twenty years, all the spe-cialists from Alfa and Audi to SAAB and Volvo have sought the pro-tection of larger assemblers with whom they share the cost of floor pans and major mechanicals; the only exception to this rule is BMW whose creditable but not outstanding performance will be briefly considered in the second half of this chapter when BMW and Volvo are compared.

– 176 –

Table 9.8: Major Industry and Major Assembler Car Output 1973–1989.

	1973 output	1989 output	Percentage change	Change in units
Germany	3,649,880	4,563,673	25.0%	913,793
France	2,866,728	3,409,017	18.9%	542,289
Italy	1,823,333	1,971,969	8.2%	148,636
UK	1,747,321	1,299,082	-25.7%	-448,239
Renault	1,292,991	1,446,669	11.9%	153,678
PSA	1,262,364	1,189,925	5.7%	-72,439
VW	1,364,154	1,463,991	7.3%	99,837
Fiat	1,390,251	1,968,094	41.6%	577,843
Ford Europe	1,230,962	1,662,269	35.0%	431,307
GM Europe	1,315,804	1,568,506	19.2%	252,702
Rover	875,839	466,619	-46.7%	-409,220

Source: SMMT, various years.

But if the minors lived in an unstable world of change, the major assemblers were considerably luckier; most of the European major assemblers, like the major national industries which they dominated, survive twenty years of weakness with remarkably few adverse consequences. The British assembler Rover (formerly BL) has never recovered from its loss of output in the later 1970s and early 1980s and the British national industry has never recovered from the combined effects of decline of its indigenous major and the coincident sourcing decisions of Ford and GM who supplied many of their British customers with product from their European factories. But Rover and the British industry is the exception because as Table 9.8 shows the other major assemblers and major European industries all increased their volumes over the decades of the 1970s and the 1980s. Between the cyclical peaks of 1973 and 1989, the French, German and Italian industries achieve volume increases of 11–28 percent. The major assemblers listed in Table 9.8 do rather better partly because most of them have branch assembly operations in the rapidly growing Spanish industry: and all the major assemblers show output gains of at least 30 percent between 1975 and 1991.

For the weak European industry over the past twenty years, growth in overall market size and an expansion in the available market space has served as a lubricant which prevents breakdown of an otherwise fragile and highly-stressed industrial structure. As Table 9.9 shows, the overall EC market for new cars expanded by almost exactly 50 percent from 8.5 to 12.4 million between the cyclical peaks of

1973 and 1990. The assemblers based in the mature markets of Northern Europe faced year-on-year home-market fluctuations in demand of up to 20 percent. But the effects of such fluctuations were damped for assemblers who had a reasonable export-market spread. The cycles in different national markets were not synchronized and the overall fluctuations in the EC market as a whole were much more modest with peak-to-trough falls of 5–13 percent in three successive cycles. After the 1973 and 1979 downturns, EC market growth was resumed within two to three years and within four years the previous peak level of demand had been surpassed.

Table 9.9: EC Market Cycles, 1973–91.

Years	Peak sales	Trough sales	Percent Fall
1973–4	8,503	7,424	-12.7
1979–81	9,426	8,722	-7.5
1990–1	12,400	11,822	-4.7

Source: SMMT, various years.

A significant feature was that the benefits of favorable overall market trends accrued to EC-based assemblers who were able to claim most of the increased market space. This was another piece of good fortune because the EC assemblers were ill-placed to hold market share against product originating from American or Japanese factories. This point is powerfully indicated by the European industry's poor direct export performance on the American market where producers and product from the three regions meet in open competition; in the 1985–91 period the Europeans sold just 300,000 to 500,000 mainly German luxury cars on the US market while Japan exported between 2.0 and 2.5 million cars a year to the United States where they were also rapidly expanding transplant production. If the European industry was desperately vulnerable to lower-cost competition from America and Japan, the American challenge was averted by corporate strategy and the Japanese challenge was postponed by national regulations which hindered Japanese imports. As the trade chapter observed Ford and GM preferred to run independent operations on either side of the Atlantic; this corporate choice was the legacy of an earlier period of autarchy and persisting differences in dominant product type. Ford and GM played an internal game of exploiting relative costs of production within the EC; they were pioneers of Spanish branch assembly which was an economically sensible choice given their unsuccess with the larger, more expensive cars which the indigenous German firms produced. As for the Japanese, their exports to Europe were effectively restrained by national governments. The big four national markets (Germany, France, Italy and UK) accounted for some 80 percent of the new cars sold in the EC; national governments effectively excluded the Japanese from the Italian and French markets and restricted them to under 15 percent of the German and British markets. The growing EC market space was thus substantially reserved for indigenous producers.

The weak industry's problem is that its long period of good fortune is over; the major assemblers and the national industries must now face much more adverse market trends as they confront the complex problems posed by a saturated market for new cars and a growing park of cars in use against a background of intensifying competition which diminishes the market space available to them. The industry's short-term economic problem is a saturated and increasingly cyclical market for new cars which makes it more difficult to realize the exchange value to cover costs of production. In the medium and longer term the industry's social problem is the contradiction between car use and urban life which threatens to undermine the use value of its product with unpredictable consequences for consumer demand.

In terms of the overall EC market for new cars, the industry is now entering a new period of zero growth punctuated by intermittent market collapse of (replacement) demand; it is a disturbing prospect for an industry whose weakness was covered in an earlier period by forty years of continuous unsteady increase in demand. The growth in the West European market for new cars has reached its limit because new cars are relatively expensive big-ticket items which can only be considered by the better paid amongst those in employment. This point is established by Table 9.10 which relates new car sales to the number of economically active individuals in various West European countries and in the EC as a whole; the data covers the period 1982–9 over the upswing of the most recent cycle and it also includes data on Japan and the United States as a point of reference.

Table 9.10: New Car Sales as Percent of the Economically Active Population 1981 to 1991.

	1981	1983	1985	1987	1988	1989	1990	1991
France	9.3	9.9	8.8	10.5	10.9	11.1	10.9	9.8
Germany	8.9	9.0	8.7	10.6	10.1	10.1	10.4	11.6
Italy	8.6	7.1	7.9	8.8	9.7	10.5	10.4	10.2
UK	6.5	7.8	7.8	8.4	9.1	9.4	8.0	6.2
Spain	4.4	4.8	4.9	6.8	8.5	9.1	8.1	7.3

Table 9.10 (*continued*)

	1981	1983	1985	1987	1988	1989	1990	1991
EC12	7.5	7.7	7.7	8.9	9.3	9.6	9.3	8.9
Japan	9.0	9.1	9.2	9.9	10.9	11.6	12.2	11.6
USA	9.6	10.5	13.4	12.5	12.7	12.1	11.1	9.9

Source: ILO and *SMMT*, various years.

The message is relatively straightforward; even in the most affluent advanced countries, only just over 10 percent of the economically active become purchasers or users of new cars in any one year. Most new cars are replaced with another after two or three years, so the proportion of the economically active who directly purchase or use new cars is no higher than around 25 percent; even if we include the partners of (mainly male) purchasers and users as participants, the percentage of direct and indirect purchasers and users is still no higher than some 40 percent. The Japanese and American experience strongly suggests that this level is an upper limit: in America cars are relatively much cheaper while in Japan the distribution of income through waged employment is much more equal and yet in the best year new-car sales accounted for only 13.4 and 12.2 percent respectively of the economically active. Whilst the averages for these years were just 11.5 and 10.4 percent. The problem of the EC cars industry is that the whole of its market is at or near this point of saturation; the south European markets are less mature but the largest of these markets, Spain, matured rapidly over the 1980s to the point where, by 1989, it is statistically indistinguishable from its northern counterparts. From this point of view we can only endorse the European Parliament report which states that 'A Community wide fail-ure of recovery in demand would increase problems of overcapacity and excessive competition' (*European Parliament Draft Report*, COM 92 0166). Market saturation coupled with longer car-replacement cycles all point towards a more or less flat market of around 12 million new cars in the EC for the rest of the 1990s. The US experience of saturation suggests that fluctuations caused by collapses in replacement demand are likely to get worse in these circumstances; in each of the three major downturns since 1973 the US car market shows peak to trough sales declines of more than 25 percent.

In broader social terms, the industry will also need to face the social consequences of car use which it has been able to ignore for the past forty years. Throughout this earlier period automobility took the pri-vate form of the purchase of a car which the individual was then free to use in the hope that it would take him/her wherever s/he wanted

to go. The major social intervention required was that of road building which had double-edged effects because good roads generate
short-distance commuting, shopping and leisure movements which
hinder long-distance trunk traffic. The end result is a 'drive to work'
society. As Table 9.11 shows, the park of EC cars in use has increased
rapidly and now includes more than 135 million cars or roughly one
car for every economically-active individual so that it is at least statistically possible for everybody to drive alone to work. The question is
whether in the next period the car park will continue to increase in a
way which creates gridlock in the urban centers of the densely populated North European countries. The increase in the size of the EC
car park has certainly been phenomenal over the past 25 years; it grew
three-fold from 46 million cars in 1967 to 135 million cars by 1991.

Table 9.11: Park of Cars in Use in EC and Major European
Countries, 1967–91.

EC 12 park

	Vehicles in use	Cars in use	Cars per economically active person	Cars per square kilometer
1967	53,325,963	45,952,454	0.37	20.5
1971	70,321,989	62,414,757	0.49	27.8
1975	86,171,341	77,007,125	0.65	34.3
1979	103,319,112	91,445,912	0.65	40.7
1987	131,837,917	116,004,474	0.67	52.1
1991	153,001,809	134,790,178	0.94	60.1

Source: ILO and *SMMT*, various years.

'Big four' park (Germany, France, Italy, UK)

	Vehicles in use	Cars in use	Cars per economically active person	Cars per square kilometer
1967	45,318,575	39,575,326	0.42	33.6
1971	58,237,051	52,313,473	0.55	44.3
1975	69,496,397	62,770,844	0.75	53.1
1979	80,371,232	73,090,079	0.74	61.5
1987	99,683,651	93,379,698	0.90	80.0
1991	119,545,411	106,671,306	0.90	91.0

Source: ILO and *SMMT*, various years.

Although the rate of increase has slowed in recent years, the
absolute increase in numbers is still alarming; the EC park increased
by 48 percent from 91 to 135 million over the twelve years from 1979
to 1991. This growth rate is threatening because the EC is relatively

densely populated; a European population roughly equal to that of the United States is concentrated in an area which is one-quarter of the size of the US landmass and three-quarters of that EC population is urbanized. The pattern of car use is relatively stable; the average EC car covered 13,000–14,000 kilometers a year or 35 kilometers a day through the 1980s (*World Road Statistics, International Road Federation*, various years) and most of these miles were racked up on short-distance commuting, shopping and leisure trips. The problems created by such usage were most acute in the North European countries, especially the 'Big four' countries which account for 80 percent of the total park; by 1991 these countries had more than 100 cars per square kilometer.

Table 9.12: Average Distance Travelled Per Passenger Car in Kilometers.

	1982		1991	
	Per year	**Per day**	**Per year**	**Per day**
France	12,400	34	13,700	38
Germany	13,600	37	13,000	36
Italy	11,200	31	10,800	30
UK	13,000	36	17,200	47
EC 12	12,887	35	13,928	38
Japan	9,843	27	9,861	27
US	14,750	41	17,200	47

Source: International Road Federation, World Road Statistics, various years

On present trends, the mushrooming growth in the North European park will continue until well into the next century. The flat demand for new cars and a constant flow of new cars into the park will not automatically solve the problem of park growth because the flow out of the park through scrappage is slowing. European cars are increasingly rust proof and mechanically durable so the poor can join the drive to work society by buying bangers: no less than 27 percent of the cars in use in the EC in 1992 were more than nine years old and that percentage is likely to increase over the next fifteen years towards the American level where almost 40 percent of cars are more than nine years old (*SMMT*). Equally, the current EC density of one car per economically active person does not represent a natural upper limit on user demand. As multi-car households increase so Europe will generally move towards the US pattern of three cars for every two economically active persons; by 1991 only (West) Germany had reached this three for two level and that fact alone implies a 30 percent or more increase in the fleet as the rest of Europe catches up.

Only the exercise of government power can save the EC car industry from the consequences of a saturated market and a growing park. The EC needs regulation to stabilize and safeguard the market for new cars and to integrate urban transport systems so that the demand for personal mobility does not clog the roads. Such policies would not be anti-car or anti-freedom because they would seek to establish the conditions under which the largest number of individuals can own and use cars without frustrating each other and thereby incidentally and unintentionally undermining the value-added and employment base in the supplying industry. It is of course possible to repress the problems of car use by adopting the road-pricing policies which are everywhere favored by right-wing think tanks. We would reject this kind of solution because it redefines personal mobility as a positional good whose enjoyment by the affluent depends on the exclusion of poorer citizens who would otherwise clog the roads; road pricing which allows the self-important business middle classes to speed between meetings is not a social solution worthy of the region which invented the welfare state and decent minima for all. The intellectual challenge is to devise alternative policies and the political problem is that the European Community lacks the political power to confront these issues and implement appropriate policies.

As Machiavelli observed in *The Discourses* (1970, p.145) 'no country has ever been united or happy unless it has been under the jurisdiction of one republic or one prince'. The EC is not under one jurisdiction; it remains in Machiavellian terminology a confederation or league of small independent states (on the Swiss or Tuscan model) where none have precedence over others and all must live in the shadow of more powerful unitary states. Up to 1989 it was politically defined within the system of military alliances imposed by the superpowers and economically it remains the underperforming third bloc behind the USA/North America and Japan/Pacific rim. The EC is unable to respond to this misfortune because it has no concentration of political power in a single centre: Parliament spectates, the Commission proposes and the Council of Ministers disposes, as national governments exercise their powers of veto. The Commission's plans for creating a political centre, as articulated in the Maastricht Treaty, were always fatally flawed because they proposed economic union as a means to political union and then got blown off course by discrepancies between national economic conditions and policies; the collapse of a fixed-rate ERM has postponed monetary union for an indefinite period of time and the EC is unable to develop any other way of building Europe. So what we have is a confederation that is slow to take decisions because 'a league is governed by a council which needs to be slower in arriving at a decision than those who dwell within one and the same circle' (*The Discourses*). The quality of these decisions is poor because it involves an endless reinscription of the liberal-market principles which were enshrined in the Treaty of Rome and embodied in the customs union which was completed in the 1960s. The trajectory of the EC is not Machiavellian 'corruption of original principles' but neurotic repetition and reinscription of those principles regardless of conditions and circumstances; the achievement of customs-union was followed up by the single market plan for removing non-tariff barriers and that in turn was succeeded by the plan for monetary union through ERM which would remove currency fluctuations.

All of these structural and ideological limits condition EC policy on cars where the EC's liberal-market neurosis leads to vestigial and atrophied industrial and transport policies combined with an overdeveloped competition policy whose naive pursuit of consumer welfare threatens to have disastrous consequences for the EC car industry. The EC's industrial policy for cars is no more than a few high-tech projects and some noises about training. The EC's transport policy is equally irrelevant; as part of its regional policy of improving infrastructure, the Commission subsidizes road building in underdeveloped peripheral areas. By way of contrast, competition is actively addressed in many ways which threaten the EC car industry. To establish this point we will briefly consider the EC's position and policies against national differences in new-car prices and against government subsidy of loss-making car manufacturers.

The European Commission's DG 4, largely responsible for competition policy, has an obsession with differentials in the prices paid for equivalent new cars by consumers in different national economies. The obsession reflects a narrow and naive definition of purchaser welfare which presumably can be attributed to the activity of consumer groups who represent the middle-class interests of those who, like the Commission's civil servants, are sufficiently well paid to be able to afford new cars. On most estimates there are 3-4 used car sales for each new-car sale and, as we have seen, only a minority of the economically active population ever buys a new car. For most British consumers the question of whether they might pay 20 percent more than their Belgian counterparts for the equivalent model of new car is entirely irrelevant. The used-car buyer is likely to be more affected by other trading practice issues, especially 'clocking' and revenue-based salvage disposal, which are neglected by policy makers: clocking is the practice of winding back mileometers through which the trade creates the low mileage cars which buyers are prepared to pay for; and revenue based salvage disposal sells accident damaged cars to the highest bidder who can then transfer the identity of the damaged vehicle to a similar stolen vehicle as part of a 'ringing' operation. The EC policy makers' order of priorities is all the more bizarre because some of the used-car trading practices could be fairly easily controlled but it is more or less impossible to prevent manufacturers from discriminating between different classes of customers for new cars. Clocking could be made much more difficult if road mileage was recorded whenever the car was taxed and ownership was transferred. From the manufacturer's point of view, price differentials between equivalent or identical models sold in different national markets are simply part of the opportunist detail of cost recovery. If manufacturers are prevented from discriminating between different private consumers in this way, they will still discriminate between private and corporate customers. In Britain, for example, daily-rental fleets routinely obtain cars at well below the nominal wholesale price at which dealers buy in individual units; these fleets are then sold on through auction as nearly new cars at low prices which depress the residuals on the private customer's product.

The issue of national differences in new-car prices is of more than academic interest because DG 4 takes a sledgehammer approach to the one cost-recovery detail that it is capable of identifying as an evil. The threat is always the same: unless the price differentials between equivalent models are reduced, then DG 4 will consider recommending the withdrawal of the 'block exemption' under which the EC car assemblers are allowed to maintain a tied distribution and service system of exclusive dealerships. If block exemption were withdrawn it would weaken the position of all the established European assemblers who have a strong interest in a stable distribution system where all the existing retailers with capital and sites are signed up under semi-permanent exclusive arrangements. Assemblers like Fiat with weak positions in many of their export markets would be particularly threatened and the Japanese would be particularly grateful.

If new-car prices are a sectional obsession of DG4, there is broader support within the Commission for policies which forbid subsidy of

loss-making enterprises by national governments. The EC has formulated a liberal-market economic rhetoric about creating a level field
for competition without government cash subsidy or purchasing preference for national producers; this economic rhetoric is widely
endorsed within the Commission partly because it accords with the
Commission's broader political project of building Europe by breaking down the chauvinist preferences of national governments for their
own producers. Loss-making major assemblers have traditionally been
supported with subsidies so that the banks and other creditors do not
determine the timing and form of restructuring; government subsidies, for example, covered the operating losses and the new-model
development costs of Renault and BL through the first half of the
1980s. The EC rules were effectively tightened in the mid 1980s
when subsidies were temporarily unnecessary because of cyclical
upturn. Since 1986 or thereabouts, direct and indirect subsidies (such
as debt write offs) are subject to EC approval and will normally be dis-
allowed; so far no national government has challenged this change in
the rules of the game.

Again, the EC's position is narrow and naive because it forbids
public subsidy in an economic system which is built on private subsidy. Inconsistently, the EC proposes one law for the Italian government which is forbidden from covering operating losses or
capital-expenditure requirements in any Italian auto business while
the Fiat car company operates under another law; the Agnelli family
is currently mobilizing and restructuring their interests in non-auto
activities so that they can borrow, which will then be applied to
finance new-model development in loss-making Fiat Auto. Under the
late capitalist system, diversified firms are free to cross subsidize their
loss-making businesses with cash earned elsewhere in businesses under
the same ownership; but under EC rules loss-making businesses,
which through the accident of ownership stand alone, cannot draw
support from their national governments. In a late capitalist system
with extensive private cross subsidy, it cannot be assumed that less
public subsidy delivers more economic optimality and public subsidy
should therefore be evaluated on a pragmatic basis; even without
invoking positive industrial-policy objectives, public subsidy for car
firms could, for example, be justified on the grounds that it palliates
the short-term effects of market downturn and it puts those firms
without profits earned elsewhere on an equal footing with those who
can draw resources from outside the European cars business. The

arguments against subsidy may be weak but the EC's rules against subsidy are strong; for the first time in the current downturn, major assemblers must manage operating losses without the possibility of support from their national governments.

The effects of the current downturn will aggravate because finally, the EC's preoccupation with free trade as a global as well as an intra regional principle, leads the Commission to cede market space to the Japanese thereby actively contributing to the destabilization of the EC owned car making industry. The EC assumed responsibility for external trade policy on cars under the July 1991 agreement with JAMA. The EC 'Elements of Consensus' negotiated by the Commission replaced all the previous bilateral agreements between national governments and the Japanese. The exact terms of the agreement quickly became a matter of dispute between the EC and JAMA who differed about interpreting its details. But there can be no doubt that the agreement's broad effect was to open the EC market more widely to the Japanese. Under the previous bilateral agreements, the Japanese import share of the EC had stabilized at around 10 percent. The loophole in the national agreements which dated from the 1970s was the absence of any formal restriction on Japanese transplant production within the EC; but that weakness was more hypothetical than real because the first transplant factory did not open until 1985.

Under the terms of the EC/JAMA agreement, the Japanese were to monitor imports to the Community and the five member states which previously restricted Japanese imports for a transitional period ending 31st December 1999. In a recent European Report (COM 92 0166, 30 June 1993) it is expected that Japanese transplant operations will produce a minimum of 1.2 million units by 1999 and if their direct export share of the market stays at 10 percent Japanese exports will be roughly 1.2 million units. As in the United States, the Japanese will effectively be allowed to assemble one transplant for every unit which they directly import in and, as in the United States, the import content of those transplants is not specified or even measured so that the Japanese are under no obligation to do more than final assembly and are able to exaggerate local content as they did in the United States. The concession on transplants was real because by 1985 the Japanese were investing in market access by opening transplants in the EC just as they had in the United States a few years previously; European transplant capacity was scheduled to increase from 250,000 units in 1991 to 1.2 million units by 1999. In this context, the crucial failure to impose value-added content regulation was an index of the EC's political weakness *vis à vis* national governments as much as of the EC's intellectual stupidity; effective EC wide content regulation was unacceptable to the British government which hoped to use the transplants as a way of reviving its diminished national industry and was therefore happy with a regime where the product is classified as 'European' if the last substantial operation is undertaken in Europe. There is however no sign that the EC is capable of intellectually reflecting on the futility of its liberal market obsessions which in this and other areas displace rather than suppress national sectionalism and chauvinism.

The end result within the EC is that the Japanese have been offered on a political plate most of the market access which they could hope to achieve through competition under free trade rules. The experience of the United States under a liberal trade regime and of non car producing European countries like Switzerland outside the EC suggests that the free market upper limit on Japanese market share is around 30 percent; in Switzerland the Japanese already have a 27 percent share of the market. As long as Japanese product development is primarily geared to the requirements of the Japanese and American markets, it is very difficult for them to do better and the output of the transplants within the EC simply joins that of indigenous West European producers who are forced to discount the product in an attempt to shift it; this is the strategy which Nissan is following with the Primera which has failed in the market place so that Nissan is unable to sell more than 100,000 a year in the whole of the EC. The problem is that the Japanese are better placed than most indigenous European firms to sustain a war of discounts and incentives in a flat and fluctuating market; 'the car in front is a Toyota Carina E from your local dealer with nought percent finance and two years' free servicing. The efficiency of the Japanese transplant assembly operations within the EC is irrelevant to this war; the Japanese advantage comes from cheap, high value-added components such as engines and gearboxes imported from Japan plus the fact that the product design comes free because development costs can be amortized over Japanese factory output. If the generally small Japanese branch assembly factories were stand alone operations subject to strict content regulation, the EC industry would have little to fear from their competition and the indigenous Europeans could expect overtures from the Japanese parents about cooperation and joint production of major components. As it is, the EC's political weakness and intellectual stupidity allows the

Japanese to use Europe as a way of strengthening their car companies by improving Japanese factory utilization and overall production volumes. When they come to sell their transplant product, the Japanese will do so by putting pressure on price structures and margins in the European business at the same time as increased Japanese market share in a saturated market deprives the European volume manufacturers of the capacity utilization which is the precondition for earning decent financial returns. The price and the utilization effects of one million extra transplant units by 1999 are certain to be considerable and, from this point of view, the EC/JAMA agreement can be seen as the Commission's attempt to write a suicide note for an already chronically depressed industry.

(2) Power Without Responsibility: The Renault-Volvo Case

To maintain a balance between all the different stakeholders has . . . become one of the major responsibilities of any manager or business leader in today's world. (Pehr Gyllenhammar, *People at Work*, 1977)

To enjoy continued good fortune, it is necessary to change with the times. (Niccolo Machiavelli, *The Discourses*, 1531)

The first half of this chapter argued that EC car market trends are increasingly problematic and that the Commission has removed the national ring fences which previously protected the indigenous firms from outside competition. The implication is that the EC car industry is now entering on a period of structural adjustment which has long been postponed by good fortune. A change in circumstances is an opportunity (*occasione*) but the question is an opportunity for what and for whom. Some of the major assemblers will almost certainly be subordinated and there may well be major shifts in the intra-EC location of value-added and employment. But it is impossible to predict the form, timing and outcome of structural adjustment because the fragmented EC industry includes many players who can make independent strategic moves; the effects of many of those moves are uncertain in an industry where most of the players are weak firms with no great advantage or disadvantage in terms of value-added productivity. But we can use the Renault Volvo case to illustrate and analyze the motives and mechanisms of restructuring.

The case involves an increasingly close liaison between the two car companies which climaxed in a merger proposal which was then abandoned in the face of increasing Swedish opposition. The liaison between Renault and Volvo began with their cooperation agreement of 1990 which was consolidated by a share exchange in 1991: the two companies initially collaborated on shared purchase of components, R and D and quality control; later the companies agreed to coordinate component planning and product development over the next decade and they were already working on a common product platform. In September 1993, the two companies announced a full merger of Renault with Volvo's automotive interests to create a new combine whose sales volume would make it Europe's second largest and the world's sixth largest car company. The merger was originally presented as a *fait accompli* subject to the formality of approval by the Swedish shareholders. But during October 1993, criticism from foreign researchers and increasing opposition from Swedish investors forced the postponement of the crucial shareholder meeting and then the abandonment of the merger.

The Renault-Volvo case is especially interesting because the two companies epitomize the problems of a weak industry whose cost recoverers have achieved as little as its cost reducers: so that its current options are only productionist and financial variants on the same theme of social irresponsibility. The case also nicely illustrates the way in which managerialism prefers not to contemplate these unpalatable facts. Volvo has practiced cost recovery through its safe, solid product which starts at £10,500 in the British market just as Renault has pursued cost reduction in its factories with commitment but without finding competitive advantage; neither company could sustain a decent return on sales. The achievements of both companies were invisible in managerialist books like the IMVP's *The Machine that Changed the World* which generally disparage 'European mass production' and specifically single out Volvo for criticism as an inefficient neo-craft producer. If the merger had gone through the result would have been restructuring at the expense of the worker stakeholder; a process which the business press prefers to discuss euphemistically as 'rationalization'. Here again Renault and Volvo are instructive because they epitomize the choices which the industry can now take up. For Renault, the merger was a way of strengthening its commitment to its core auto business through desperate productionism which would have been followed by large scale sacking. For Volvo the merger was an exercise in financial engineering; the aim was to exit the unprofitable auto business and recreate Volvo AB as a post-industrial investment trust.

Volvo is controversial because the company once figured as a model for the future of work in an age when Swedish capital could present itself as a humane steward of the interests of the worker stakeholder. In the 1990s the company's efficiency record has been repeatedly attacked by the current generation of managerialist researchers whose strong preference for the Japanese way is not matched by careful attention to the determinants of factory performance or the nature of working conditions. Thus for the MIT team which wrote *The Machine that Changed the World*, Volvo figures briefly as an example of inefficient 'neo-craft production' and the Udevalla plant, Volvo's most recent experiment in humanizing work by recomposing labor tasks into long cycles, is explicitly singled out for criticism. This criticism takes the form of back of envelope arithmetic which is used to set up vague (and irrelevant) hours to build a comparison between the Udevalla luxury car plant and Toyota Takaoka which produces the Corolla at forty times the volume (Womack et al., pp. 100–3). Much the same line is taken in Adler and Cole's (1993) *Sloan Review* article which makes another apples and pears comparison between Udevalla and the American NUMMI plant which is a Toyota/GM joint venture. The condescension of managerialist posterity is already being brought to bear on Volvo's two experiments in assembly without lines at Udevalla and at Kallmar; in *Personnel Management* (May 1992), these experiments were dismissed (without evidence) as attempts to control absenteeism and labor turnover 'with little regard to the effect on production, costs and efficiency'.

The 'humanization of work' has gone out of fashion just like modernist architecture. It is therefore important to make two points about the new model plants at Kallmar and Udevalla whose closure was announced by Volvo early in 1993. First and generally, assembly plant efficiency and inefficiency is not hugely important in the cars business because, as Womack et al. admit, final assembly accounts on average for just 15 percent of the labor hours in a finished car. Second and more specifically, Kallmar and Udevalla were not being closed because they were inefficient but because they were branch plants which were surplus to requirements in a firm which had excess capacity and was producing at no more than two-thirds of capacity. Both Kallmar and Udevalla were low volume plants which together produced less than 40,000 cars in recent years; the famous plant at Kallmar has employed just 800 workers. Like any other retreating company, Volvo was closing branch plants so as to load the throughput down the lines of its (underutilized) central plant: the company's main Swedish car plant, Torslanda, made less than 75,000 cars last year and is operating at less than half of capacity.

Against this background of misplaced criticism it is important to insist that Volvo is, in efficiency terms, an average firm whose record is no better and no worse than that of other European producers of specialist and luxury motor cars. All these firms put their faith in strategies of cost recovery through the 1980s; the aim was to maintain or reposition their products in the upper middle market segments so that existing costs could be recovered rather than reduced. None of the European players in this game had high levels of productivity or sustained records of productivity increase. We can demonstrate this point by comparing the productivity of BMW with that of Volvo car; BMW is an obvious point of reference because it is the most closely comparable European specialist producer and a company which is widely believed to perform better than most other specialists. The relevant data is summarized in Tables 9.13 and 9.14 below.

Table 9.13: Volvo Car Productivity.

	Output	Employees	Cars per employee	Span adjusted car per employee
1981	289,700	25,400	11.4	2.9
1982	317,000	27,950	11.3	3.4
1983	365,000	28,700	12.7	4.4
1984	387,000	31,000	12.5	4.6
1985	392,700	32,250	12.2	4.4
1986	419,500	32,850	12.8	4.5
1987	418,600	34,050	12.3	3.9
1988	400,900	34,100	11.8	3.4
1989	405,600	34,750	11.7	2.9
1990	359,600	33,550	10.7	2.8
1991	309,300	30,400	10.2	2.7
1992	303,800	28,453	10.7	2.2

Note: Process span adjustment is obtained by deflating cars per employee using the value-added/sales ratio as a proxy for process span.

Source: Annual Report and Accounts, various years.

Table 9.14: BMW AG Car Productivity.

	Output	Employees	Cars per employee	Span adjusted car per employee
1981	351,545	39,777	8.8	3.4
1982	378,769	40,738	9.3	3.5
1983	420,994	43,169	9.8	3.6

Table 9.14 (*continued*)

	Output	Employees	Cars per employee	Span adjusted car per employee
1984	431,995	44,692	9.7	3.5
1985	445,223	46,814	9.4	3.2
1986	446,438	50,719	8.8	3.1
1987	461,340	54,861	8.4	2.8
1988	484,120	56,981	8.5	2.7
1989	511,476	57,087	8.9	2.8
1990	519,660	59,544	8.6	2.8
1991	553,230	61,617	9.1	2.6

Note: Process span adjustment is obtained by deflating the cars per employee by the value-added to sales ratio as a proxy for process span.

Source: Company Report and Accounts, various years.

Using the simple and intelligible cars per employee measure, Volvo's 10–13 cars per employee is better than that of BMW in every year since 1981. If we use value-added to sales ratios to adjust for differences in the amount of each car built in house by the two companies, Volvo performs better in seven of the eleven years between 1981 and 1991 and is more or less equal in three more; BMW only pulls ahead in years like 1981 and 1992 when Volvo's output is cyclically depressed. If we look at the trend of productivity, Volvo car is apparently unable to raise productivity and build more cars per employee; in 1992 Volvo car achieved 10.7 cars per employee, slightly worse than it had achieved ten years previously in the equally depressed year of 1982. But it is worth observing that BMW had no more success in taking labor out of the product over the same time period. In retrospect Volvo car management made a major mistake on the upswing in the 1980s because it hired 8,500 extra workers between 1981 and 1987 and as a result never managed better than 12.8 cars per employee at the cyclical peak in 1986. But the broader record of Volvo Group does not suggest that this is an organization which is unable to manage auto factories: the trucks division managed a 50 percent increase in labor productivity over the 1980s.

Volvo's weakness and insecurity does not stem from productive incompetence and the largely imaginary inefficiencies of Udevalla and Kallmar but from a problem of increasingly limited market space whose effects are compounded by company specific problems about narrow market spread and wide model range. In the mid-market niches where Volvo has traditionally sold its product, the company's sales are now increasingly blocked by better resourced German and

Japanese competitors. These competitors can improve their product ranges much faster than little Volvo and do not have to persevere with products like the old 300 and 200 series which soldiered on for years after their sell by date. In the late 1970s Volvo's German competitors, BMW and Benz, consolidated their dominant position in the only two national markets, Germany and the USA, which are large and affluent enough to support volume sales of luxury cars. And by the later 1980s, Volvo like all the non-German European specialists was caught between a rock and a hard place in the US market as the Japanese moved up market with luxury ranges like Lexus and Infiniti which sold on price against the dominant German product. The Japanese effectively blocked any attempt to sell the 400 in the United States, which will make it increasingly difficult to charge premium prices for large Volvos and appears to have permanently reduced Volvo's American sales.

This is a problem for Volvo because the company has a very narrow market spread and has traditionally relied on the United States as one of its major markets. As Table 9.15 shows, Volvo's volume sales are concentrated in just three national markets. The contrast with BMW is again instructive because at this point the comparison shows difference; although BMW benefits from a large home market, the company also builds strength with a strong specialist position in its large home market and a 2 percent plus share of every other major European car market. Volvo has only a small home market in Sweden while the UK and USA are its only two significant export markets: Sweden, UK and USA were the only markets where the company succeeded in selling more than 50,000 cars a year at the height of the 1980s boom and together these markets accounted for 50–60 percent of sales in the 1980s. The company has lost market share in all three of its major markets and the problems are particularly acute in the United States where around one-quarter of Volvo cars output was sold in the 1980s.

Table 9.15: Volvo Passenger Car Registrations (000s units) by market.

	Sweden	USA	UK	France	Germany	Italy	Other
1981	49.9	67.5	44.5	9.2	13.9	15.6	89.1
1982	57.3	69.7	51.3	10.3	12.9	15.1	100.4
1983	62.1	91.8	60.9	14.1	14.6	21.1	100.4
1984	62.4	93.4	59.5	15.8	14.4	21.1	120.4
1985	71.2	109.8	60.5	17.7	14.3	17.5	101.8
1986	64.5	114.3	69.6	19.1	14.3	16.4	121.3
1987	72.4	101.8	70.5	18.9	17.5	15.8	121.7

Table 9.15 (*continued*)

	Sweden	USA	UK	France	Germany	Italy	Other
1988	74.6	94.9	79.8	17.7	16.8	15.3	101.8
1989	66.6	97.8	82.8	15.9	17.0	14.2	111.3
1990	47.6	93.0	66.3	11.5	18.4	23.5	99.3
1991	37.8	65.3	46.1	8.1	20.6	21.1	110.2

Source: Volvo Report and Accounts, various years.

If Volvo's market spread was too narrow, its model range was also too wide for the strategy of cost recovery. By any standards, Volvo is a relatively small car company; the Volvo cars division made 420,000 cars at the cyclical peak in 1986 and just 304,000 in 1992. On this kind of total volume, cost recovery for developing new models was never going to be easy because Volvo like other specialists needed to generate a large amount of cash per vehicle sold so as to cover cost of replacement every seven or eight years. BMW approached this problem by creating what is basically a two model firm where the 3 and 5 series share major mechanicals and the volume selling 3 alone generates sales of 300,000 each year; the 3, the 5 and the other specialist products share engines which are designed on a modular basis and proprietary gearboxes which are bought in from Getrag and ZF. In Volvo's case, the problem is aggravated by the way in which Volvo's output is spread over three different models in the medium, large and luxury classes: the 1992 output of 304,000 consisted of three entirely different models the 400, 850 and 900 so that Volvo's typical model volume falls closer to 100,000 each year; the cars are all so different in drive train configuration as well as size that the Volvo models share no major mechanicals. The penalty is crippling: Volvo car's most recently developed model is the 850 which cost 16.5 bill. Swe Kr. largely because the car required an all new front drive power train which was built in an all-new factory (*Financial Times*, 23 May 1991). No doubt, it is possible to develop the 850's successors more cheaply, but that should not be allowed to distract from the basic point that the arithmetic of cost recovery on three unrelated low volume models does not add up in Volvo's case.

The managerialists who have exaggerated the burden and significance of Volvo's productive inefficiency have also failed to register Renault's efficiency gains. Renault's renaissance of the late 1980s and early 1990s owes everything to the aggression and intelligence with which it pursued the objective of hours reduction. Renault claims a 50 percent improvement in labor productivity between 1985 and

1991 (*Financial Times*, 6 October 1991) and this claim is corroborated by Table 9.16 which shows how Renault built the same number of cars with an ever reducing workforce.

Table 9.16: Renault Cars Division Vehicles per Employee.

	Cars	Employees	Cars per employee
1987	1,831,400	136,646	13.4
1988	1,850,700	131,964	14.0
1989	1,966,700	129,699	15.2
1990	1,766,700	114,516	15.5
1991	1,790,700	106,223	16.8

Source: Renault Report and Accounts, various years.

Table 9.17: Renault European Sales and Market Share.

	EC (12) total market 000's units	France market share (%)	Germany market share (%)	EC (12) market share (%)
1987	2,475	32.2	3.1	11.5
1988	2,594	30.9	2.9	11.1
1989	2,668	31.1	3.5	11.3
1990	2,703	29.9	4.9	10.8
1991	2,377	29.1	5.4	10.7

Source: Renault Annual Report and Accounts.

The best efforts of car firms to reduce hours are regularly frustrated by market difficulties and cyclical declines in sales. Renault postponed this problem because the aggression it put into hours reduction was matched by the intelligence of its marketing effort which ensured that its factories were steadily loaded with throughput. As Table 9.17 shows, Renault is currently market leader in France with a steady 30 percent share of a two million per year home market; in 1991, Renault's 5.4 percent share of the German market made it that country's leading importer and Renault currently holds more than 5 percent of every other European national market, including the UK where the 5 percent target was reached in 1993. While many other European car companies talk about taking labor out and increasing market share, Renault has done the business.

If this heroic performance did not bring security that was because there was one thing which Renault could not do against the Germans; Renault could not produce a big car which sold. Renault re-entered the large car market in the mid-1970s with the 20 and since then it has followed up with two cars, the 25 and the Safrane, without finding sustained market success: each new model brings a short lived boost to sales before it goes off. Thus Renault was and is a manufacturer of small cheap motor cars which has recently adapted to its market position by introducing the Twingo as a differently packaged second small car line which complements the Clio; this does no more than take the company back to the 1970s when the Cinque and the 4 provided the basis for its European sales success. As Table 9.18 shows, Renault is trapped down market and its sales price per unit is no more than two-thirds of that realized by VW or Ford (UK) and not much better than one-third of BMW's selling price. Like other South European producers of small cars, Renault has to sell two cars to generate the same cash as the Germans get from one sale.

Table 9.18: Sales Price per Unit (in French Francs) for Various Car Companies.

	Renault	VW	Ford (UK)	BMW
1990	53,478	91,581	90,708	146,985
1991	53,283	79,307	95,105	143,507

Source: Company Report and Accounts (cars divisions).

The paradox, which again epitomizes the European industry, is that although the Volvo and Renault strategies of cost recovery and cost reduction were very different, their financial results were much the same; both companies were weak because in the turndown of the early 1990s neither could maintain a decent positive return on sales. Because their product and market portfolios were different, their weakness was exposed in rather different ways. Volvo looked good financially on the cyclical upswing and then fell further and faster into losses on the downswing; while Renault clawed its way out of operating losses and never looked impressive.

Like other weak European specialist producers, such as Jaguar and Saab, Volvo looked good on the upswing of a cycle as it moved towards full capacity utilization. Volvo made lots of money as long as the American market boomed and the dollar exchange rate was favorable; in the boom years of 1983–6 Volvo got 7–8.5 Kr to the dollar on its American sales compared with 5–6 in most other years (*International Financial Statistics Year Book*, 1992). On the downswing, fundamentals reasserted themselves and financial results became quite dire. Table 9.19 offers a reconstruction of Volvo car's finances based on assumptions detailed in the notes; in our view the imputed values are accurate enough to illuminate the transition from feast to famine.

Table 9.19: Volvo Car Division Value-added, Labor Share and Cash Flow.

	Sales revenue Swe Kr mill.	Net income as % of sales	Value added Swe Kr mill.	Labor costs Swe Kr mill.	Labor as % of value added	Cash flow per car Swe Kr
1981	13,569	1.5	3,532	2,519	71.3	2,280
1982	18,109	2.4	5,490	3,371	61.4	6,684
1983	26,262	4.8	9,210	3,960	43.0	14,383
1984	30,304	6.6	11,119	4,831	43.5	16,232
1985	33,956	7.1	12,389	5,476	44.2	17,604
1986	35,956	6.6	12,649	5,844	46.2	16,224
1987	38,523	4.7	12,093	6,376	52.7	13,664
1988	39,462	3.7	11,542	6,695	58.0	12,092
1989	42,944	2.1	10,856	7,452	68.6	8,396
1990	39,433	(1.0)	9,595	8,713	90.8	2,455
1991	36,079	(2.2)	8,104	8,442	104.2	(1,092)
1992	44,598	(2.2)	7,517	7,906	105.2	(1,280)

Notes: (1) Labor cost and depreciation figures are imputed on the basis of the car oper-ation's share of employment and capital investment in Volvo Group (i.e. Volvo's auto-motive division). (2) Value-added is obtained additively as the sum of labor costs and depreciation and net income. (3) Cash flow is calculated by adding net income and depreciation.

Source: Volvo Report and Accounts, various years.

In the years from 1983–7, Volvo car managed a return on sales of 5–7 percent. Labor's share of value-added was in the range of 45–55 percent and, if we define cash flow as sales minus labor costs, the com-pany gushed cash; in a good year like 1985, the company had a cash flow per unit of 17,600 Swe Kr (or $US 2,060). In this exceptional period model replacement was not a problem; the cash of the boom years covered the development expense of the 400 and 850 models. But in the later 1980s, boom turned to slump and the cars business made losses in the years 1990–2. As sales turned down, labor's share rode up as it always does in car companies on the downswing. In 1991 and 1992 labor costs accounted for more than 100 percent of the value-added fund, leaving nothing over for depreciation, or any form of new investment in plant, tooling and development. It was possible to envisage an improvement which would reestablish labor's share around the level of 70 percent which is normal in manufacturing com-panies; the lever of head count reduction in association with market recovery and an easing of exchange rate pressures could almost cer-tainly deliver that result. But on the evidence of years like 1981 or 1989, a normal share of 70 percent would mean a cash flow of 3–8,000

Swe Kr and that would leave Volvo car with too little cash to cover replacement expenditure. For this purpose, Volvo car needed a labor share of nearer 50 than 70 percent and 50 percent was inconceivable.

As Volvo moved from feast to famine, Renault managed financial improvement but never achieved financial results that were anything better than mediocre and precarious. After 1986, Renault did succeed in putting six consecutive years of losses behind it and, by the early 1990s, the record 1984 loss of FF 12.6 bill. was a fading memory. But net income as a percent of sales reached the respectable level of 5 percent for only two years in 1988 and 1989 before collapsing to 0.7 percent in 1990 and then rebounding to 3.2 percent in 1992. The precariousness of Renault's financial position emerges very clearly from Table 9.20 which analyzes the financial ratios in the (non-consolidated) accounts of Regie Nationale which is Renault's core operating business; the Regie accounts for nearly 70 percent of total Renault sales and car sales account for around 75 percent of the Regie's turnover.

Table 9.20 covers the period when the financial benefits of productivity improvement should have been coming through. But cash recovery was always mediocre largely because Renault sold small cheap cars. In the two best years, 1988 and 1989, Renault did no better than realize FF 5,200. (about £500) per vehicle sold; in its hey day in the mid-1980s Volvo could realize three times as much. 'Small car small profit' was an industry adage of the 1960s; twenty years later Renault's cash recovery still depended on its ability to shift large numbers of small cars. Worse still, Renault was conceding nominal wage increases in the late 1980s so that the financial benefits of head count reduction were very modest. Thus, only in two years, 1988 and 1989, did Renault succeed in getting labor's share of value-added below 70 percent; the very modest fall in the Regie's output after 1989 bounced the labor share back up above 70 percent. This kind of variation suggested that a further output reduction of around 10–15 percent would create real problems (as it soon did). In the mature cyclical car markets of Western Europe, peak to trough demand falls of 20 percent plus are the norm: thus Renault had not created a robust firm because it never achieved the financial ratios which would allow the firm to ride out an average European downturn.

Table 9.20: Regie Renault Value-added, Labor's Share and Cash Flow.

	Income pre tax depreciation F/mill.	Employment costs F/mill.	Value added F/mill.	Labor share of Value added (%)	Vehicles 000's	Cashflow per vehicle FF.
1987	3,620	14,165	17,785	79.7	1,831	1,977
1988	8,201	13,850	22,051	62.8	1,851	4,431
1989	10,166	14,287	24,453	58.4	1,967	5,169
1990	4,745	14,331	19,076	75.1	1,777	2,671
1991	5,768	14,527	20,295	71.6	1,791	3,221

Source: Annual Report and Accounts and Renault Economic Atlas, various years.

By autumn 1993 when the merger was announced Renault was in the middle of an average European downturn; in the first eight months of 1993 the EC car market was thirteen percent down on the previous year. Renault's output in the first six months of 1993 was 19 percent down on the comparable period in 1992; we estimated that if this sales loss was sustained, labor's share of value-added would rise to 90 percent in the Renault group and cash flow would be halved. Renault had already suffered a profits collapse; when Renault announced its provisional results for the first half of 1993, the company, which had been in loss in the final quarter of 1992, announced an 87 percent year on year drop in pre tax profits to Fr 730 million (123.93 mill. $US) in the first half (*Financial Times*, 27 August 1993). As Renault hovered around break even in the first half of 1993, it was performing better than competitors like VW, Ford of Europe or Fiat (which were incurring losses) and PSA (which was predicted to make a loss). But the newly elected centre-right French government had scheduled Renault for privatization some time in or after the second half of 1994 and privatization requires a track record of profits rather than the avoidance of loss. By autumn 1993, Renault was not a strong car company, in terms of cash flow, but a desperate one, trying to do better.

If the two companies were equal in financial failure, Volvo was the first to lapse into operating losses in 1990 and the parent company Volvo AB was unable to cross subsidize its automotive operations from other businesses. Thus, Renault was temporarily stronger when the merger was being planned in 1990–2 and this temporary disparity in financial power determined the terms of a deal which was to Renault's advantage. Under the terms of the merger announced in September 1993, Renault would have paid nothing in cash for Volvo car and truck interests and, through share exchange, would have obtained 65 percent of the equity plus management control of the merged combine. The proposed merger could also be represented as the nationalization of Volvo by the French government; there was no definite timetable for the privatization of state owned Renault and the French government proposed to retain a golden share which would block changes in ownership of Renault. This was all too much for the Swedish institutional shareholders whose growing opposition provoked a boardroom and management revolt which led to an internal coup against the chairman, Pehr Gyllenhammar, and the collapse of the merger.

While this drama was unfolding in October and November 1993, the business press, except for *Affars Vareldn* in Sweden, took an overwhelmingly managerialist line. At the press conference which launched the merger, Renault claimed that the combined automotive operations could make savings of FF 30 bill. (£3.4 bill.) before the year 2000 through rationalization and integration of overlapping activities. The press questioned only whether Renault management was up to the task of realizing these savings: commentators noted the disappointing results of many giant mergers and observed that Renault-Volvo faced particular problems about the culture gap between the two companies. Our own Machiavellian interpretation was different and harder because we saw the merger as an abdication of responsibility for the worker stakeholder in a corporate world where the shareholder interest must now be privileged. (Williams et al., 1993a and 1993d)

One of the most fundamental rules of modern business is that the balance between worker and shareholder interests in individual firms and sectors depends on whether cost recovery can be assured. When cost recovery is assured, as it was for Volvo and Sweden in the 1970s and 1980s, the result is strong companies which can satisfy the conflicting interests of the different stakeholders. In this context, the Volvo chairman Pehr Gyllenhammar could in 1977 write about the importance of 'balancing the different interests'. When cost recovery fails, as it has failed differently in the 1990s for Volvo, Renault and for most of the rest of the European car industry, then the interests of the shareholder-stakeholder are privileged over those of the worker-stakeholder; companies and sectors which cannot realize a surplus for shareholders must try to reduce their headcount and/or their wages bill. As the same Pehr Gyllenhammar said nearly twenty years later at the press conference which announced the merger; 'there can be no guarantees about on jobs' (*Guardian*, 7 September 1993). Against this background, the irony of the affair is that Swedish resistance to the merger was led by the shareholders while the blue collar workers who stood to lose most were acquiescent. The explanation for this paradox is that the shareholders could make an independent judgement of the plan for protecting their interests whereas the blue collar unions had been co-opted by management in the earlier period of prosperity.

Volvo managers planned the merger as an exit strategy for quitting their unprofitable core auto business. It was an exercise in dealing of the Hanson or Goldsmith kind: the aim was to turn low yielding and illiquid capital assets into cash which could then be reinvested in more lucrative assets that offer a higher yield or capital gains. Before Renault came along, Volvo AB had large amounts of capital tied up in auto factory assets that nobody wanted to buy for cash; worse still the nature of its auto business was such that it offered no prospect of decent returns and was cash hungry in a way that required cross sub-sidy from other activities. If the merger had been completed, Volvo would have successfully turned its assets into paper which gave it a shareholder's claim on Renault's earnings when Renault made a profit without any downside risk because Volvo has no responsibility for Renault's operating losses or cash requirement. The Renault paper which Volvo AB would have gained through the merger might not of course offer a decent rate of return but, after Renault was privatized, the paper would have become tradeable and that opened up the prospect of a second phase of transformation whereby Volvo gets back to cash by selling its paper.

However, all of this was a financially risky game in the long term. The only certainty was that the game began with the distress sale of Volvo's automotive interests on disadvantageous terms at the bottom of the cycle. Volvo's institutional shareholders could see that this was not how Lord Hanson played it. Furthermore, the whole longer term plan raised the issue of whether Volvo's management would make a success of additional dealing as it moved further into financial engineering. If the merger had gone through, Volvo AB would have become a rather peculiar holding company whose portfolio include too many loss mak-ing and low yielding problem investments alongside a couple of cash cows. By 1994 the investments would have included a 35 percent stake in Renault Volvo; 25–35 percent of Pharmacia, the pharmaceuticals business of Procordia; a 100 percent share of Branded Consumer Products, the consumer goods business of Pharmacia; and a rag bag of investments mainly in property and oil. The cash cows are Pharmacia and BCP both of which have a starry return on sales of 10 percent. The problem investments include everything else because Renault Volvo was never going to generate half of that return on sales and because Volvo had showed very poor judgement in picking non-auto investments which generally perform badly: Volvo's oil trading and investment subsidiary Beijerinvest cost it money for most of the 1980s and Beijerinvest was in many ways the symbol of a decade-long unsuccessful diversification strategy. The Swedish shareholders did not vote against the mutation of Swedish capitalism towards the Anglo American form of dealing; however, they did register their doubts about whether the Volvo management was up to dealing and thereby incidentally saved the workforce from the attentions of Renault.

Renault is an altogether more traditional productionist capitalist enterprise for whom the merger was a way of strengthening its commitment to its core auto business. But that hardly makes it virtuous because it was a weak firm which needed to make rationalization savings through merger. And Renault's rationalization savings would undoubtedly have been made primarily at the expense of Swedish workers, managers and suppliers whose production and development jobs and supply contracts were all at risk. The Swedish problem was not the burden of inefficiency but the benefits of a progressive social settlement which, thanks to cost recovery in an earlier period, offered the highest wages and the shortest hours in the world auto industry. In any merger with Renault the crucial consideration was the gap between Swedish and French wages and conditions. Table 9.21 presents basic data on motor industry employment costs per hour in France and Sweden taken from the standard German VDA source. The VDA series shows that French hourly employment costs are broadly comparable with those paid in Italy or Britain but Swedish employment costs are much higher; in recent years, Swedish hourly costs have been about 45 percent higher than in France. Swedish labor costs are much higher partly because the Swedish social settlement imposes a large mark-up for social welfare benefits.

Table 9.21: Hourly Labor Costs in Sweden and France (in Swe. Kr.).

	France	Sweden
1980	45.8	66.6
1983	69.7	83.6
1986	74.6	113.7
1989	83.9	143.7
1991	96.5	169.4

Source: VDA, Frankfurt.

The burden of social charges is increased by the very short hours which are typically worked in the Swedish auto industry; short hours mean more workers and more per capita social charges to deliver a given quantum of assembly or supplier factory labor. This problem is a real one, not because the standard working week is very short in Sweden but because the social welfare system offers an assortment of leave arrangements for responsibilities such as parenting which are worse provided for in other advanced capitalist countries. According to Riegler and Auer (1991, p.234) Swedish blue collar workers in car and engine production actually worked an average of less than 1,400 hours in the period from 1981 to 1986. Renault's workers in France and Spain are on a standard worked year of around 1,650 hours and most of those hours are actually worked. In Renault Volvo, the underlying social issue is the competition between social settlements.

In an earlier generation, the Swedish government could have used its power to protect its workers: until the mid-1980s national governments routinely used subsidies to prop up loss-making national champions like Volvo and thereby clumsily palliated the consequences of market failure. Now, even if the Swedish government had wanted to subvent Volvo it could not do so because the option of Swedish government aid for Volvo is blocked by EC competition policy under Article 92 of the Treaty of Rome. The fact that Sweden is not a member of the EC makes no difference because the power of EC competition rules now extends well beyond the boundaries of the EC. From a Brussels' point of view, Swedish government aid for Volvo would, under Article 92, be a subsidy that distorted competition and the Commission would be prepared to retaliate with import duties against the products of the Volvo company. This point is illustrated by the 1992 dispute between the EC and the Austrian government over state aid for the new Chrysler plant at Graz which will produce MPVs for the European market. The EC threatened 10 percent import duties on the vans until the Austrian government climbed down and reduced its subsidy from 33 to 14 percent of the cost of the plant 'in line with rules on state aid applied in the wealthiest EC countries' (*Financial Times*, 10 September 1992; 26 November 1992).

The problem is one of negative integration whereby national governments lose power or are denied powers which the EC refuses to assume. In the name of liberal market ideology, the EC prevents national governments from supporting their national manufacturing sectors and opens the EC to world competition which intensifies the pressures; thus, the EC is the villain of our story because it creates the unregulated free for all which allows desperate productionists to prey on weaker corporations and indirectly encourages the mutation of productionism into financial engineering. It is politically and intellectually difficult to resist the powerful ideologies of competition and free trade. But the Renault Volvo affair may serve a useful purpose in mobilizing opposition to these ideologies because it highlights the underlying social issues and the inadequacy of a free market response which relies on the best efforts of corporate management.

Competition and free trade does not simply expose technical inefficiencies which could and should be rectified by virtuous management efforts to improve productivity. As the Swedes are finding out, it is also, and maybe mainly, a misfortune which undermines the social settlements of the more privileged. And what needs to be propped up is not companies like Volvo Car but social settlements which are collapsing because the Swedes, like the Germans, can no longer recover the costs of high wages and short hours by selling middle class products to the rest of the world. As the French are finding out, the answer to these problems is not taking hours out of the product because most competitors can do that and, as in the case of Renault, hours reduction therefore produces no competitive advantage. So what was Renault supposed to do after axing Swedish jobs and reducing its French payroll: was Renault to shift all its jobs to Poland where wages were less than $2 (US) an hour and then face the double problem of low wage competition from China and limited demand from an impoverished Western Europe? Many would argue that this intellectualism is irrelevant because the EC will not, in our life times, become a strong political federation which has the power to confront these issues, and liberal market ideology will inevitably dominate a community which can be no more than a customs union and free trade area. We are not convinced by these defeatist arguments. If the EC does not exist as a strong federation, it is partly because nobody at Maastricht or anywhere else had any clear concept of what they wanted the EC to do. The lesson of the Renault Volvo affair is that the EC's prime task should be to put a floor under destructive competition between social settlements.

❖ ❖ ❖

10
America versus Japan:
Bad Companies or Different Social Settlements

❖

This chapter considers the contest between the American and Japanese car companies and the sectors which they represent. Japanese success was unthinkable thirty years ago when American big business was universally regarded as a paragon of corporate efficiency and a model for the rest of the world. But, if we look at trade flows and market shares at the beginning of the 1990s, the Japanese victory was overwhelming. Through imports and transplants, the Japanese product held 30 percent of the American market whereas the American product had a negligible share of the Japanese market; while the *yakuza* transferred their loyalty from Cadillac to Benz, the American middle class made the Honda Accord America's best-selling car. The question that we wish to ask is why did the Japanese car companies succeed and the American car companies fail? The conventional business–school answer is that the Japanese succeeded because their companies made good management choices. Against this we argue that the Americans failed because their sector had structural handicaps.

In *The Machine that Changed the World* market-place success is the just reward for good companies whose managers choose 'lean production', a set of high-productivity practices which dramatically reduces physical hours and costs. If an earlier pre-modern age believed in miracles through divine intervention, our own post-modern period believes in excellence through management action. Thus, in the Womack et al. book, as in the consultancy reports of Harbour and Andersen, management is a privileged social actor that can always or usually deliver heroic changes that transform hours, costs and competitivity. This 'excellence with enthusiasm' position meets its political opposite in 'excellence with regret' which accepts the orthodox economic premise about increased efficiency and competitivity through management action but complains about the social cost in terms of labor intensification and increased management prerogative. In our view, this is not radical enough because the orthodox economic premise could and should be questioned.

In our alternative conceptualization, cars represent a set of social choices or, more exactly, structural values and institutions which are embodied in the product; where Marxists would have argued a labor theory of value, as radicals we now offer a congealed social-choice explanation of international competition. To encapsulate the idea of a set of choices, we introduce the concept of social settlement which includes structural variables on both the cost-incurring and the cost-recovery side: wages and hours, social charges, supply-chain segmentation, wage gradient, pricing structure and market space are all relevant. The important point is that the value of most of these variables are fixed beyond management control and thus the connection between 'good management' (or Japanese factory practices) is much less direct and positive than the business-school professors and the consultants suppose. As in the Book of Ecclesiastes, 'the race is not to the swift, nor yet riches to men of understanding'. And because settlement variables rather than chance determine the outcome, we believe the appropriate response is political intervention.

The choice between the two interpretations depends on the outcome of an argument about measurement. The pro-management case is that the Japanese won because they were better and that case rests on the evidence of orthodox productivity comparisons which allegedly show a large efficiency gap which is directly attributable to the adoption of Japanese-style factory practices; this is argued in the IMVP papers by Krafcik which provide the scholarly support for Womack et al. and it is asserted or assumed in subsequent reports for managers like the Harbour report which ranks American assembly factories or the Andersen report which promotes 'bench marking'. The social settlement case is that the Americans lost because they were different and that case rests on different measures which show a much smaller gap and disclose a structural handicap. This chapter is therefore organized into two main sections that deal separately with measuring the performance gap and identifying the determinants of success and failure. Readers who are persuaded by our arguments on these points can draw their own conclusions; we do not aim to replace one emphatic dogma with another. A third section does however present our own understanding of the implications of the problem shift which we propose in sections one and two; if the problems of the average (American) car company are beyond management, political intervention and regulation should be considered.

Section one begins by questioning the methods and results of orthodox productivity measurement before going on to provide some alternatives by using a range of disparate sector and company measures taken from the first analysis section of our book. The alternative measures show fluctuating gaps between America and Japan which are much smaller than 2:1. Equally important, the measures suggest that best to worst comparisons are fundamentally misleading because most American and Japanese car assemblers are average performers which share common problems about cost recovery. Section two on the causes of success and failure begins by arguing that orthodox productivity analysis fails to identify the causes of performance differences. It then draws together evidence from the earlier analysis chapters to establish two crucial points about the contest between the Americans and the Japanese: first, many costs are effectively fixed and beyond management control; second, the American social settlement imposes a structural handicap of extra costs which arise from the distribution of employment, social charges, and exposure to cyclicality.

(1) 2 to 1: Now You See It / Now You Don't

The Machine that Changed the World, like the various *Harbour Reports*, and the Andersen *Bench Marking Project Report* all encourage us to think about measurement in a stereotyped one-dimensional way in terms of the efficiency gap. The comparisons, league tables and quadrant diagrams encourage a basic dichotomy between good and bad sectors, companies, and above all, plants. The good and the bad are distinguished by one supposedly invariable characteristic; the good need a low labor input to assemble a vehicle or complete a given task whereas the bad need a high labor input for the same operation or task. This position is associated with claims about a large performance gap between Japanese and Western firms which is dramatized by best to worst comparisons, such as Krafcik's notorious 2 to 1 comparison between GM Framingham and Takaoka. And it is garnished with the rhetoric of excellence; 'world class' is used no less than 79 times in the twenty page Andersen report. What we want to do is to question this established way of thinking about performance differences.

The business–school academics and consultants who promote these measures have borrowed the techniques of comparative physical-productivity analysis which were first used in applied economics in the late 1940s. Efficiency gap means differences in physical productivity at line and plant level which are measured using comparative ratios of (labor) input to physical output as in vehicles per employee or hours to assemble. The comparison is usually made in the form of net ratios which correct for differences in output characteristics and in the amount of work undertaken; this complication cannot be ignored when there are, for example, large differences both in the span of process operations undertaken by different assemblers and in the size and complexity of the vehicles produced. The process of correction involves moving from gross to net by correction that takes the form of cumulative subtraction. Step by step the calculation strips out the differences between the cases that are being compared and, on the bottom line, isolates the residual net difference in efficiency. The common-sense case for adjusting gross ratios is overwhelming but the question is whether it is possible to construct valid like for like comparisons by correcting for the many differences in internal organization and external conditions. In raising this issue, we are developing points made in existing critical literature; Nichols (1986) and Cutler (1992) in different ways both suggest that physical process comparisons do not deliver precise results because it is impossible to correct or control for all the differences in capital equipment, process task and market requirements which jointly influence the amount of labor which is used in the process. In Cutler's view, the effects of differences in the pressure of market demand cannot be taken into account because the method rests on the premise of an abstracted sphere of production where a supply-side production function determines output as the result of varying inputs (when the process task is the same).

The control problems can be illustrated by considering Krafcik's IMVP 'hours to build' assembly-plant comparisons whose method (Krafcik, 1988) and results (Krafcik, 1986, 1989, 1990) provide the scholarly support for the Womack, Jones and Roos bottom-line claim that lean producers do it with 'half the human effort' and that therefore the Japanese deserve to win. Krafcik's results are important because they have been widely accepted as authoritative and the methodological issues remain topical because the IMVP is continuing to use the Krafcik method and will in due course publish updated assembly-plant comparisons. The method offers corrected labor hours to assemble which are calculated in an entirely orthodox way. Process span is standardized by including only workers employed in weld, paint and final assembly. Gross figures, obtained by dividing employee total into vehicles assembled, are corrected for the difference of product size, for the process-task differences of weld number and equipment-options content, and for work-practice differences which influence actual working time within the shift (Krafcik, 1988). The variable pressure of market demand is cancelled by bringing all plants to the same standard of full utilization using engineering estimates of their throughput capacity (Krafcik, personal communication).

Krafcik's results are difficult to interpret because his later studies do not clearly and separately focus on individual plants, companies or sectors. Instead, the later studies (Krafcik, 1989; Krafcik, 1990), which take in fifty or more plants, present results for bundles of plants grouped by region of operation and by region of origin of the company which owns the plant. Krafcik, thus compares American-owned plants in America with Japanese-owned plants in America but does not identify or compare individual plants, companies or sectors. His bundling creates problems because each of the 'bundles' contains a wide dispersion of good and bad performers. As Krafcik (1990, p.9) recognizes, there is a 'wide range of performance in each regional grouping and . . . overlapping performance across regions'. Thus, although European plants generally perform worse, 'at least two plants in Europe achieve productivity levels superior to some Japanese parent plants . . . [and] the best performing North American plant . . . is not a Japanese transplant but a traditional Big Three plant' (Krafcik, 1990, p.9). This kind of blooming, buzzing confusion is by no means unusual in large-scale productivity studies and the classic response is to concentrate on some detailed part of the overall picture which provides a suitable illustrative bottom line.

So it is in this case where the Womack et al. claim about 'half the effort' is based not on groups or averages but on Krafcik's earliest (1986) pilot study of just two plants, General Motors Framingham against Toyota Takaoka. This gives Womack et al. (p.81) the result that they want; according to Womack et al., 'Takaoka was almost twice as productive . . . as Framingham' because sixteen corrected build hours were required to weld, paint and finally assemble at Takaoka compared with thirty-one at Framingham. What this proves is not so clear because GM Framingham was in 1986 America's worst plant and Takaoka was the volume plant of Japan's best company; the gap between average American and Japanese plants is presumably very much smaller than 2 to 1. Furthermore, the gap between Takaoka and

Framingham reported in the Womack et al. book is very much larger than in the original Krafcik research paper; presumably some undisclosed adjustment has been applied to obtain a final figure. According to Krafcik (1986, Table 2), whose results are summarized in Table 10.1, the difference in corrected build hours is not 2:1 but around 50 percent between 18 corrected build hours at Takaoka and 27.6 at Framingham. If we examine Krafcik's assumptions, then we can see that this 50 percent difference almost certainly overstates Takaoka's margin of superiority. Takaoka's performance is flattered because Krafcik assumes that the two plants were working at the same level of capacity utilization for the same forty hour week. But, in the mid-and late-1980s, Takaoka was, like much of Japanese industry, working well above notional full capacity thanks to bottleneck breaking and long hours of overtime; when we visited Takaoka in 1988, we observed the employees were working a ten-hour shift and a six-day week. If we correct for Takaoka's higher capacity utilization, the gap between America's worst and Japan's best is considerably smaller than 50 percent and that implies that average plants in both countries may well be fairly evenly matched.

Table 10.1: Krafcik's Comparison of Takaoka and Framingham Build Hours.

	Takaoka	Framingham
Overall productivity (hours)	18.0	40.7
Corrected productivity (hours)	18.0	27.6

Notes:

Krafcik's method

(1) Overall productivity means gross assembly hours per car which are calculated by dividing total plant hours by number of cars produced.

(2) Corrected productivity incorporates adjustments for product, process and working practice differences at Framingham as detailed in assumptions below.

Krafcik's assumptions

(1) Working week of 5 days, each of 8 hours, at Takaoka gives 10.8 million hours with workforce of 5,410.

(2) The implied capacity utilization at Framingham is 87.6 percent with 368 units per shift against stated capacity of 420; at Takaoka the implied capacity utilization is 85.7 percent with output of 1,200 units per shift against capacity of 1,400.

(3) Correction factor of 32 percent applied to Framingham hours to build for weld number, product size, relief time and option content.

Source: Krafcik (1986, Table 2).

But we do not believe that this important point can be established by IMVP-style process comparisons because there are fundamental problems about the whole procedure of correcting for differences. To begin with, what correction factor should be applied where, as in the case of volume plants like Takaoka and Framingham, there are large differences in product type and process task? Krafcik's (1986) original study applied a large correction factor of 32 percent to Framingham's actual hours to build. The later, large group studies (Krafcik 1989, 1990) appear to have applied a much more modest correction factor; that seems to be the implication of the 'methodology' paper (Krafcik, 1988, p.13) which reports a simple correlation of $R = 0.924$ between corrected and uncorrected productivity. The problem is that large or small adjustments are equally unjustifiable because both rest on the assignment of arbitrary weights. In the 1988 paper, for example, the labor-hours correction for extra option content is calculated (for all options in all countries) by taking the retail price of the options and dividing by the $25 (US) per hour wage that prevails in the American industry. Almost anything can be operationalized and measured using procedures of this sort but the quality of the results will be very low. These difficulties are compounded by the practical impossibility of correcting for differences in market pressure. The procedure of crediting all plants with their estimated maximum throughput does not control for variability in market demand because throughput and capacity respond dynamically to demand pressure; when demand pressure is intense and sustained, maximum throughput can usually be raised by putting modest extra resources into breaking bottlenecks.

Our criticism so far discredits the Womack et al. claims about the gap but is otherwise ambiguous because it could be read as a plea for better productivity studies with more sophisticated controls; on this issue we side with Cutler against Nichols who concludes by asking for better studies and praising the National Institute's Anglo German comparisons. In our view, the problem is not imperfect execution but the inherent problems of the method which moves from gross to net by cumulative correction for differences; cumulative correction has never, and will never, produce a precise bottom line for processes, plants or companies. Our general argument is fully developed in *Deconstructing Car Assembler Productivity* (Williams, et al., 1994b) and it can be briefly summarized by presenting four strong reasons to doubt the method and its results.

Reason 1

The calculation quickly cumulates uncertainty because the individual corrections at each step are not precise and independent. The process of adjustment only works if each step adds a precise adjustment, but many of the adjustments are necessarily imprecise either because they take an observable difference as proxy for an unobservable difference or because they involve imputed relations of variation which are beyond the realm of the observable. So, for example, differences in product type and complexity can only be roughly proxied by taking a related variable such as weight or number of welds. Nor is it easy to disentangle and separately allow for conceptually-distinct variables like hours worked and capacity utilization which are variably intertwined in different advanced economies.

Reason 2

The individual adjustments, which are typically made for less than five or six differences, correct for an arbitrary sample of the infinite number of differences that separate individual cases. If, for example, we correct for span of operations, product type, option content, hours worked and capacity utilization, why not consider manufacturability and length of model run. Those who have done such calculations know the list of corrections must be short; if the list is extended, overlapping imprecise corrections generate wildly-implausible bottom lines. But, logically, the list of variables to be controlled stretches out beyond five or six towards infinity.

Reason 3

Step by step correction makes the individual plant or company cases more alike at the expense of creating an increasingly implausible and bizarre counterfactual world. Suppose, for example that we want to correct for GM's capacity utilization which averaged no better than 60 percent in the early 1990s. In that case, we are obliged to assume counterfactually that GM can take a 70 percent share of the American car market or find large new export markets in Japan or Europe.

Reason 4

The bottom line result is ambiguous because it typically corrects for supply-side differences but ignores the effects of variable market demand pressure which is a powerful pull-through influence on factory flow and labor utilization. Market pressure cannot be safely ignored because there is no simple positive relation between productive excellence and the ability to sell product. For assemblers, the relation is mediated by product design, distribution and market maturity; while many component manufacturers face a derived demand which depends on the success of one or two assemblers.

If these general problems arise whenever net-productivity ratios are compared, their effects are compounded in management discourse by the recent tendency to make opportunist comparisons across short spans of the productive process and an increasingly-cavalier attitude to the business of adjustment. Krafcik is representative of the recent trend towards focus on plant (rather than company) productivity; the bench marking in the Andersen report is largely concerned with process comparisons. Against this we would argue that the first law of productivity measurement is 'the shorter the span, the more dubious the measure'. In our discussion of the early 1980s 'productivity miracle' at BL, we showed that almost anything can be proved by selective citing of process productivity figures which may well not represent the plant or the company as a whole (Williams et al. 1983, 1987a). Vehicles per employee comparisons for major plants or companies are more interesting. Even then, bottom-line comparisons of individual assembly plants are not necessarily representative of company differences and assembler company differences are a poor guide to sectoral differences because final assembly typically accounts for only 15 percent of the value of the vehicle.

The other worrying tendency is the literature's increasingly cavalier attitude to the essential step by step adjustment for difference. In this respect, the recent degeneration of the method can be traced on a slide downwards from Krafcik's IMVP papers of the late 1980s, through the Harbour Report to the Andersen bench marking report. As we have seen, Krafcik's IMVP research papers make a serious but (necessarily) unsuccessful attempt to correct for differences using a methodology where the assumptions are generally explicit and the basis for correction is usually disclosed and justified. By way of contrast, the plant league tables in the Harbour Report (1992) are the result of arbitrary decisions. In the case of American Big Three assembly plants, Harbour makes no adjustment to the gross scheduled output per employee obtained by dividing employees into vehicles. In the case of the Japanese transplants, this procedure discloses mediocre productivity, a result which does not fit the consultant's story line about the Japanese. Harbour conjectures that this mediocrity is caused by plant-level employment of a substantial staff engaged in purchasing and distribution and then, without any hard information about numbers, applies heroic adjustments which correct for this disadvantage and incidentally nearly double Toyota Georgetown's productivity. In the Andersen bench marking study (1992), the individual component plants are not identified and it is simply not clear how much adjustment has been applied, and for what reasons, to individual plants and lines.

The new combination of increasing assertiveness and diminishing care reflects a slippage. In the applied-economics texts by Rostas (1948) and others in the late 1940s, the productivity gap was the object of the discourse and everything depended on getting high quality measures. But this is not necessarily so in management texts where measurement serves an illustrative rhetorical function in persuading the non-numerate. This is the function of the Takaoka and Framingham comparison in Womack, Jones and Roos. And standards are still lower in studies such as the Andersen Report which is produced for a business audience with a short attention span and an aversion to long words. In the Andersen Report, the productivity comparison really exists only as a bottom line which serves as input for the 'executive summary' claim that 'world class plants' have 2 to 1 productivity superiority and 100 to 1 quality superiority. Illustration in the form of the quadrant diagram also plays an important role in the Andersen report because it is a way of interpellating the business subject who can immediately see that his/her company is the cross in the upper left-hand corner. Firms like Andersen and Harbour are really in the business of selling representations of difference to the unsuccessful in league table, bar chart and quadrant diagram form. Like other consultants, who are judged by the amount of new business or sales revenue which each report generates, they are unlikely to spend much time worrying about the intellectual deficiencies of their methods.

Against this background of defective method and increasingly opportunist measurement, we can understand more about the extent, variability and multi-dimensional nature of the performance gap by presenting three different comparative measures from the analysis chapters. Our aim is not to construct the gap using one measure but to construct a multi-dimensional profile of the American and Japanese sectors and companies using several measures which show different and changing gaps; the profile has two dimensions because we include time series as well as snap shot comparisons. The particular measures we use are not chosen because they fit the existing *a priori* of economics or any other established discourse; they are chosen because the analysis chapters indicate that these measures are relevant to the activity of car manufacture. Our argument is simply that if the measures are laid out in this way they can generate new insights into an important real world case. First, at a sectoral level the difference between the American and Japanese industries is illustrated in terms of sectoral hours to build; this series shows us that the hours gap between the two national industries is, and for over twenty years has been, considerably less than 2 to 1. Secondly, there is considerably more variation in company performance which can be approached by considering value-added per employee on a company basis; this series gives us a league table of companies which is instructive because it shows the limits of best to worst comparisons when most Japanese and American assemblers cluster around an average and change position over a decade. Finally, the complex and multi-dimensional character of any performance gap can be explored further by introducing cash flow per vehicle produced as a third performance measure; this series shows us the limits of Japanolatry because, on this measure, average car companies in Japan as well as America have real problems.

The physical gap between the Japanese and American industries is best illustrated by calculating sectoral hours to build and Table 10.2 presents the results of a calculation of build hours per vehicle for the French, German, Japanese and American motor sectors which was initially presented in Chapter 4. As was then explained, sectoral hours to build are calculated by multiplying the number of employees in the national motor sector by realistic estimates of average hours worked which is then divided by vehicles produced.

The Table 10.2 series is interesting because it shows that it is possible to find a major national motor sector which currently does take twice as many hours as the Japanese to build a vehicle; in the latter half of the 1980s, the Germans took around 260 hours to build a vehicle against just over 130 hours in Japan. But, the physical gap between the Japanese and the American motor sectors was much smaller especially in years like 1985 and 1986, when demand was brisk in America and the American sector could build a vehicle in just over 150 hours; between 1983 and 1989, the American industry took between 12 and 32 percent more hours than the Japanese. Because the hours gap is so much narrower than the exponents of lean production suggest, relative wage levels and structural differences are of considerable importance in determining the balance of competitive advantage between Japanese and American based producers. We will return to this important theme in the second section of this chapter.

Table 10.2 is also instructive because it provides a time-series perspective on differences which the existing management literature constructs in snap-shot form. The time series in Table 10.2 is important because, like all our other time series, it shows substantial changes in relative positions over the past twenty years. Management rhetoric about Japanese *kaizen*/continuous improvement is seriously misleading insofar as it implies or assumes that change takes the form of the Japanese sector opening up an increasing advantage over all the others.

Table 10.2: Motor Sector Build Hours Per Vehicle.

	France	Germany	Japan	USA
1970	267	278	254	189
1971	257	270	224	162
1972	241	268	217	169
1973	238	266	203	167
1974	248	308	200	182
1975	292	279	176	174
1976	254	246	173	163
1977	251	258	158	165
1978	253	278	146	170
1979	241	294	147	179
1980	252	318	139	202
1981	260	271	138	204
1982	243	267	140	204
1983	225	262	139	163
1984	237	266	141	165
1985	220	258	139	155
1986	197	266	133	154
1987	175	255	132	173
1988	162	256	132	174
1989	n/a	286	132	170

Sources: Automotive News Market Databook, Crain Publications Inc, *Labor Statistics Yearbook*, ILO, *Industrial Statistics Yearbook*, United Nations.

If we consider the four national sectors, it is possible to find one sector which is stuck on high hours because the Germans have managed no improvement on 260 hours over the past twenty years. The American industry illustrates the opposite case of a sector stuck on low hours because the Americans have managed no improvement on 160 hours over the past twenty years; cyclical fluctuations of demand are the main influence on build-hours variation and the opening of Japanese transplant factories in America since 1983 has had no discernible effect. Stability in Germany and America is balanced by two cases of dramatic hours reduction; in the 1970s, the Japanese sector managed to halve its hours to build from an initial level of 250 hours and the French industry managed the same feat a decade later. Both industries performed very strongly in the late 1980s and early 1990s with the Japanese sector building increasingly sophisticated cars in the same hours and the French sector extracting further hours reductions; our work on Renault (Williams et al. 1992b, 1993a, 1993d) shows that Renault has a 25 percent improvement in vehicles per employee since 1988. The achievements of the French industry are real, but France is not Japan and it does not figure in the management literature.

Any national sector is of course an average of companies and plants which perform at different levels. On the whole, company performance comparisons are more interesting than plant analysis because every company is a collection of plants which perform differently because of differences in the saleability of their product lines which feed through into variable capacity utilization. The Harbour league tables of American assembly plant productivity are little more than translations of capacity utilization into a different language; if we take Harbour's recent (1992) productivity ranking of thirty-one Big Three car assembly plants, on our calculations, the top quartile have an average utilization of 87 percent and the bottom quartile an average utilization of 55 percent. If we are concerned with company-level differences in performance, the best single measure is value-added per employee which uniquely takes account of company-level differences in vertical integration. The adjustment is automatic because value-added equals sales minus purchases of materials, components and services; companies which buy-in more have a lower value-added to sales ratio. International comparisons of value-added per employee require translation into a common currency and we have chosen to translate into US dollars. Variation in exchange rate does influence company ranking; but we would argue that in the Table 10.3 comparison below, between Japanese and American companies, the exchange rate is less a source of bias and more a fact of life for Japanese companies which export components and finished cars to America and repatriate the proceeds. As long as cars are internationally traded, exchange rates are as relevant as factory efficiency in determining cashflow and profitability.

The problem of course is that American and Japanese owned companies manufacture and assemble in more than one country so that companies are not the same as national sectors. Companies can only be appraised on the basis of their consolidated accounts which report results from their global operations; in the case of the major American or Japanese owned companies it is either very difficult or impossible to strip out the results of operations within the boundaries of different national sectors. This slippage does not, however, completely undermine the possibility of comparisons between companies because as we observed in the analysis chapters, most of the world's major car companies are centered in one region. Thus, in the cases of Toyota, Nissan, GM and Chrysler, 80 percent or more of their total sales turnover originates in factory operations within either Japan or north America. In these four cases, the company is a fair proxy for the national sector. In the case of the two Japanese companies, exports from Japan account for around 50 percent of their volume so that their financial results do depend on the exchange rate of the yen, but that is a complication which arises wherever national sectors are dependent on export sales. The inclusion of Ford and Honda will be more controversial because neither company has much more than 50 percent of sales turnover originating from its home base. Ford's results are influenced by its relatively large European operations just as Honda's results are influenced by its commitment to American transplant operations. In the case of Ford, we are, however, convinced that the inclusion of its European operations does not massively bias the result because our calculations show a value added per employee in recent years of around $75,000 in the Ford UK operations which is not greatly out of line with the consolidated result. It is also true that in the case of Ford, the bias arising from the inclusion of European operations is negative. In most years the American operations tend to perform rather better and thus Ford's consolidated results usually gently understate American performance. With these points made, we will now turn to company comparisons.

Table 10.3: Company Value-added Per Employee in $US.

	Honda	Nissan	Toyota	Chrysler	Ford	GM
1983	38,329	27,950	41,085	53,962	43,632	44,379
1984	40,542	26,284	41,816	43,386	49,815	44,369
1985	59,302	37,806	59,601	67,080	56,084	45,385
1986	83,533	47,580	71,339	69,939	60,743	42,709
1987	87,368	62,951	85,668	75,526	77,736	44,868
1988	84,227	63,329	90,663	65,312	86,484	53,738
1989	68,247	59,881	83,932	73,078	83,516	53,143
1990	73,661	65,179	103,794	68,107	76,142	44,307
1991	79,473	69,489	112,859	70,040	68,861	44,433

Note: Value-added is calculated additively by summing the distributions.

Source: Consolidated Company Report and Accounts, various years.

Here again we can begin by considering the snapshot for the most recent year. It is true that the difference between best and worst is substantial, but in a cyclical peak year not 2 to 1. Toyota's value-added per employee is 70 percent greater in the peak year of 1988. But it is doubtful whether this is a very interesting or illuminating observation because it tells us nothing about the broader distribution of performance which shows a strong tendency towards clustering around the average with Toyota as an outlier. Toyota is in a class of its own because c1990 it added 20,000 more US dollars per employee than its closest rival; on a company workforce of around 100,000 this translates into a lump-sum advantage of 2 billion dollars in one year. As for the rest, most of the other assemblers, Japanese as well as American, in a cyclical peak year, are clustered in the range 60,000 to 85,000 dollars per employee. And the Japanese companies do not consistently occupy the upper positions in this central range; the worst performer is (unsurprisingly) GM but the next worst performance is turned in by Nissan which adds 10,000 dollars more value-added per employee, in a cyclical peak year, than GM but is still below that generated by Ford and Chrysler. From this point of view, we find it hard to see why 'Japanese' transplants or manufacturing techniques should transform American performance because the Japanese have only one super-company, Toyota; all their other assemblers do no better at adding value than their American counterparts.

As usual, the time-series view changes the picture. It shows all the Japanese assemblers improving their position relative to the Americans in the 1980s; in 1983 the three Japanese assemblers in Table 10.3 occupied the bottom three positions and only Toyota was within sight of adding as much value as the American Big Three. Whether this amounts to a dramatic improvement in relative efficiency is altogether another matter; in all the companies except Toyota, labor accounts for a normal 70 percent of value-added and thus rising real wages have increased Japanese value-added and diminished the relative advantage of the Japanese. Toyota has usually been the best of the Japanese companies; Honda's flash in the pan performance of the mid-1980s owed much to the exchange-rate effects of its early shift into American transplant production. For a time in the late 1980s Toyota turned its Japanese lead into a world supremacy not seen since Henry Ford at Highland Park. This lead could be attributed to the combined effects of Toyota's productive techniques and its strong domestic sales performance against companies like Nissan and Honda who, like the Americans, appear to be stuck on a value-adding plateau. The two effects (techniques and market success) cannot be disentangled using a value-added measure which shows market place ability to recover costs incurred in the factory. In this respect, the measure faithfully reflects the complexities and interconnections of the real world; and the implication is that where market space is limited it is not possible for all companies to be equally excellent. For the other Japanese assemblers, the road block problem has been Toyota's dominance of the Japanese market where it sold 43 percent of passenger cars. As we observed in Chapter 7, the lesser Japanese companies have responded, not by imitating Toyota's techniques, but by shifting into export sales and transplant production which was an attempt by the Japanese also-rans to find market space elsewhere; the Japanese also-rans must then have to suffer the effect of Yen appreciation which depressed their value-added in a way which was beyond management.

The argument so far suggests that it would be useful to shift the focus of analysis onto the average assembler companies, Japanese as well as American. In considering the average car company, a discussion of performance in terms of hours to build and quantum of added value is inadequate because for all companies the crucial issue is whether, at existing costs and prices, they can recover their conversion costs in the market place and generate a surplus for product renewal which maintains or increases volume; cashflow from existing operations is the parameter which determines whether and how assemblers can stay in the business. To explore these issues, Table 10.4 presents a simple analysis of cashflow which is calculated crudely by subtracting labor costs from value-added; to put all the assembler companies on a near equal footing, we calculate cashflow per vehicle produced and express the results in US dollars. The results are important because Table 10.4 shows that, whatever the differences between assemblers, they do not translate into financial advantage in terms of cashflow. Furthermore, average car assemblers, Japanese as well as American are mostly weak; the average assembler can recover its labor costs which account for a normal 70 percent of value-added but cannot steadily generate a substantial cash surplus over and above labor costs. This problem is likely to have knock-on effects for the whole sector because component firms which supply cash hungry assemblers are unlikely to have fat margins on their Original Equipment (OE) contracts.

Table 10.4: Company Cashflow Per Vehicle Produced ($ US).

	Honda	Nissan	Toyota	Chrysler	Ford US	GM US
1981	n/a	429	n/a	n/a	424	835
1982	n/a	430	n/a	574	697	921
1983	830	464	546	917	901	1,424

Table 10.4 (continued)

	Honda	Nissan	Toyota	Chrysler	Ford US	GM US
1984	1,025	395	558	455	1,033	1,294
1985	1,401	508	812	1,403	1,185	1,198
1986	1,917	604	970	1,452	1,327	1,084
1987	1,486	735	1,126	1,527	1,744	1,204
1988	1,552	931	1,140	1,307	1,984	1,677
1989	1,110	703	1,087	948	1,945	1,540
1990	1,220	790	1,312	936	1,574	699
1991	1,323	770	1,434	537	925	565

Note: Cashflow is defined as value-added less labor's share.

Source: Consolidated Company Report and Accounts, various years.

The snapshot for the most recent year shows a very interesting dispersion of performance which needs some commentary and explanation. Two Japanese assemblers, Toyota and Honda, are strongly cash generative with cash of more than $1,400 per vehicle in 1991. So is one of the American Big Three because Ford managed approximately a thousand dollars per vehicle in 1991. The rest, (Nissan, Chrysler and GM) turn in much weaker performances with between $540 and $770 per vehicle. The immediate puzzle is why Toyota cannot turn its otherwise super performance into a cash gusher. Toyota does have a strong cashflow from the operations it does undertake in its own factories. This is a matter of simple arithmetic when labor's share of value-added at Toyota is consistently below that of other car companies; Toyota's labor share of value-added was 44 percent in 1991 and substantially lower for much of the 1980s. But Toyota, like the other Japanese assemblers is much less vertically integrated than its American Big Three counterparts; as Table 10.7 in the next section demonstrates, in recent years Toyota's value-added to sales ratio averages 14 percent against 19-20 percent in the case of Nissan and Honda and 34–38 percent in the case of the American Big Three. The problem is not that Toyota's vehicles do not generate cash but that a large part of the cash is generated inside Toyota's supplier network which does most of the work. It is hardly surprising that the upper tiers of this network are dedicated to supplying Toyota at prices which Toyota sets as it struggles against the consequences of vertical disintegration.

The time series again supplies a different, complementary perspective. The first interesting point is that the burden of vertical disintegration has been too much for Nissan; the Japanese home-market boom of the late 1980s did no more than raise cash per vehicle to a cyclical peak of $931 in 1988 and the subsequent mild market downturn damaged Nissan's cashflow and in 1992 forced the company into operating losses. The news since then has been of Nissan's intention to postpone model replacement and rationalize componentry. In a broad historical perspective there is an obvious analogy between Nissan in Japan now and BMC/BLMC in Britain thirty years ago; like BMC, Nissan has high-volume, substantial market share and an unusually wide model range whose regular replacement is problematic because the company only generates the cash for new models in unusually favorable market circumstances. Nissan's only consolation in the early 1990s was that some other major players were now worse off; two of the American Big Three were even weaker. The problem of the American-owned assemblers is that their cashflow fluctuates dramatically according to cyclical movements in a saturated and mature American market. In a good year all three American companies can realize more than $1,300 on each vehicle and the strongest of them, Ford, realized $2,000 at its peak in 1988; in a bad year the two weaker American companies (Chrysler and GM) realize a surplus over labor costs of $600 or less per vehicle and then have to borrow to cover the costs of model replacement. The regular alternation of cash on the upswing and debt on the downswing leaves all the American Big Three with a burden of short-term debt: worst placed around 1990 was GM; according to GM's 1991 report, the company's current debt was then $95 billion of which $51 billion was due within the year (*GM Report and Accounts*, 1991). If Nissan was weak it was not yet dynamically unstable like GM, and (like Ford and Chrysler) Nissan could hope that GM will create market space for competitors' products by downsizing.

(2) Causes of Success / Conditions of Failure

In *The Machine that Changed the World* differences in performance are confidently attributed to one active cause, differences in management practice. 'Lean production' is a cluster of management practices and the Andersen Report takes up the Womack, Jones and Roos argument that these practices improve organization of the labor process in development, production and distribution and realize better materials flow inside and outside the assembly factory. The connection between productive excellence and market-place success is taken for granted so it is simply assumed that firms which adopt these practices will be rewarded with high performance; firms with poor performance have simply not made what we would call the right productive interventions. This position is broadly coherent with the more general *a priori* of the business school and consultancy where management figures as a purposive social actor whose rational decision-making or, more recently, commitment to excellence, brings success. What we want initially to do is to question this model of cause and effect.

We can begin by observing that orthodox productivity measurement techniques do not identify the causes of observed differences in efficiency. The procedure of cumulative subtraction leaves a residual, the bottom-line efficiency gap which supposedly reflects the influence of an X variable whose presence/absence generates the difference. The X variable is identified by a process of addition which brings an external discourse to bear in a way that generates explanation or, more exactly confirms what the discursively orthodox knew all along. *Deconstructing Car Assembler Productivity* (Williams et al. 1994b) showed that engineers and accountants identify X as production techniques and management accounting; economists identify X as quantity or quality of factor inputs; and business-school professors identify X as management practices. These confident explanations cannot all be correct and they are all equally speculative. Attempts to vindicate particular explanations through empirical work on the co-variation of different variables does generate some insight; Fuss and Waverman's (1990) econometric work confirms our own less systematic conclusion that capacity utilization is an important influence on performance. But empirical work seldom vindicates the *a priori* identification of X and we can illustrate this point again by considering Krafcik's research which is important for two reasons: first, it is the only attempt to identify the causes of high performance/low labor input at plant level which focuses directly on factory practice; second, Krafcik's results undermine the interpretation advanced by Womack, Roos and Jones.

The Krafcik research papers (1989, 1990) which measured assembly labor hour variation also tested a causal hypothesis that '"the management policies inherent in a fragile/lean production system lead to high performance manufacturing' (Krafcik, 1989, summary). To test this hypothesis, Krafcik constructed a list of possible causal 'independent variables' which might influence labor input: the 1988 list included scale, product age, model mix, automation/level of technology and 'factory practice' which was specified so as to capture 'lean' characteristics (Krafcik, 1988). Each variable was assigned a numerical value and in the case of factory practice (as with technology) a 'management index' was constructed by assigning numerical values of one to three for each of four subvariables; thus firms could score between four and twelve according to Krafcik's rating of floor space given to rework, visual control of the production process, team working, and average level of unscheduled absenteeism (Krafcik, 1988, p.18). Krafcik then crunched the numbers, examined the correlations and thereby hoped to identify the causes.

The investigation was ill conceived because most of the sub-variables in the 'management index' were not independent and because manufacturability was not included in the list of putative causes until the last phase of the study. Three of the four 1988 management-index subvariables (team working, visual control of production and low absenteeism) are generally present in Japan and absent elsewhere. Their 'independent' status is very dubious if the plants with low assembly labor hours are also Japanese. In this case the result will be a respectable positive correlation which tells us nothing about causal relations because the work is only exploring an identity with Japan redefined in different ways on either side of the correlation. The propensity of the workforce to eat raw fish and read comic books or any other set of peculiarly Japanese characteristics would produce an equally impressive positive correlation and of course imply nothing about the causes of low assembly labor hours.

The other problem concerns manufacturability whose exclusion from the list of putative causes in the earlier papers (Krafcik, 1986, 1989) is entirely inexplicable because the principal researchers in the IMVP project clearly accept the general industry view that manufacturability is an important determinant of build hour requirements; Womack et al. (p.96) actually report the results of a General Motors tear-down study which found that manufacturability accounted for 41 percent of the 'productivity gap' between two comparable Ford and General Motors cars. In the 1990 paper, manufacturability is for the first time included as an independent variable and measured opportunistically by assigning a 50 percent weight to the age of model and a 50 percent weight to the judgement of eight manufacturers who were asked in a questionnaire to rank competitors' products for manufacturability. The result is a low-quality measure because there is, for example, no reason to suppose that age of model is a good cross-section predictor of differences in manufacturability between manufacturers and the measure is clearly biased towards the Japanese who have more recently introduced product ranges. The questionnaire rankings are impressionistic and show only that the industry believes manufacturability is, like capacity utilization, an advantage for the Japanese against the Americans; the Japanese Big Four occupy four of the top five places in the questionnaire based ranking for assembly manufacturability.

The research project design was such that it could never positively establish what caused the variation in labor assembly hours. It did however suggest negatively that the connection between management/factory practice/lean production and low labor hours was nowhere near as strong as Womack et al. assert and most consultants assume. There is a large reporting gap between Krafcik's findings and the line which Womack et al. take in their chapter on 'running the factory' (Womack et al., pp.75–103) where the causal privilege of lean production is maintained rather than questioned. In summarizing his own research findings, Krafcik generally takes the position that lean production is a joint and necessary condition but not in itself a sufficient cause of high manufacturing performance. The 'executive summary' in the 1989 paper concluded,

> the level of automation and the degree to which a plant uses a fragile/lean production system are important determinants of manufacturing performance *separately* but contribute most significantly to high productivity and high quality when they occur *together* . . . . Achieving top performance requires *both* continued investments in technology and a fragile/lean production system. [Emphasis in original]

The 1990 paper introduced manufacturability or product design as a third joint cause,

> our essential message now reads: the world's most productive, highest quality automotive assembly plants have three things in common-high levels of automation, lean production systems and product designs that are easy to build. The data show that those plants lacking even one of those characteristics suffer significant competitive disadvantages in cost and/or quality. [Emphasis in original] (Krafcik, 1990, p.4)

The qualified privilege of lean production as joint cause is further eroded by the explicit conclusion that good design plus automation *'allow Western companies so far unable to implement lean production systems to at least approach the performance levels of the best Japanese producers'* [Emphasis in original] (Womack et al., 1990, p.6). If Womack, Jones and Roos had seriously considered the findings generated by their own researcher, they might have retitled their book; *More than One Way to Skin a Cat* would be an altogether more appropriate title than *The Machine that Changed the World.*

If the Krafcik investigation disproves conventional assumptions, it provides no basis for developing an alternative understanding of the causes of success and failure. We can begin to do this negatively by questioning the whole model of management activity, the concept of the firm and the assumptions about management competence which underlie texts like *The Machine that Changed the World*. It is, for example, doubtful whether management is a cost-reducing activity because much management is cost-increasing; the general law of capitalist management is that 'the number of suits expands to claim any surplus created in production'. The American Big Three carry a burden of staff employment in head office and in divisional functions like financial control. As we observed in Chapter 7, if the Japanese owned firms do not employ these supernumaries in production, their extravagant systems of home-market distribution incur large staff costs. Table 10.5 makes this point again by presenting data on Toyota which in 1991 employed 30,000 in distribution and Nissan which has half Toyota's market share but employed no less than 81,000 in distribution; the reason is simply that Nissan (unlike Toyota) owns a large part of its (unsuccessful) dealer network. Clearly Nissan is a company which is struggling not to sink under the burden of unproductive white–collar employment which is difficult to reduce without undermining an already weak home-market performance.

Table 10.5: Comparison of Manufacturing and Sales Employment in Toyota and Nissan.

	Toyota					Nissan			
	Motor Corp.		Motor Sales		Total employ-ment	Motor Corp.		Motor Sales		Total employ-ment
	No.	%	No.	%		No.	%	No.	%	
1985	61,665	77	18,236	23	79,901	58,925	54	49,575	46	108,500
1991	72,900	71	29,523	29	102,423	56,873	41	81,453	59	138,326

Source: Company corporate profiles, various years.

Western business-school analysts might argue that what the Americans and Europeans need is Japanese-style production without the burden of unproductive Japanese distribution. But it is doubtful whether all or many Western firms can be redirected in this way because many of them are not unitary, controllable entities and management is often not capable of defining and executing new strategies. Many firms are divided on functional or geographic lines into competing or semi-independent centers of power. Thus GM figures as the textbook example of M-form organization but it does not have a single assembly division or central management group like Ford and

Chrysler (Harbour, 1992, p.38). When eight different organizations manage GM assembly plants, it is hardly surprising that GM's downsizing is always too little and too late. Furthermore, in most firms managers are generally concerned with the routine business of incremental decision making in firms moving along well defined trajectories of possibilities. When that is not enough, management often does not innovate in the Schumpeterian sense but behaves like turkeys voting for Christmas. Mercedes Benz has discovered that it is a high-cost producer of luxury cars; the company is now considering whether to build a car smaller than the existing 190/ C class and has already decided to open an American factory which will produce a four-wheel-drive utility vehicle (*Financial Times*, 6 April 1993).

Even if management controls its own firm in a purposive way, all management must face the fact that bought-in materials and components, whose costs are largely beyond internal management control, account for a substantial part of total costs. In any individual firm the bill for purchases is a major constraint on the possibility of cost recovery and on value-added productivity because value-added equals sales minus purchases. Even in a relatively integrated Western manufacturing firm bought-in materials and components typically account for more than half the value of sales; the components come from smaller suppliers inside the sector and the materials from outside the industrial sector in which the manufacturer operates. If we consider the motor sectors of the industrially advanced countries, external costs are important because purchases from outside the auto sector account for a substantial proportion of the total cost of each car and because the conversion costs in the lower tiers of the supplier network cannot be managed by assemblers and upper tier suppliers.

Car production is often discussed as though what happened inside the auto sector was the only influence on performance and competitiveness. Because our analysis chapters focused on the internal logic of the activity, they did not question this assumption; so at this point it is important to emphasize that the availability of cheap high-quality inputs from outside the auto sector is a crucial determinant of competitiveness. If this point has been lost in the literature, it was appreciated by new entrants like the Japanese in the 1960s and the Koreans in the 1980s. And its importance is underscored by Table 10.6 which estimates the relative importance of non auto-sector purchases in America and Japan by subtracting the average value-added per vehicle realized in a national sector from the sales revenue per vehicle realized by the two largest domestic manufacturers (GM and Ford in the United States, Toyota and Nissan in Japan). In both countries, purchases from outside the auto sector account for an estimated 40 percent of the sales revenue per vehicle realized by GM and Ford in the US and Toyota and Nissan in Japan.

Table 10.6: Non Auto-Sector Purchases in Japan and America.

	Major manufacturer sales revenue per vehicle	Motor sector value added per vehicle	Imputed non auto sector purchases per vehicle	Non auto purchases as percent of selling price
United States	12,142	7,471	4,671	39%
Japan	12,559	7,367	5,192	41%

Note: Column 4 is calculated by subtracting column 3 from column 2.

Sources: Company Report and Accounts, various years; *Industrial Statistics Yearbook.*

If we now turn to consider costs within the car sector, the central point is that conversion costs in the lower tiers of the supplier network are always beyond the control of upper tier management. The Japanese assemblers do, of course, organize their upper tier suppliers into unitary *kieretsu* networks. But, as was emphasized in Chapter 7, these Japanese firms are substantially less vertically integrated than their Western counterparts; all these Japanese firms buy in sub-assemblies and the most vertically disintegrated assembler, Toyota, sub-contracts the final assembly of nearly half its vehicles. Table 10.7 summarizes again the contrast in value-added/sales ratios which we used as a proxy for process span.

Table 10.7: Value-added to Sales Ratios for Japanese and American Companies.

	Honda	Nissan	Toyota	Chrysler	Ford US	GM US
1983	18%	17%	14%	40%	38%	37%
1987	21%	19%	13%	39%	38%	32%
1991	20%	20%	15%	29%	35%	32%

Source: Company Report and Accounts, various years.

Toyota's value-added accounts for only 14 percent of the sales value of each car, against an average Western ratio of around 35 percent. Even if Toyota controls its first and second tier suppliers, it gains little more leverage over costs than the average Western firm which undertakes many more processes in its own factories. And Toyota's choice of a vertically disintegrated structure is itself significant; it still might be asked if Toyota's manufacturing techniques are so wonderful, why don't they do it all in-house? On this point, the Chapter 7 contrast between Ford and Toyota is really telling; Ford at Highland Park chose vertical integration and brought work in-house because he could produce parts at half the cost of outside suppliers, even though Ford workers had the highest wages and the shortest working hours in the industry. The implication is that Toyota lacks or cannot practice Henry's virtuoso technical ability, and instead chooses vertical dis-integration which allows Toyota to exploit a steep wage gradient into the supplier network whose positive effects on costs partly compensate for the negative effects on cash.

At this point in the argument we can turn from making negative points and advance a more positive conceptualization. Because management does not control many of the costs, conversion efficiency and cost recovery are powerfully influenced by a set of structural variables which have different values in various national economies and car-producing regions. On the supply or cost incurring side, these variables include enduring conventions about wage levels and hours worked, national systems for allocating social charges like retirement costs to firms and a pattern of supply-side segmentation into differently-sized firms with a definite wage gradient between large and small firms. On the cost-recovery side, assemblers and their suppliers need a pricing structure and the market space to recover the costs incurred in production. In mature markets, where demand is cyclical, the pricing structure should allow a margin to cover the extra costs of capacity underutilization in demand troughs. The concept of social settlement is no more (or less) than a synthesis of the structural variables whose importance was demonstrated in our analysis chapters. But it is crucial to our distinctive analysis of the cars business; where the business-school literature and the consultants see managers actively creating the conditions of success for companies and sectors we put much more emphasis on the way in which, under a particular national settlement, indigenous firms can exploit or must suffer the values of different structural variables which are embedded in institutional structures and enforced by social actors like trade unions. Rather than change settlement variables, it is now often easier for management to shift production or try and find market space elsewhere so as to exploit a different national or regional settlement.

We expect some resistance to this idea of settlement from those who are taken by fashionable ideas of globalization. All we would say in response is that, as with much recent social science, the totalising idea runs ahead of the patchy reality. Maybe, at some distant point in the future, all the major car companies will have gone global so that they have a balanced portfolio of regional production bases and markets; but, for the time being, as Chapter 6 demonstrated most of them are strongly centered, and exposure to different social settlements is a powerful influence on competitive advantage and disadvantage. The general rule about companies being centered on one production area is broken mainly by two American companies (Ford and GM) which, as Chapter 6 noted, have long had independent volume-production bases on either side of the Atlantic. We would be more sympathetic to those who respond to social settlement by observing that the idea of management agency should not be evicted. That is because, in general, we do not want to spoil a good argument by pressing it too far and, in particular, we recognize that our analysis in this second half of our book shows that management often can make a difference. The historical studies in Chapters 7 and 8, demonstrate this clearly; they show how the good manager, Kamiya, checkmated the opposition for Toyota, and bad managers at BLMC/BL hastened the collapse of their firm. Equally, the analysis of the European industry in Chapter 9 shows that, with output flat, French managers reduced build hours in a way which transformed the cost-recovery position of the French industry. The lesson of these cases is that in any individual case of success and failure the role and relative importance of management action and structural variables should be carefully considered; all we are saying is that the structural variables are usually important and in many cases of success and failure these structural variables are necessary and sufficient determinants of the outcome (regardless of management action). So it is in the case of America versus Japan and we will now review the evidence on this point.

The concept of social settlement is flexible enough to accommodate variable sources of advantage and disadvantage because it provides a basic checklist of supply and demand side variables which will have positive and negative values in different cases of success and failure. If supply side structural variables have an obvious relevance to failing industries, the same variables do not always play the same role. Thus, as Chapter 9 has shown, the German industry is in the middle of a cost-recovery crisis and the Swedish firms have collapsed because of the burden of a wages and hours package which cannot be sustained. In the case of America versus Japan, the American firms do have a moderate disadvantage in terms of hours worked which we estimate at 2,150 in 1990 on the basis of the United Auto Workers estimate for the Big Three; against this the Bosch and Lehndorff studies, which are cited in Chapter 4 Table 4.2, estimate Japanese blue collar hours worked, before the recession of the early 1990s, at 2,250–2,300 in the case of Nissan and Toyota and around 2,050 in the case of Honda. If the hours differential does not translate into overwhelming disadvantage that is mainly because in recent years, hourly earnings in Japan and America have been fairly evenly matched and the mark up for social charges is roughly similar in both America and Japan and certainly much smaller than in Germany where it adds nearly 75 percent to gross hourly earnings. Table 10.8 reprises the basic information about relative wage costs and earnings from Chapter 4.

Table 10.8: Hourly Wage Costs in the Automotive Industry, 1991 (US$).

	Germany	Japan	US
Employer wage costs	26.95	20.52	21.24
Gross hourly earnings	15.59	15.70	15.41

Source: VDA communication.

Table 10.9 on wage gradient illustrates another set of supply side structural peculiarities which is relevant to the competition between America and Japan. This table re-emphasizes the point, from Chapter 4, Table 4.3, that the Japanese motor sector has a steep wage gradient between large and small firms and a large percentage of employment in small and medium firms. In 1987, no less than 26.5 percent of total Japanese motor-sector employment was in small establishments employing less than 100 workers and, on average these establishments paid wages which were just 56 percent of those paid in large firms employing more than 1000.

Table 10.9: Wage Gradient and Employment Structure in the Japanese and American Motor Vehicle Manufacturing Sector.

	Japan (1989)		United States (1987)	
	Wage gradient	Share of employment	Wage gradient	Share of employment
1–99	56.4	26.5	51.5	7.9
100–499	72.4	20.3	59.3	18.0
500–999	86.2	12.6	68.3	9.7
1000+	100.0	40.6	100.0	64.0

Source: Statistical Yearbook, Japan; *Bureau of the Census,* US.

No other major national motor-vehicle industry operates with this double structural advantage; all the rest either have a shallower wage gradient and/or a smaller proportion of employment in small firms. Table 10.9 illustrates this by presenting comparative data on the American motor sector which has a wage gradient just as steep as in Japan but only has 7.9 percent of employment in firms employing less than 100. Here we have a second indication of why the Americans are bound to lose.

On the other side of the social settlement, the demand-side variables influencing cost recovery are important and diverse. Not least, there is the question of relative prices; the Ludvigsen report (1992) demonstrates that retail prices for comparable or identical products are typically 25 percent higher in Europe than in America or Japan. The German industry's nightmare is competition from the Japanese who can live with substantially lower prices than those needed by the Germans to recover costs. This is not the American problem because prices are similar on either side of the Pacific and if market conditions were the same the Americans and Japanese would be competing on a level playing field. But, as Chapter 5 demonstrated, market conditions are not the same and Table 10.7 restates this difference.

The Japanese Big Two assemblers and the American Big Three assemblers face very different home-market conditions. As we emphasized in Chapter 7, both markets behaved very similarly in the rapid growth period of early motorization. But that period ended in 1929 in America and market growth was much more modest in the maturing years of the 1950s and 1960s. Subsequently the American manufacturers have faced a mature home market with no sustained growth since the early 1970s combined with vicious cyclical fluctuations as volatile replacement demand is brought forward or postponed. In popular imagery, the Detroit manufacturers are still associated with the excess and profligacy of long discontinued product, which is ironic when these manufacturers have been living with zero growth for the past twenty years. By way of contrast the Japanese home market was emerging from initial rapid growth in the early 1970s and subsequently shows the maturing pattern of sustained but unsteady volume growth with fewer, weaker downturns. Overall, the Japanese home market doubled in size between the early 1970s and 1990 in a way which made life easier for all the domestic players.

As Blake observed in the most poignant of his *Songs of Experience*, 'it is an easy thing to triumph in the summer sun'. Much the same perception was articulated by the GM US executive, quoted in Womack, Jones

and Roos, who said that when the Japanese hit cyclicality they would become like everybody else. The recent experience of profits collapse after
a home-market downturn suggests that the Japanese trajectory is past its
peak and the long descent into ordinariness has begun. Whether this is
in itself enough to relieve the Americans may be doubtful.

Table 10.10: Car Registrations and Market Cyclicality 1970-92.

	Japan		United States	
	Car registrations	Year on on year (%)	Car registrations	Year on on year (%)
1970	2,379,128		8,388,204	
1971	2,402,757	1.0	9,729,109	16.0
1972	2,627,087	9.3	9,834,295	1.1
1973	2,933,590	11.7	11,350,995	15.4
1974	2,286,795	-22.1	8,701,094	-23.4
1975	2,737,595	19.7	8,261,840	-5.1
1976	2,449,428	-10.5	9,751,485	18.0
1977	2,500,095	2.1	10,826,234	11.0
1978	2,856,710	14.3	10,946,104	1.1
1979	3,036,873	6.3	10,356,695	-5.4
1980	2,854,176	-6.0	8,760,937	-15.4
1981	2,866,695	0.4	8,443,919	-3.6
1982	3,038,272	6.0	7,754,342	-8.2
1983	3,135,610	3.2	8,924,186	15.1
1984	3,095,554	-1.3	10,128,729	13.5
1985	3,104,074	0.3	10,888,608	7.5
1986	3,146,023	1.4	11,139,842	2.3
1987	3,274,800	4.1	10,165,660	-8.8
1988	3,717,359	13.5	10,479,931	3.1
1989	4,403,745	18.5	9,852,617	-6.0
1990	5,102,660	15.9	9,159,629	-7.0
1991	4,868,000	-4.6	8,175,582	-10.7
1992	4,454,000	-8.5	8,210,627	+0.4

Source: Automotive News Market Databook; Company Corporate profiles, various years.

But emerging cyclicality in the Japanese market will serve to undermine their distinctive production systems just as it has inhibited their
adoption in the West. As was argued in Chapter 7, the idea of a distinctive Toyota production system is something which should be
treated with some caution because there are so many ambiguities about
its nature and extent. But there can be no doubt that, in Toyota's case,
stability of demand is a crucial precondition for the application of its
distinctive techniques of productive intervention; as demonstrated in
Chapter 7, stable demand allows production smoothing which is the
essential precondition for instruments like *kanban*. More fundamentally, if the basic objective of intervention in repetitive manufacture is

to improve flow so that less labor sticks to the product, that objective can only be attained when demand is brisk: as the case of BMC shows, flow cannot be sustained against market restriction.

After all the qualifications have been stated and all the complexities have been laid out, the fact remains that reducing motor-sector labor hours is potentially a powerful instrument of cost reduction which can transform the cost-recovery position of a sector that takes out labor. If we take, for example, the industry's most recent success story, as was observed in Chapter 9, the French reduction of sector build hours by some 100 hours since the early 1980s takes around $US 2,000 out of each product and safeguards the French position within the West European industry as producers of small cheap cars which the Germans cannot profitably produce. But labor hours reduction is, as Tom Waits observed in a different context, 'not for everyone' because it depends on initial conditions which are often not satisfied and the reduction is ultimately self-limiting.

The earlier analysis of Ford Highland Park and of Toyota, as well as later Chapter 9 discussion of the French, suggests that two crucial internal preconditions must be met before hours reduction can be achieved. The first precondition is a large management prerogative over the labor process in factories where unions have little power; this condition is satisfied in all three cases and it is crucial for the Ford and Toyota style of productive intervention which depends on endless recomposition of the labor process. The second initial condition is the market: both Ford (Highland Park) and the Japanese operated with increasing market shares of growing markets and French firms like Renault have pulled the hours reduction trick with stable demand. Even more fundamentally, there is the external condition of the market. The reduction in labor hours is ultimately self limiting because all successful car firms sooner or later encounter market limits. Thus Ford in the 1920s built the new Rouge factory which was probably the most perfect conversion apparatus that the world had ever seen: but, as was argued in Chapter 7, market limitations prevented Ford from exploiting Rouge's full potential. The other relevant limit on hours reduction is technical because as long as car manufacture involves fabricating and assembling thousands of different parts into bodies, interiors and major mechanicals there is an apparently irreducible minimum of well over 100 motor-sector labor hours in any car. Ford, at Highland Park around 1915, like Toyota in the late 1980s was never able to build a car with a negligible labor content: on our calculations, in 1915 Ford took 123 internal hours to add value equal to 40 percent of Model T selling price; and, more recently, if we exclude distribution employees, Toyota has taken 70 hours to add value equal to 15 percent of the value of a much more complex car. Beyond a certain point, it is simply impossible to find large, continuous reductions in motor-sector hours to build; the game becomes rather like serious competitive running where huge amounts of effort are required to obtain small improvements on last year's record.

All these arguments imply that, for the American Big Three, hours reduction through adoption of 'lean production' techniques is irrelevant and largely unattainable; in the American case, the internal labor control and external market conditions are not satisfied and there is no gross excess of hours to be eliminated. The American and Japanese national industries have been fairly evenly matched on motor-sector hours to build since the mid 1970s when, as Table 10.2 shows, the Japanese reached parity with the Americans at around 170 hours. As the same Table 10.2 also showed, the Japanese sector then moved into a position where it had a small hours advantage which varied between 16 and 42 hours, according to market conditions, between 1983 and 1988. But the unionised Big Three operating in a saturated and cyclical car market are unlikely to be able to close that gap by management action. The only relevant management action is downsizing which Ford US used in the last major recession to transform its performance. The candidate for downsizing then became GM. But GM executives would do well to ponder the lessons of Chapter 8 on BL; downsizing is immediately attractive because it promises to remove a burden of unproductive excess capacity but that does not produce a significant hours improvement if, as in the case of BL, a narrower range of cars captures a smaller market share.

If hours are effectively fixed beyond management control, the gap between the American and Japanese industries can be re-interpreted as a cost gap which is determined by structural variables that are beyond management. In many ways, this is only restating the obvious: as 150 +/- 20 motor-sector build hours is around the irreducible minimum, the outcome of any contest, between two national sectors operating around this level, is always likely to depend on relative wages and other structural variables. And if we review the evidence, this is what we find.

The structural sources of Japanese advantage do change over time. In the first decade after the Japanese had achieved parity, their relatively low wage levels were crucial. Table 10.11 presents the basic data, from Chapter 4, on relative labor costs since 1980 in the two national sectors; the Japanese figures broadly represent cost per hour in the major assemblers rather than their lower wage suppliers. In the first decade after the Japanese industry had achieved parity with American build hours, they were absolutely unstoppable because their labor costs per hour in major assemblers were half or less those of the Americans and in small suppliers the ratio was even more favorable to the Japanese. Yen appreciation and rising real wages only slowly eroded the advantage of the low wage competitors: as late as 1985, according to VDA, the Japanese hourly cost was $11 against $23 in the US. Although wages in large Japanese assemblers have been close to American levels since 1990, the low wages paid by the sector's many smaller suppliers remain a potent source of advantage for the Japanese.

Table 10.11: Employer Labor Costs per Hour in the US and Japanese Motor Manufacturing Sectors, 1980–91 in $US.

	Japan	United States
1980	7.40	12.67
1985	11.15	22.65
1990	18.03	20.22
1991	20.52	21.24

Source: VDA Frankfurt.

From an American perspective, we would now identify this as one amongst several major structural handicaps which have disadvantaged the American industry since the late 1980s. Table 10.12 presents the results of an illustrative calculation of the relative weight and importance of the three most important structural variables for one recent year.

Table 10.12: US Motor Sector Structural Cost Handicaps per Vehicle against the Japanese Motor Sector, 1988.

(1)   Extra American wage cost arising from an industry structure which displaces less employment into small firms paying lower wages   **$543**

(2)   Extra social charges arising from American requirement for extra workers because each American worker supplies 2,000 hours against 2,300 hours in Japan   **$321**

(3)   Cyclicality burden arising because fall in demand from cyclical peak of 1986 raises sector build hours by 20 hours per vehicle   **$505**

Source: VDA; *Statistical Yearbook of Japan; Industrial Statistics Yearbook,* SMMT, *International Financial Statistics Yearbook,* various years.

The calculation in Table 10.12 does not have an additive bottom line because that would be misleading when the relative importance of the variables shifts from year to year with changes in the market and capacity utilization and when an exhaustive structural analysis of all the differences can never be made. But we cannot help observing that in an average year like 1988 the three structural variables in Table 10.12 together account for nearly $1,400. In the same year, after allowing for wage gradient and the distribution of employment between differently-sized firms in the two economies, we estimate that the American motor sector had an actual internal labor cost per vehicle which was some $1,500 higher than the Japanese sector's internal labor cost per vehicle. Thus, the three structural handicaps account, in that particular year, for almost all of the observed difference in labor cost per vehicle.

This kind of comparison of national sectors is illuminating but incomplete when the American industry now includes many Japanese owned transplants as well as American owned factories: in 1991 Japanese transplant assembly plants in the United States produced 1,500,000 cars and this transplant sector will have a capacity of 2,500,000 vehicles by 1994. In the conventional view, the transplants represent the migration of superior production techniques; as we have argued elsewhere (Williams et al., 1992a), there is little evidence of superior performance. In our alternative view, the transplants are significant because they represent a form of internal competition which avoids many of the structural handicaps that afflict the Big Three's long-established American plants. As new entrants with young work-forces and no retirees, the transplants avoid many of the social costs which the Big Three must pay: according to the OTA (1992), the hourly wage of $15 is the same in the transplants and the Big Three, but employer labor costs per hour are $22.50 in Big Three plants against $17.50 in the transplants (OTA, 1992). As minor players with low market shares, the transplants are often able to avoid the worst effects of market downturn which always hurts major players with large market shares. And because the transplants are branch-assembly operations operating under a free trade regime, they can access cheap parts from the low-wage supplier networks back home in Japan. Chapter 6 reported the results of the UMTRI study which showed that 38 percent of the value of the best-selling Honda Accord came directly from Japan and also reported our own work on Bureau of Commerce data which shows that in 1989 the Japanese transplant auto sector had an overall import to sales ratio of 48 percent (Williams et al., 1992a). It is not necessary for the transplant factories to be super-productive because their structural characteristics give them a large advantage over their American owned competitors.

Finally, we would observe that the American Big Three are, in the current idiom, challenged because they have fewer defensive and offensive options than their Japanese counterparts; for a variety of reasons, the Japanese are likely to find it easier to reduce break-even and increase volume so that they generate the cash to stay in the business. The Japanese can save costs by reducing their broad model ranges and lengthening their short model lives; the Americans, especially GM, which is too big, cannot take this option without risking market share and Chrysler, which is too small, has the additional problem that every new model must be a winner. The Japanese can access cheap components from small Japanese suppliers while they slowly develop low-wage Asian alternatives; low-wage Mexico is half a continent away from the traditional Big Three plants in Michigan. Japanese companies together export half their output and can increase sales of components at the same time as they send higher value-added cars to America and Europe; Big Three exports from American factories are negligible and will remain so when they have no distribution in Japan, and GM or Ford exports to Europe would cut across the interests of their local manufacturing operations. Japanese companies operate in an environment where financial institutions have modest expectations of short-run profit and approach restructuring in a constructive way; whereas GM and Ford must rely on size to protect them from the financial engineers who buy and sell assets.

Emulation versus Regulation

The argument about measurement may appear to be arid and technical but it has interesting and important implications. In this third and final section of the chapter we draw out these implications for readers who have followed the argument of the previous two sections which deconstruct the appearance of technical efficiency and reconstitute it as being largely social difference. Our measurements as much as our concept of social settlement challenge the business world taken-for-granted notion that all problems can be solved by appropriate management action, and support a new politics of regulation against the old politics of emulation.

The old politics of emulation date from the decade 1945–55 when comparative efficiency measures began to circulate in a newly-constituted popular discourse about national success and failure; productivity moved out of the *Economic History Review* and into official and unofficial reports, political speeches and editorials in the quality press. This was the period of the productivity missions to America; the Anglo American Council on Productivity and the OEEC (precursor to OECD) both produced influential best-selling reports on why American productivity was higher. Of course, the general concept of productivity as the (efficiency) relation between inputs and outputs has a much longer pre-history which stretches all the way back to classical political economy. But the post-1945 literature introduced the novel ingredient of international comparison using new kinds of comparative efficiency ratios, such as hours to build.

The discovery of comparative productivity was part of the post-1945 policy revolution which constituted the firm, the sector and the national economy as manageable objects. Much of the intellectual apparatus of post-war management has been discarded but productivity is still very much with us; we have entered a post-Keynesian era but not a post-productivity era. Far from being eclipsed or superseded, comparative productivity has consolidated its position as an important weapon in the armory of agenda-setting and attention-getting social science and management. Thus, for example, many believe that the National Institute's studies of productivity differences between UK and German manufacturing somehow or other prove that poor training is a major cause of British economic failure. Just as many believe that Womack, Jones and Roos have proved that Japanese-style lean production is twice as efficient as Western productive systems.

The continuing popular success of comparative productivity is a function of the derived demand which arises from the pressure of intensifying international and inter-regional competitive trade in finished manufactures. It was discovered in the post-war period when the rest of the world, for the first time, had to face the prospect of competition with America under a pax Americana with liberal trade rules. The expansion of competitive trade through the whole post-war period gradually broke down national manufacturing autarchy and increasingly exposed hitherto sheltered producers to competition from the apparently more efficient. Thus the British were increasingly exposed to competition from Germany under free-trade rules as British trade inevitably shifted away from Empire/Commonwealth to European partners. American compacts drove the European car importers back into the sea in 1959, but the American Big Three could not resist the next wave of Japanese importers. The European car manufacturers now fear that they too will lose against Japanese competition. All these developments stimulated the demand for productivity-gap studies.

Productivity measurement has become a compulsory activity for the fearful and dispossessed; it is the British who must study German productivity and the Americans who now study Japanese productivity just as the rest of the world once studied America. Productivity discourse is powerful because it speaks to the unsuccessful through stereotyped discursive mechanisms, the bottom line and the promise of transformation, which figure prominently in Womack et al. as in other business texts. The bottom line is important because it can be separated from the technicalities of calculation and used as a headline 'analysis' by popularizers: 2 to 1 or 'half the human effort' objectifies difference and spreads panic by defining a gap which is so large that it requires the response of action. As for the promise of transformation, that provides a reassurance that if the subject's technical deficiency is remedied, then the reward will be an improvement in performance: thus, Womack, Jones and Roos insist that lean production is not the prerogative of the Japanese because all companies can improve performance by becoming lean and they cite the success of Ford US and the transplants to support their position.

Since the beginning of productivity discourse there has been a tension between the two roles of diagnosis and prescription; those who study productivity both measure the gap and act as agents of change. This point is made by MacSweeney in his critique of the British Audit Commission and it indicates a serious problem for critical social science which requires a certain independence. But as management discourse increasingly appropriates productivity measurement, the problem becomes an opportunity because the tension is resolved in favor of enthusiastic promotion of change; business school gurus and management consultants build their reputations and make their living by selling interpretations and telling other people what to do. In 'the executive summaries' at the beginning of the consultants' reports, measurement itself functions as a rhetoric of change. Thus, in Andersen's bench-marking report, the first recommendation is 'find out how far behind world class you are . . . ' and the second recommendation is 'use the resulting crisis to commit the firm to closing the gap'. (Andersen, 1992, p.5).

Thus productivity has a curious double existence; it is both discursively conservative and really radical. The discursive effect is conservative because, as we have already observed, the explanation of the efficiency gap is usually derived from an external discourse so that the diagnosis and prescription only confirm what the discursively orthodox knew all along. At the same time, productivity promotes radical real-world change because the bottom line and the promise delegitimize the national social settlements of the unsuccessful who can and must change their ways if they are to succeed against 'new competition'. The discursive world is congenially familiar but the real world has changed utterly so that managers and workers must learn to behave in new ways.

Not surprisingly, this kind of position attracts centrist politicians and bureaucrats who instinctively favor training and industrial policy to rectify 'market failure' so that the nation can succeed against the new competition; Michael Heseltine or Robert Reich only represent transatlantic variants on this theme. More cynically, senior managers see the utility of efficiency measures and concepts which establish the necessity for change; the huge sale of *The Machine that Changed the World* within the car firms represents a case of academic supply meeting an insatiable industrial demand. The measures and concepts are often used in bad faith by management which knows that Japan is not the answer. One French assembler tells us privately that its gap against Japanese best practice varies between 20 and 80 percent 'depending on the measure and the year'. The same firm organizes conferences where it publicly endorses 2 to 1 because, we are told, that is an effective way of persuading managers and workers to accept the objective of competitiveness and the instrument of changes in organization and working practice.

Against this background our argument so far demonstrates the futility of a politics of emulation and, in these last few paragraphs, we will draw out the implications of our argument. To begin with we have argued that precise comparisons of the efficiency of different plants, firms and sectors are illusory because it is not possible to correct precisely for all the differences that separate the cases; any achieved level of efficiency is the result of intertwined supply and demand side conditions whose joint effects can never in practice be separated. The implication is that we can never know the extent of the 'efficiency gap' to be closed nor can we know the causes of the gap; emulation is hardly a very attractive public policy option if it rests on an assertive identification of relevant levers whose movement has an uncertain effect on performance. Furthermore, the idea of an efficiency gap collapses a complex multi-dimensional financial and physical reality into a coarse one-dimensional representation; some companies and sectors score well on some measures and badly on others and most are distressingly average on many measures. No single, straightforward one-dimensional ranking can capture this complexity and unevenness which makes it more difficult to identify the appropriate action or remedy at the same time as the whole project of emulation becomes problematic because it is no longer clear who or what is to be emulated. The project of emulation rests on one-dimensional simplifications and, as soon as these are questioned, the discourse and politics of emulation must fail; it is impossible to construct a business best seller or a political campaign around the idea of following different firms for different reasons in the hope of improving some indicators.

If these arguments against emulation are negative and rest on observing the deficiencies of orthodox productivity thinking, we also offer a more positive concept of the limits on what management can achieve through productive intervention. The focus of productivity thinking is always on changing supply-side variables, whereas we have drawn attention to the demand-side variables of market access and market conditions on cost recovery; the lesson of Ford and Toyota is that excellence comes to those who achieve dominating positions in growing markets. As for productive intervention, that is a difficult game which most can play without achieving sustainable advantage through cost reduction. Furthermore, the effects of management action are bounded by the extent to which, as we have demonstrated, many costs are fixed or at least determined by the structural variables within particular social settlements; on a broad front. The lesson of Japanese competition up to the mid-1980s, and of Korean competition in the 1990s, is simple: *the advanced countries which pay high wages and work short hours are threatened by low-wage competition which cannot be met by any conceivable form of productive intervention to improve efficiency.* Such considerations encourage us in the view that there should be a problem shift from encouraging management action to defending social settlements. This would carry with it implications for the direction and nature of public policy where we propose a shift from emulation of efficiency to regulation of low-wage competition.

The issue is free trade or, more exactly its benefits, costs and the paths of adjustment for those who lose out under a free trade regime.

International trade is important, necessary and wealth-creating but global free trade between high and low wage countries is likely to have unacceptably high social consequences for all the advanced countries in the next generation. Economic models of the benefits of trade depend on restrictive assumptions which are not met – indeed, cannot be met. The reality of trade in cars is unbalanced flows which will not be corrected under free-trade conditions. In the loser countries, car-induced balance of payments deficits inhibit their ability to pursue expansionary macroeconomic policies at the same time as the need for such policies is increased when the losers suffer employment losses. If wages and costs of living flexed downwards in loser countries and if labor flowed smoothly into alternative employment, then there might be little cause for regret. But the fact of the matter is that the burden of adjustment falls on tradeable goods producers in manufacturing and displaced labor flows into the pool of unemployment or into low-wage service employment. The consequence is a polarized society with haves and have nots determined by the accident of their social position and economic relation to competitive trade.

Gains in consumer welfare provide the ideological justification for unimpeded free trade and individual consumers do benefit from free access to the goods of low-wage producer areas which clearly stand to gain employment from what amounts to a transfer of production. But the question we would ask is whether such gains represent net social gain for the advanced countries if they have a high cost in terms of producer welfare. The cost that concerns us is the expulsion of a section of producers into an underclass of the displaced and dependent. Under current social conditions this has further inevitable long-term consequences for family structure, crime and all the other problems which are met ideologically by political scapegoating of the victims and practically by fitting alarms to every house and car; the middle classes in comfortable service employment may retreat to the suburbs but they cannot escape the consequences of social disintegration. It could be argued that our observation reflects a reactionary preference for misery at a convenient distance somewhere in South China rather than the inconvenient misery of inner Birmingham or Detroit which is within travel to crime distance for many of our readers. But this travesties and misrepresents our position. We are not opposed to the extension of the process of development from which all the advanced countries have benefited; all we are saying is that we are fearful of the consequences of competition between low and high wage countries in some lines of manufacture such as motor cars. And our concern with this competition does not simply reflect a selfish preoccupation with defending the living standards of those privileged enough to live in the advanced countries. Under current market conditions, the new competition also threatens the liberal achievements of the advanced countries which fuse political democracy with a set of defensive institutions that set limits on the arbitrary exercise of power by employers and other powerful social groups. We have long been accustomed to thinking about the institutions of model advanced capitalist countries, like Germany and Sweden, as causes of superior economic performance; in the next generation we must consider the possibility that their institutions like secure employment, generous welfare, unionism and participation can be undermined by competition which management can meet only by shifting production offshore. This book has not been written to advocate any particular set of policy measures but we have presented evidence and argument which encourages a problem shift and reduces the inhibitions on using instruments of policy to regulate the competition between social settlements with large differences in wages and conditions.

✤ ✤ ✤

References

--- ❖ ---

AACP (Anglo-American Productivity Council), (1948–51), various reports, AACP, London, United Kingdom.

Auer, P. (ed), (1990), *Workforce Adjustment Patterns in Four Countries: Experiences in the Steel and Automobile Industry in France, Germany, Sweden and the UK*, WZB Discussion Papers on Labour Market and Employment, Berlin.

Austin Rover Group, (1983), *Historical Production Figures*, Austin Rover, Oxford.

Autocar, various dates, London.

Abramovitz, M. (1993), 'The Search for Sources of Growth', *Journal of Economic History*, Vol 53, No.2, June.

Adler P.S. and Cole R.E, (1993), 'Designed for learning: A tale of two Auto plants', *Sloan Management Review*, Spring, pp 85–94.

Altshuler, A. et al., (1984), *The Future of the Automobile: The Report of MIT's Automobile Programme*, Allen and Unwin, London.

Anderson Consulting (1992) *The Lean Enterprise Benchmarking Project Report*, London.

Arnold, H.L and Faurote,F., (1915), *Ford Methods and the Ford Shops*, Engineering Magazine Co., New York.

Automotive News, *World Automotive Statistics Market Data Book*, Crain Communicator Inc, Detroit, various issues.

Berggren, C., (1993), 'Lean Production: The End of History?' *Work, Employment and Society*, Vol.7 No.2.

BMC World, (1960), September and October, Oxford.

Bonazzi, G.(1992), *A gentler way to total quality: The case of the integrated factory at Fiat Auto*, Mimeo, University of Torino.

Bornholt, O.C. (1913), 'Placing machines for sequence of use: The trucking involved when machines are grouped by classes', *Iron Age*, pp 1276–1277, Dec. 4th.

Bosch, G.(1991), *Working time and operating hours in the Japanese automobile industry*, Institut Arbeit und Technik, Berlin.

Boston Consultants, (1975), *Strategy Alternatives for the British Motorcycle Industry*, H.M.S.O, London.

Bryan, F.R. (1990), *Beyond the Model T*, Wayne State University Press, Detroit.

Chandler, A. (1962), *Strategy and Structure*, MIT Press, Cambridge (Mass).

Clark, K. et al. (1982), *The Competitive State of the U.S. Auto Industry*, National Academy Press, Washington.

Coffey, D. (1992), *Cost Determinants in the Car Industry*, Mimeo, University of Leeds.

Colvin, F.H. (1913), 'Building an automobile every 40 seconds', *American Machinist*, June 5, pp. 757–762.

Commission of the European Communities, (1992), *The Future Development of the Common Transport Policy*, (Com 92, 494, Final), The European Commission, Brussels.

References

CPRS (Central Policy Review Staff), (1975), *The Future of the British Car Industry*, H.M.S.O, London.

Cusomano, M.A. (1985), *The Japanese Automobile Industry: Technology and Management at Nissan and Toyota*, Harvard University Press, Cambridge, Massachusetts and London.

Cutler, A. (1992), 'Vocational Training and Economic Performance', *Work, Employment and Society*, Vol 6. No.2.

Encyclopedia Britannica, (1925), article on Mass Production, London.

Edwards, M. (1983), *Back From The Brink: An Apocalyptic Experience*, Collins, London.

Financial Times, various dates, London.

Ford Times, July 1908 and January 1913.

Friedman, A. (1977), *Industry and Labour*, Macmillan, London.

Fucini, J. and S. (1990), *Working for the Japanese: Inside Mazda's American Auto Plant*, Free Press, New York.

Fuss, M. and Waverman, L. (1992), *Costs and Productivity in Automobile Production*, National Bureau of Economic Research, New York.

Galbraith, J.K. (1992), *The Culture of Contentment*, Sinclair-Stevenson, London.

Garrahan, P. and Stewart, P. (1992), *The Nissan Enigma: Flexibility at Work in a Local Economy*, Mansell, London.

The Guardian, various dates, London.

H.M.S.O, *UK Census of Manufactures*, PA1002, various years, London.

Harbour and Associates Inc. (1992), *The Harbour Report: Competitive Assessment of the North American Automobile Industry*, 1989–92, Michigan.

Hartley, J. (1981), *The Management of Vehicle Production*, Butterworth, London.
___, (1986), *Fighting Recession in Manufacturing*, IFS Publications, Bedford.

Hounshell, D. (1984), *From the American System to Mass Production*, Johns Hopkins Press, Baltimore.

IBJ Monthly Report, *Economic and Industrial Trends in Japan*, various issues, Tokyo, Industrial Bank of Japan.

International Financial Statistics Yearbook, various years, International Monetary Fund, New York.

International Labour Office, *Yearbook of Labour Statistics*, various years, Geneva, Switzerland.

International Metalworkers Federation, (1992), *Toyota Motor Towards 2000. A report for workers and their unions*, International Metalworkers Federation, Geneva.

JAMA, *The Motor Industry of Japan*, Japanese Automobile Manufacturers Association various dates, Tokyo, Japan.

Jones, D. (1985), *The Import Threat to the U.K. Car Industry*, Science Policy Research Unit, Brighton.

Kamata, S. (1983), *Japan in the Passing Lane: an insider's account of life in a Japanese auto company*, Allen and Unwin, London.

Kamiya, S. (1976), *My Life With Toyota*, Toyota Motor Sales Company Ltd, Japan.

Klann, W. (1955), *Oral Reminiscenses*, Ford Archive, Oral History Section, Detroit.

Krafcik, J. (1986), 'Learning from NUMMI', *IMVP Working Paper*, MIT, Mass. September.
___, (1988), 'A methodology for assembly plant performance determination', IMVP Research Affiliates, MIT, Mass. October.

___, (1989), 'Explaining high performance manufacturing', *International Policy Forum*, MIT, Mass. May.

___, (1990), 'The effect of design manufacturability of productivity and quality', *IMVP Working Paper*, MIT, Mass. January.

Lee, E.S. et al., (1957), *Population redistribution and economic growth in the United States 1870 to 1950*; The American Philosophical Society, Philadelphia.

Lehndorff, S. (1991), *Operating time and working time in the European car industry*, Institut Arbeit und Technik, Berlin, June.

Lewchuck, W. (1987), *American Technology and the British Vehicle Industry*, Cambridge University Press, Cambridge.

Ludvigsen Associates, (1992), *Report on European Car Prices*, London.

McAlinden, S.P. Andrea, D.J. Flynn, M.S. and Smith, B.C. (1991), T*he US Automotive Bilateral 1994 Trade Deficit*, Transportation Research Institute (UMTRI), Ann Arbor, University of Michigan.

The Machinist, various dates, Michigan.

Maxcy, G. and Silbertson, A. (1959), *The Motor Industry*, Allen and Unwin, London.

Machiavelli, N. (1531), *The Discourses*, Penguin Classics, London.

MacSweeney, B. (1988), Accounting for the Audit Commission, *Political Quarterly*, Vol. 59, No.1, pp.28–43.

Melman, S. (1956), *Dynamic Factors In Industrial Activity*, Blackwell, Oxford.

Meyer, S. (1981), *The Five Dollar Day*, State University of New York Press, Albany.

Monden, Y. (1983), *Toyota Production System*, Industrial Engineering and Management Press, Norcross, Georgia.

Nevins, A. (1954) *Ford: The Times, The Man, The Company*, C. Scribner and Sons, New York.

Nevins, A. and Hill, F. (1962), *Ford: Decline and Rebirth, 1933–62*, Scribner and Sons, New York.

New, C. and Myers, C. (1986), *Managing Manufacturing Operations in the UK*, British Institute of Management, London.

Nichols, T. (1986), *The British Worker Question*, Routledge, London.

Office of Technology Assessment (OTA) (1992), *US-Mexico Trade: Pulling Together or Pulling Apart*; US Government Printing Office, Washington.

Ohno, T.(1988), *The Toyota Production System,* (Diamond, Tokyo, 1978), English translation, Productivity Press, Cambridge, Mass.

Oliver, N. et al. (1993), *World Class Manufacturing: Further Evidence in the Lean Production Debate*, Mimeo, University of Cambridge.

Piore, M. and Sabel, C. (1984), *The Second Industrial Divide: possibilities for Prosperity*, Basic Books, New York.

Porter, M. (1985), *Competitive Advantage: the creating and sustaining of superior performance*, Free Press, New York.

___, (1990), *The Competitive Advantage of Nations*, Free Press, New York.

Preston, B. (1990), *The Impact of the Motor Car*, Brefi Press, Wales.

Rhys, D.G. (1972), *The Motor Industry: An Economic Survey*, Butterworths, London.

Riegler, C. and Auer, P. (1991), *Workforce adjustment and labour market policy: Sweden*, Research Area and Labour Market and Employment, Report No.FSI 91–4, Berlin.

Rosenberg, N. (1982), *Inside the Black Box: Technology and Economics*, Cambridge University Press, Cambridge.

Rostas, L. (1948), *Comparative Productivity in British and American Industry*, NIESR, Occassional Papers, no.15, London.

Ryder Report, (1975), *British Leyland: the next decade*, HMSO, London.

SMMT (Society of Motor Manufacturers and Traders), *Motor Industry of Great Britain*, various dates, London.

Schonberger, R. (1982), *Japanese Manufacturing Techniques: nine hidden lessons in simplicity*, Free Press, New York.

Schonberger, R. (1987), *World Class Manufacturing*, Free Press, New York.

Seltzer, L. (1928), *A Financial History of the American Automobile Industry*, Houghton Mifflin, New York.

Sloan, A. (1967), *My Years with General Motors*, Pan Books, London.

Sorenson, C. (1956), *My Forty Years with Ford*, Norton, New York.

Statistical Yearbook of Japan, Statistics Bureau, Management and Co-ordination Agency, Tokyo.

Toyota Motor Corporation, (1985), *Toyota: A History of the First Fifty Years*, Toyota Motor Corporation, Japan.

___, (1992), *Report on Toyota and the Japanese Car Industry*, Toyota Motor Corporation, Japan.

___, *The Wheel Extended*, International Public Affairs Division, Toyota City.

___, *The Automobile Industry: Toyota and Japan*, Toyota Motor Corporation, various years, International Public Affairs, Tokyo.

United Nations, *Annual Trade Statistics Yearbook*, various years, United Nations, New York.

United Nations, *Demographic Yearbook*, various years, United Nations, New York.

United Nations, *The Growth of World Industry*, Volume 1, United Nations, New York.

United Nations, *World Programme of Industrial Statistics*, United Nations, New York.

United Nations, *Yearbook of Industrial Statistics*, various years, United Nations, New York.

Ure, A. (1835), *The Philosophy of Manufactures*, Charles Knight, London.

US Department of Commerce, *Foreign Direct Investment in the US: Operations of US Affiliates of Foreign Companies*, various years, Washington DC.

Van Deventer, J.H. (1923), various articles, Ford Principles and Practice at River Rouge, *Industrial Management*, Vols. LXV and LXVI.

Verband der Automobilindustrie (VDA), (1991), *Tatsachen und Zahlen: aus der Kraeftverkehrswirtschaft*, No 55, Frankfurt.

Williams, K., Williams, J. and Thomas, D. (1983), *Why are the British Bad at Manufacturing?* Routledge and Kegan Paul, London.

Williams, K,. Haslam, C., Williams, J (1987a), *The Breakdown of Austin Rover*, Berg, Oxford.

___, (1987b), 'The end of mass production?' *Economy and Society*, Vol. 16, No.3, pp.405–438.

___, (1989), 'Do Labour Costs Matter?' *Work, Employment and Society*, Vol.3, no.3, Sept, pp. 281–305.

Williams, K. Mitsui, I. Haslam, C. (1991) 'How far from Japan: a case study of Japanese press shop practice and management calculation'. *Critical Perspectives on Accounting*, No.2, pp. 145–169.

Williams, K. Haslam, C. Williams, J. Adcroft, A. Johal, S. (1992a) *Factories V Warehouses: Japanese Foreign Direct Investment in the UK and America*, University of East London Occassional Paper No.6.

__, (1992b) *Tout Va Bien*, Mimeo of report given to Renault, University of East London.

Williams, K. Haslam, C. Williams, J. Cutler, A. Adcroft, A. Johal, S. (1992c) 'Against Lean Production', *Economy and Society*, Vol.21, No.3, pp.321–354, August.

Williams, K. Haslam, C. Williams, J. (1992d) 'Ford versus Fordism: The Beginning of Mass Production?' *Work Employment and Society*, Vol. 6, No. 4, pp. 517–555, December.

Williams, K. Haslam, C. Johal, S. (1993a) *Machiavelli not MIT*, Arbetslivcentrum, Stockholm, April, mimeo.

Williams, K. Haslam, C. Johal, S. Williams, J. Adcroft, A. (1993b) *Beyond Management: Problems of the Average Car Company*, paper presented at the Lean Production and Labor Conference, Wayne State University, May, mimeo, University of Manchester.

Williams, K. Haslam, C. Williams, J. with Adcroft, A. Johal, S. (1993c) 'The Myth of the Line', *Business History*, Vol. 35, No.3, pp.66–87, June.

Williams, K. Haslam, C. Johal, S. (1993ii) *Fait Accompli?: A Machiavellian Interpretation of the Renault-Volvo merger*, International Labour Studies Centre, University of Manchester, October.

Williams, K. Haslam, C. Johal, S. (1994) Who's Responsible? BAe, BMW, Honda, Rover, *University of East London Occassional Paper No.13*.

Williams, K. Haslam, C. Williams, J. Johal, S. (1994) 'Deconstructing car assembler productivity', *International Journal of Production Economics*, forthcoming.

Woollard, F. (1954), *Principles of Mass and Flow Production* , London, Iliffe.

Womack, J. Jones, D. and Roos, D. (1990), *The Machine that Changed the World,* Rawson Associates, New York.

Index